RAFFLES
AND THE
GOLDEN OPPORTUNITY

ALSO BY VICTORIA GLENDINNING

NON-FICTION

Elizabeth Bowen: Portrait of a Writer
Vita: A Biography of V. Sackville-West
Edith Sitwell: A Unicorn Among Lions
Jonathan Swift
Trollope
Rebecca West: A Life
Leonard Woolf: A Life

FICTION

The Grown-Ups
Electricity
Flight

RAFFLES
AND THE
GOLDEN OPPORTUNITY
1781–1826

Victoria Glendinning

P
PROFILE BOOKS

First published in Great Britain in 2012 by
PROFILE BOOKS LTD
3A Exmouth House
Pine Street
London EC1R 0JH
www.profilebooks.com

Copyright © Victoria Glendinning, 2012

1 3 5 7 9 10 8 6 4 2

Typeset in Bell by MacGuru Ltd
info@macguru.org.uk

Printed and bound in China
Through Asia Pacific Offset

A CIP catalogue record for this book is available from the British Library.

ISBN 978 1 84668 6030
eISBN 978 184765 8241
Export edn ISBN 978 1 78125 025 9

Contents

For Kevin O'Sullivan
who had the idea

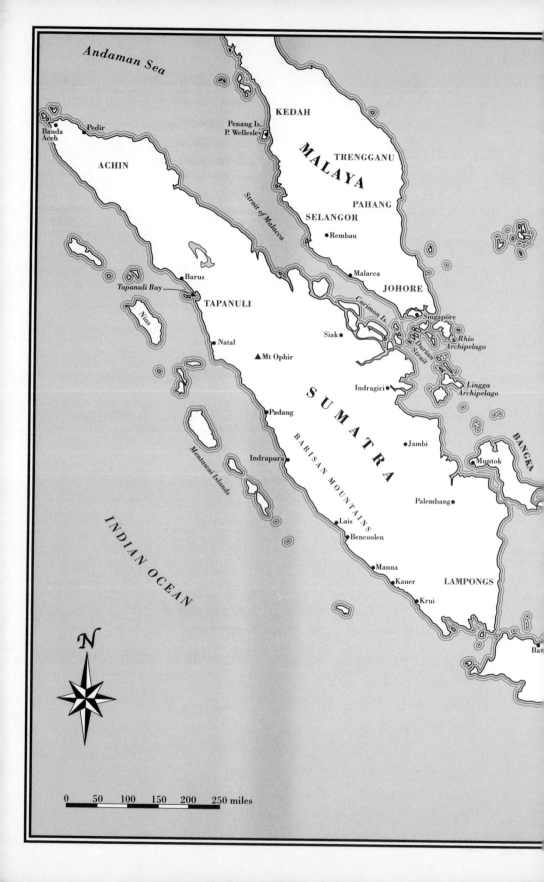

The East Indies

South China Sea

Balambangan

Jesselton

NORTH BORNEO

SARAWAK

Sambas   Sarawak

Pontianak

B O R N E O

Penebangan

Karimata
Archipelago

Pasir

Karimata Strait

Strait of Macassar

BELITUNG

Banjermasin

Java Sea

CELEBES

MADURA

Cheribon   Rembang
     Pekalongan   Samarang   Sumenep
JAVA   Surakarta   Surabaya
     Jokyakarta   Pasuruan   BALI   Bali Sea

Mt Tomboro

Banu Wan

Taliwang

LOMBOK   SUMBAWA

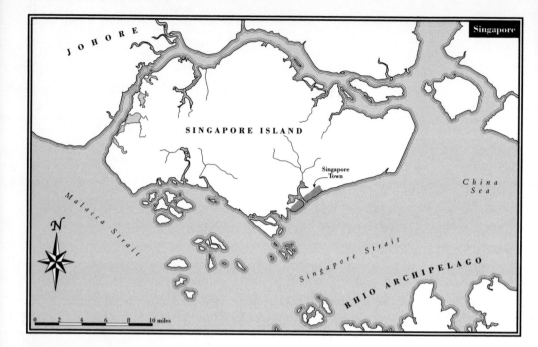

Singapore

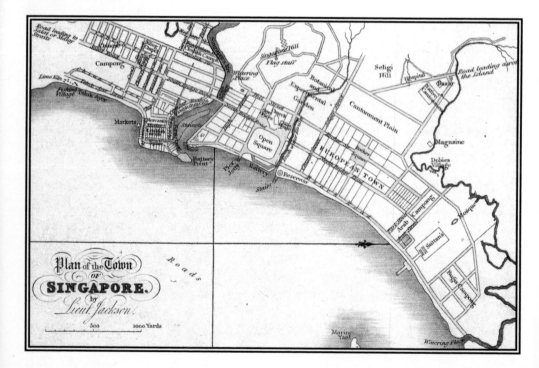

Introduction

Everyone has heard of Raffles Hotel in Singapore. There are also in Singapore schools, colleges, businesses, medical centres, auctioneers, investment management companies, shopping malls, clubs, streets, squares, landmarks and serviced apartments all bearing the name 'Raffles' or 'Stamford'. Until recently Singapore Airlines called their Business Class 'Raffles Class'. 'Raffles' is a brand that belongs to no one and everyone in Singapore. The name delivers an instant message: exclusive, probably expensive, uniquely Singaporean, 'heritage' – though the branding becomes stretched at the lower end of the commercial spectrum.

This is all because in 1819 Sir Stamford Raffles raised the British flag on a small jungle-covered island and founded a settlement which became the city state of Singapore. He was also Lieutenant-Governor of Java and of Bengkulu in West Sumatra. That is not all that he did in the East Indies – the Eastern Archipelago – and only a part of what he was. The reality of him has been submerged by his image and his name.

He has been re-imagined by history-writers both as a hero and as a villain of the British Empire. The fiction writer E. W. Hornung, at the turn of the nineteenth century, borrowed the name Raffles for his gentleman thief. Raffles appears as himself, a fictional presence, in three of Patrick O'Brian's seafaring sequence of novels. There is even a musical, *Raffles of Singapore*, last performed in 2010 in Henley-on-Thames – fortuitously, where Raffles and his second wife spent their honeymoon in 1817.

Raffles' story, in a work of fiction, would strain credulity. His good fortune and his ill fortune were both of an extreme kind. Many times, learning about him, I felt I recognised him. At any period, such people erupt. Born with no advantages, he took his chances and strove to realise his visions. He became the entrepreneur of his own ideals and a utopian imperialist. He wanted fame, and he wanted to do good.

From the age of fourteen he was an employee of the East India Company – a two-hundred-year-old, hydra-headed commercial entity, administering the British Empire in fractious partnership with Parliament. The Company's arcane practices and cronyism had something in common with dysfunctional global corporations today, and was called by Adam Smith 'an absurdity' five years before Raffles was even born. The Company contained and constrained Raffles and finally spat him out, while reaping the benefits of his greatest achievement: Singapore. He was not an organisation man. For him, the status quo was never an option.

His way, which is the way of all impatient innovators, was to do something first and seek approval from the proper authority after-wards. Usually what came was a directive *not* to take the measure in question, by which time it was too late. In the days of sail it could take up to ten months each way for despatches between the Eastern Isles and Company headquarters in London. The history of political activism, then as now, is the history of communications.

Raffles' career was played out in the East, but the backdrop was European. The Portuguese, then the Dutch, the British and the French were involved in the lucrative spice trade in the Eastern Isles for two centuries, before the wars between Britain and France (each in shifting coalitions with other European states) injected a strategic and military dimension into the commercial rivalry. Apart from a shaky one-year peace in 1803, Britain was at war with France on land and at sea from the time Raffles was twelve until he was in his mid-thirties.

In the year that Raffles met his first wife Olivia, Napoleon was proclaimed Emperor and was massing troops in Boulogne to invade England. By the time Raffles and Olivia set sail for the East the following year, 1805, Spain too was at war with Britain. They reached Penang, Raffles' first posting, about a month before Nelson's victory and death at Trafalgar, though that news would not reach Penang for several further months. The vicissitudes of war in Europe, and hostile French incursions in the East, determined British policy in India and the Archipelago. Almost nothing that Raffles wanted to do was judged on its intrinsic merits, but in the light of the European conflict, in dismal combination with the Company's entrenched caution and conservatism.

Napoleon's defeat at Trafalgar put a stop to his invasion of England, but his ambition to gain control over continental Europe was not abated. After France conquered the Low Countries, Dutch possessions in the Archipelago were taken over by the French, so that when Raffles and the Governor-General of India, Lord Minto, invaded Java, they were ousting the French not the Dutch, though the Dutch were still there. After the defeat of Napoleon by Britain and her allies there was a reshuffling of territories, and the Dutch were given back most of their possessions in the Archipelago. Restitution to the Dutch in the event of British victory had been foreseen. Raffles' radical reforms in Java needed far more time to see through than he had, or was ever likely to have. This did not deter him.

Raffles was high-strung, clever, articulate, impetuous, charming, small in stature and physically fragile. He had unusual resources of energy, curiosity and resilience. He had a loving heart. He was loyal, supporting and promoting his friends to an extent that was injudicious even in a time of accepted patronage and nepotism. He inspired profound devotion in some colleagues, and made enemies of others, especially military men. He loved his mother and sisters and looked after them financially. He loved his wives, both of whom were remarkable women. Coming to fatherhood relatively late, he adored his children. Writing about their deaths has been painful, as was writing about the fire on the *Fame* – which he and his second wife Sophia survived, but which saw one of his precious collections of natural history drawings, animal specimens, manuscripts, Javanese artefacts and his professional and personal papers all lost at the bottom of the Indian Ocean.

This is not a rags to riches story. It is more interesting than that. Raffles was never much good at making money, either for himself or for the East India Company. He died at forty-five under a dreadful burden of debt, in semi-disgrace with the Company, while paradoxically lionised by the scientific community in London.

His second wife, Sophia, rescued his reputation as a colonial administrator. Her monumental *Memoir* of him laid the foundations of a somewhat fantastical critical heritage. Between the last decade of the nineteenth century and the middle of the twentieth, most accounts of Raffles were heroic and uncritical. It is possible to take a long step back from all that. It is equally possible to take a long step back from the weight of the post-colonial guilt (on the one hand) and the post-colonial revisionism (on the other) of the last half of the twentieth century. It would be as easy to paint a black picture of Raffles as a golden one, and neither would show him as he was, or just what it was like to be that particular person in that region at that time. This book seeks to demythologise him without diminishing him. He was not a genius but, like all ambitious visionaries, he had a streak of genius.

Those who ran the expanding Empire did not really know what it was for. The East India Company was interested in making profits for its shareholders. Its senior civil servants out East were interested in getting home as soon as possible with enough money to support them for the rest of their lives. The Company was generally against acquiring territory other than for strategically essential commercial settlements because administering territory cost money.

Raffles' vision, on the other hand, was of bringing together the countries of the Archipelago in a romantic reconstitution of ancient indigenous kingdoms, under benign British rule. In this respect he was closer to the Victorian idea of Empire, the *Pax Britannica*, but with a difference. When in Java, he sought to promote the value and beauty of the indigenous culture and its pre-Islamic Hindu heritage. That was the driving force behind his collection of antiquities and anthropological artefacts. Similarly, his plans for education in Singapore prescribed the teaching of students through their own languages and literature.

Some of his ideas changed. Sumatran civilisation was not so evolved as Javanese. In Sumatra, he said he would (had he had the time) be a benevolent despot. His idea of civilisation was based on human development – that is, that all societies grow from a state of infancy to maturity. (He did not take into account that any society at any time is advanced in some respects while 'barbaric' to outsiders in others.) He was beginning, too, to advocate colonisation – the permanent settling of Europeans under a British flag, as in the lost American colonies – again, to be a feature of the later Empire. He was inconsistent, like everyone except religious fanatics. But on certain essentials he never wavered – an absolute intolerance of slavery, the banning of gaming (cock-fighting) and opium-farming, and his insistence on free trade.

Writing about him has been an act of concentration, in both senses. There are a great many strange characters churning around in this book, and a great many more clamouring outside it, shut out for reasons of space and focus. Similarly, many episodes, sideshows, back stories and circumstantial details have been consigned – not to oblivion, but to the shadows – and a website tsraffles.co.uk. Raffles' energies were never confined to his reformist administrations.

A whole book could be written on Raffles the natural historian, another on Raffles the ethnologist and collector.

During the war with Napoleon, and in armed conflicts in the East, defeats and victories were reported vividly in the British and Indian public prints. Successful naval and military commanders became national heroes. Company civil servants did not get the same press, yet the civil branch was senior to the military branch. The military, however, did not always see it that way, which caused problems for Raffles. He did not have the social clout or the experience to deal wisely with an uppity colonel.

Raffles was English. But whether from great families or, like himself, from unprivileged backgrounds, virtually all his superiors, colleagues, subordinates, friends and enemies were Scottish. Those that were not were Irish, mostly from the north of Ireland. The Act of Union of 1707 provided unprecedented career opportunities for the Scots, not only in England but in India and the Eastern Archipelago. Scotland, with one-tenth of the population of England, was massively over-represented in the East India Company and on the ground out East – Scots army officers, naval captains, doctors, administrators, engineers. Sometimes it will seem, in these pages, that among the British, Thomas Stamford Raffles is the only Englishman around, and even he may have had distant Scottish origins: there are small places called East and West Raffles near Mouswald in Dumfriesshire.

Note on the Text

The period 1783–1815 is often referred to as the Second British Empire. I have called it the 'early Empire', as being less laborious.

Raffles and his contemporaries used capital letters for common nouns in a completely random manner. To follow this slavishly in quoting from letters and despatches, makes for a distracting kind of 'period' distancing. I have behaved in an equally random manner, leaving capitalisations only when they seem to add an intentional or particularly graphic emphasis. Capital initial letters were always used for titles and official positions, all the way from 'President of the Board of Control' to 'Master Attendant and Storekeeper'. Against all modern practice and my every inclination, I have felt compelled to follow this. In the hierarchical structure of the Company, these were more than just job descriptions: they defined a man.

In quoting from letters I have substituted 'and' for the crossed squiggle – a reduced ampersand – which everyone uses, then and now. An ampersand in print looks heavy and intrusive.

So far as place names are concerned, I have used the forms and spellings used by Raffles, putting in brackets at the first mention the modern form, as for example, 'Bencoolen (Bengkulu)'. Raffles and his contemporaries transcribed Malay and Arabic proper names more or less phonetically, and they did not all hear the same phonemes. I have followed Raffles' usage, rather than duplicate every proper name according to the conventions and accompanying diacritics of modern scholars. Raffles' time, in this book, is real time.

It is notoriously hard to establish today's values for the varied and variable currencies of India and the Eastern Isles between 1800 and 1825. The most stable unit in the Archipelago was the Spanish dollar, generally worth then about five English shillings – twenty shillings to the pound (£), or just under five US dollars ($) or, probably, twenty pounds or thirty-three dollars today.

The value of £1 in Raffles' lifetime equates to between £80 and £95 in today's money.

Raffles in romantic mode, with an arm resting on his book *The History of Java*. This was painted in London by the fashionable portraitist James Lonsdale in 1817.

Chapter 1

The Boy from Walworth and the Circassian Bride

London 1781–1805

எஃஃஃஃஃ

Raffles had brought the red carpet with him.

He knew the importance of ceremony and etiquette when treating with the rulers of the Indian Archipelago. There were about one hundred and fifty people living on the island of Singapore: a few Chinese settlements in the forest and, on the shore, the Malay sea-gypsies who subsisted on fishing and piracy and whose activities were evident from the human skulls bobbing around in the shallow waters. A larger dwelling, back from the river which debouched into the bay, was that of the local governor, Temenggong Abdul Rahman of Johore. The ground beyond the sandy beach was partially cleared. All the rest was smothered in jungle.

The squadron of eight vessels anchored offshore on 27 January 1819. Wa Hakim, a sea-gypsy boy, remembered watching the landing of two white men, a short one and a tall one, escorted by a sepoy. The tall man was Major William Farquhar. The short man was Sir Stamford Raffles, Lieutenant-Governor of Bencoolen (Bengkulu). Raffles made a provisional treaty with the Temenggong, and gained permission to land troops with building materials, arms and stores, to pitch tents and lay out a fort.

Tunku Long was one of two rival Sultans of Johore with pretensions to sovereignty over the island of Singapore. He arrived, was escorted out to the Raffles' ship, and was received with every honour by Raffles who, according to a Malay historian, 'told him everything, using courteous words, advising him, and paying him delicate compliments. And Tunku Long agreed to whatever Mr Raffles proposed.'

On 6 February the Sultan and his party attired themselves for the Treaty ceremony, while Raffles, Farquhar, and all the military and ships' officers gathered on the shore. Guns were fired, flags flew, sepoys were drawn up under arms. A hundred feet of the red carpet were unrolled. The Treaty document was read aloud, in English and then in Malay, signed by Raffles in the name of the East India Company, and sealed by the Sultan and the Temenggong.

In the name of the Governor-General of Bengal, Tunku Long was declared to be 'Sultan Hussein Shah in the state of Singapore and all its subject territories', with the promise of five thousand Spanish dollars a year and the protection of the British. In return the British Government was granted exclusive rights to establish a settlement or 'trading factory' on the island. It was not a conquest. It was more like a leasehold purchase.

This brief account of the founding of Singapore gives no idea of the political and personal machinations leading up to what seems a smooth operation, nor of the political storm which it caused. It does not convey the importance to the East India Company of establishing a safe haven and a profitable trading post midway on the trade route between India and China; nor the vision and verve which had made it possible. Raffles and Farquhar had brought it off. Given their different skills and temperaments, neither could have done it without the other.

Major Farquhar remained on the island as Resident, with full authority and a raft of instructions from Raffles. He, the very next day, sailed away up the Strait of Malacca to another island, Penang, where his pregnant wife Sophia was waiting for him.

Raffles was born on a different ocean, on 6 July 1781, off Port Morant on the south-east coast of Jamaica. His father, Benjamin Raffles, aged forty-two, was the English master of the West India-man *Ann*. The trade with Jamaica and the Caribbean, familiar to Benjamin Raffles over many years, was in sugar, rum, and slaves.

His mother was Anne Lyde, in her mid-twenties. Her new baby was baptised when the *Ann* put in at Port Royal, further west on the Jamaican coast. He was christened Thomas Bingley Stamford: Thomas was the name of his paternal grandfather, Thomas Bingley was a London merchant friend and the boy's godfather, and Thomas Stamford a doctor friend in Jamaica. The boy was called 'Tom' in the family.

His mother's eldest sister, Harriet, was married to John Linde-man. Of Dutch descent, with connections in the East Indies, he was rector of Eaton Bishop in Herefordshire. On a visit with his mother to the Herefordshire Lindemans when Tom was rising three, the boy – along with a younger sister, christened Harriet after her aunt Lindeman – was re-christened by his uncle and registered simply as 'Thomas' this time. Tom himself dropped 'Bingley' but always retained 'Stamford'.

After Tom and Harriet came Leonora, Maryanne (or Mary Anne or Marianne), Elizabeth (who died when she was four), another boy, Benjamin, who did not survive his first year; and Ann, who was always a problem. Maryanne was the prettiest and the most fun, and the closest to Tom. Thus he grew up the eldest and only boy with four younger sisters.

Benjamin Raffles seems not to have made money by private trading, as most sea captains did. He had a good enough start in life, enter-ing Christ's Hospital, the 'Blue Coat School', in Newgate Street in London at the age of ten. The school was free, with a reputation for discipline and high standards, and admission was through recom-mendation from the parish of St Ann's, Blackfriars, where he was baptised in 1739. He left at sixteen to become apprenticed to the master of a ship engaged in the slave trade, bound for Antigua. Ten years later, he was a ship's master himself.

The Raffleses were ordinary people with no family money and few influential connections. Tom's paternal grandfather, Thomas Raffles, was for thirty years a clerk in Doctor's Commons, which administered ecclesiastical and Admiralty courts. But the genes on each side produced eccentric talents, and Tom was one of three extraordinary first cousins born within a few years of each other. All three were intelligent, full of nervous energy, and ambitious to the point of assuming entitlement.

One cousin was Elton Hamond, born in 1786, son of Elizabeth Lyde – another sister of Tom's mother – married to Charles Hamond, a tea dealer in Milk Street, off Cheapside in the City. Elton had intense literary aspirations and was a compulsive unpublished autobiographer. Strikingly handsome and a seductive talker, he sought, successfully, the acquaintance of writers. He knew the poets Robert Southey and Samuel Taylor Coleridge, the novelist Maria Edgeworth, and the diarist Crabb Robinson, who was fond of him but thought him insane. Elton believed that only he possessed the secret of rendering mankind perfect. At the age of thirty-five, deluded and depressed, he killed himself.

The other significant cousin was another Thomas Raffles, born 1788, son of Captain Benjamin's half-brother William, a solicitor, and his wife Rachel. They lived in east London in Princes (later Princelet) Street in Spitalfields, where William was a vestry clerk at Christ Church. Theirs was a religious household, and Thomas joined the ministry of the dissenting Congregational church, having a startling gift for oratory at a time when evangelical preachers were celebrities, attracting huge followings. Based at the Great George Street Chapel in Liverpool, the Rev. Thomas Raffles D.D., LL.D, travelled throughout Britain and abroad, often preaching three times in one day for an hour and a half at a time. Cousin Thomas performed in the pulpit like an actor. 'Oh! what a vapour is popularity!' he wrote, inhaling, and praying for humility. He wrote books, had a fine library, antiquarian interests, and was a collector of manuscripts and of autographs.

The destiny of Thomas Stamford Raffles was unlike that of either of these younger cousins, to both of whom he was close. But there is something visionary and driven in the nature of each of the three which resonates disturbingly.

When they were all young, Tom's family lived in Walworth, a Surrey village south of the City of London across the river. East Street (or East Lane), off the village street, was part of a development which, in the course of the nineteenth century, would see Walworth join up with Camberwell and both become swallowed up by the capital – its population under one million in 1801, in a country of just over eight million. Tom Raffles' childhood was about thirty years earlier than the period in which Dickens's *Great Expectations* is set, but when Pip walks out from the City to have supper with Mr Wemmick and his Aged Parent in Walworth, the village still 'appeared to be a col-lection of back lanes, ditches, and little gardens, and to present the aspect of a rather dull retirement.' But just north of Walworth, the Elephant and Castle coaching inn presided over a congested traffic junction where converging horse-drawn vehicles clattered into the capital over Blackfriars Bridge, or through the Southwark tollgate up the Borough Road and over London Bridge.

East Street petered out towards the Thames through farms and market gardens, and Tom will have seen sheep and cows from the back windows. Cousin Thomas remembered visiting when he was a boy of nine or ten and Tom a teenager, and 'flying my kyte with him in the neighbouring fields.' The main street was 'lined by elegant mansions.' Walworth Common provided nineteen marshy acres of green space.

'As a schoolboy, his garden was his delight: to this was added a love of animals,' wrote his second wife Sophia Raffles in her *Memoir* of her late husband, reporting what Cousin Thomas had told her. There were people in Walworth to sow the seeds of Tom Raffles' later passion for natural history. James Maddock, the author of *The Florist's Directory: or Treatise on the Culture of Flowers*, had a famous plant nursery there. Another local florist – 'florist' being the contemporary term for 'horticulturist' – was Samuel Curtis, a couple of years younger than Tom, who had acquired his own nursery in Walworth by the time he was twenty-one. Curtis became the proprietor of the *Botanical Magazine*, and in 1810 – six years sooner than Raffles – a member of the Linnean Society.

Tom Raffles would have known the Cuming family, and handled the strange objects in their house just across the road from East Street, on the corner of Manor Row. Richard and Henry Cuming, father and son, were amassing a collection of curiosities – a jumble of old bones, teeth, coins, ornaments, textiles, animal skulls and skeletons, fossils, artefacts and weapons, from all over the world. Raffles, in an age of collectors, was to become a collector of distinction.

Further afield, for an entrance fee of one shilling, a curious wandering boy could see wild animals from faraway countries – another personal passion when he himself was in the East – by crossing the Thames and visiting Edward Cross's menagerie in Exeter Change on the Strand, where a tiger, a hyena, and other beasts were kept in iron cages on an upper floor, their howls audible from the street.

Tom had almost no formal education. When he was twelve he went to the Mansion House Boarding School on King Street in the village of Hammersmith. It was a typical small, inexpensive private school of the kind which prepared boys for clerkships, or the armed services or, at a pinch, Oxford or Cambridge, offering Latin and Greek, French, arithmetic, book-keeping and geography. Tom was only there for two years. In a long autobiographical letter to Cousin Thomas (henceforth cited as 'the letter of 14 October 1819'), he admitted: 'The deficiency of my early education has never been supplied, and I have never ceased to deplore the necessity which withdrew me so early from school.' It was a question of money.

His father Benjamin seems to have sold the *Ann* the year after Tom's birth. Ships' captains were young, and getting younger.

Something went very wrong in later life for Captain Benjamin Raffles. Tom was devoted to his mother, but not a single written word about his father, by him or anyone else in the family, has survived. The Captain or his wife must have found other sources of income, as the girls had some education. They wrote good letters in good handwriting, and had the necessary refinement as they grew older to mix comfortably with privileged people.

There were seafaring people on their mother Anne (Lyde)'s side as well as their father's, but it seems not to have been suggested that Tom should go to sea. He was small and slight and not robust. He had to get a job.

Uncle Charles Hamond, Elton's father, through his tea business had contacts in India House, the headquarters of the East India Company on Leadenhall Street in the City. Another connection was his godfather Bingley, whose son – another Thomas – was an insurance broker with enough shares in the East India Company to qualify him for a vote in the General Court of Proprietors.

There were no formal qualifications for employment in the Company. The only way in was through patronage – who you knew. To solicit employment for one's sons, brothers, brothers-in-law or nephews was perfectly acceptable. There were multi-generational Company dynasties, such as the Dundas family.

Uncle Charles Hamond, probably with Bingley's aid, paid the necessary bond and secured for Thomas Stamford Raffles the position of 'Extra Clerk' in India House. With a salary of £50 a year, this was a precarious position, the lowest step on a ladder which rose to heights far beyond the line of sight of the boy from Walworth who entered the portals of India House for the first time in 1795. He was fourteen, which was young but not unusually so. In 1809 the Company opened their East India College at Haileybury to prepare boys for service out East. The idea was that the students, nominated by Directors, should be either from families already connected with the Company, or fine examples of young British manhood from the landed gentry. Tom Raffles, on the face of it, was not the sort of youth anyone in the Company would expect to be a high-flyer.

Queen Elizabeth I had granted a Charter in 1600 to a group of London merchants, guaranteeing them a monopoly on all English trade east of the Cape of Good Hope. The most valuable trade from the East was spices, for which Dutch traders were charging exorbitantly on the European market.

The Dutch East India Company – the *Vereenigde Oost-Indische Compagnie*, or VOC, was established two years after the British East India Company, and was a larger organisation in terms of shipping and tonnage. The VOC had its own East Indian capital on the coast of Java, at Batavia (Jakarta). The VOC crashed, and was dissolved in 1800, but with no diminution to Dutch trading activity and territorial ambition in the East Indies. There was also a French East India Company, and a small Danish East India Company.

The main spices were, from the beginning, nutmeg, clove, mace, cinnamon. Of these nutmeg, *Myristica fragrans*, was originally the most expensive and the most desired. Pepper became equally important. Although spices remained a core trade, by Raffles' time tea had taken over as the most profitable commodity (with opium, exported to China from Bengal, an uneasy second). Tea came only from China, and the China trade was expanding – East Indiamen brought back not only tea but also silks and porcelain, painted wallpapers, ivories and lacquered objects, fuelling a fashion for *chinoiserie*.

By the turn of the nineteenth century there was a trade gap. Private fortunes could still be made, but for the Company there was a limited market in South Asia and China for British woollens and metals, which was all that the Company could think of sending out. So its operations required huge injections of capital. Money made trading from Bengal, and quantities of silver bullion from London, financed goods from China which were wanted at home. Indian cottons and muslins were re-exported from London to China and West Africa, but did not close the gap.

The Company, too big to fail, continued to expand. In the years immediately after Raffles came to work there, India House was remodelled and enlarged. The facade was widened and a pillared portico added, topped by a pediment embellished with a statue of the reigning monarch, George III, flanked by emblems of commerce and topped by Britannia. Off the central corridor on the ground floor was the Court Room, a thirty-foot cube with double tiers of windows, where the Court of Directors met every Wednesday, sitting round a horseshoe-shaped table.

Another large room off the corridor was the Proprietors' General Court Room. The Proprietors were the shareholders – people in banking, shipping and commerce, and retired 'nabobs' who had made their pile out East. To the left of the corridor was the Sale Room, where imported commodities were auctioned to dealers and wholesalers; and committee rooms for the thirteen committees, of which the three-man Secret Committee was the most prestigious.

Grandiosity was defying decline and loss of independence. For in 1784 the Government imposed upon the Company a seven-man Board of Control, with statutory access to its reports and accounts, in order to restrict its geopolitical autonomy. The East India Company's powers were eroded with every statutory renewal of its Charter, although in Raffles' time there was still an inextricable co-dependency between Company and Crown. The Company was also the largest single employer in the country. In 1785 it employed over fifteen hundred in London alone, which doubled by 1813: not only clerks and administrators but labourers, cleaners, porters, packers, watchmen, warehousemen, chandlers, carters and carriers, dockers and shipbuilders. The Cornish tin and copper mines depended on the Company for its markets. It has been estimated that as many as thirty thousand people in Britain were in some way dependent on the Company.

The Chairman of the Government-appointed Board of Control had a seat in Cabinet, thus acquiring political clout while subjecting the Company's affairs to supervision. Company interests were heavily represented in Parliament. Company and Crown wrangled over which had legal right to the revenues of Bengal, Bihar and Orissa. The Government, which depended on the Company's experience and establishments, had no wish to take over the administration of Company possessions in India and the Indian Archipelago, but the Chairman of the Board of Control influenced the appointment of new Directors. Crown approval was required for the appointment of Governors-General. The Board of Control had the right to communicate directly with the Secret Committee, and with India, without going through the usual channels.

India House extended three hundred feet behind its frontage, terminating in warehouses. Somewhere in the rambling complex was the library, and from 1801 a museum, or 'Oriental Repository', open to visitors. On the upper floors of the four-storey building were the Departments, with warrens of offices divided into cubicle-like compartments, off dingy passages. The clerks, six to a compartment, sat hunched over their desks on uncomfortably high stools. (Raffles developed a pronounced stoop.)

The essayist Charles Lamb, diminutive and fragile, joined the Company as a clerk in the Accountant's Department at the age of seventeen, three years before Raffles arrived. He called India House 'a drear pile' with its 'labyrinthine passages and light-excluding, pent-up offices, where candles for one half of the year supplied the place of the sun's light.' Outside work, Lamb combined a febrile social and literary life with caring devotedly for his sister Mary, who was intermittently psychotic. Mary had a bad turn at dinner-time on a Monday in September 1796. She killed their mother with the carving knife. Everyone knew, so probably fifteen-year-old Raffles did too. Some men broke down, others turned to drink. In 1800 the clerk to the Committee of Buying threw himself out of his office window. Lamb worked in India House for thirty-three years, becoming, he said, as most clerks did, 'doggedly contented, as wild animals in cages', and retired with a pension two-thirds his salary. 'Doggedly contented' would never describe Raffles.

The actual work, unless like Lamb in the Accountant's Department one were dealing with figures, was copying letters, reports, memos, drafts, abstracts and despatches, with quill pens taken from bunches, hour after hour, day after day. Raffles and his fellow clerks were human word-processors. The Company generated mountains of written material, as every document had to be copied and recopied many times.

Official letters arriving from India were first read by the Court of Directors then distributed among the relevant offices of the Examiner's Department, where abstracts were drawn up to be reconsidered by the twenty-four Directors. Meanwhile the Examiner's Department collected up all the documentation which might be relevant in drafting replies, and 'narratives' were composed, providing the context or back-story for any given problem.

Draft replies were circulated to the members of the Board of Control who scrutinised them at their leisure and returned them to India House with emendations. Revised drafts were submitted to the Committee of Correspondence, where they were approved – or not. The final drafts became despatches and were sent to India. Copies of every document generated were filed in leather-bound folio volumes.

Lord Minto, Governor-General of India from 1807 to 1813, writing to his wife from Calcutta, described the process in reverse. He had not only despatches and letters from London to deal with, but also from the other two presidencies, Madras and Bombay, and from lesser settlements, out-stations and factories. (Not factory as in manufactory, but as in an entrepôt overseen by a factor.) At the twice-weekly Council meetings in Calcutta, which lasted from ten in the morning till three or four in the afternoon, the secretaries read aloud the substance of each paper. Lord Minto found it hard to stay awake.

These procedures took months at each end. Add to that the six to ten months it took for a ship to reach England from Calcutta and vice versa. If a despatch from London was destined for, say, Malacca

(Melaka), there was further delay. By the time it reached its destination, either some course of action, whether proposed or deplored, had become irrelevant owing to changed circumstances, or had been implemented months before.

The surreal time-lags, which were later to get the impatient Raffles into hot water, applied not only to official despatches, to news of changes in Company policy and of defeats and victories in the war against Napoleon. Personal letters, bringing news of marriages, births and deaths, of safe arrivals of loved ones or of tragedies at sea, were all subject to displacement in time. All stories were back-stories, all responses retrospective. Out East, one lived in the present, waiting for the past to catch up. The resulting psychological dislocation contributed to the often irrational behaviours of the servants of early Empire.

India House was the hub of that Empire, in prickly partnership with Parliament. The Company had its own army for defending and securing its settlements in India and around the fringes of the East Indies – 'the Eastward' – today's Indonesia and Malaysia. The Company appointed its own surgeons, chaplains, police and law officers in its settlements. The Company had its own civil service, abroad as at home. The Company both chartered and built its own fleet of East Indiamen, flying in Eastern seas the Company flag – red and white lateral stripes with the Union Jack in the upper corner nearest the flagstaff. The ships' officers wore the Company uniform – blue coat with black velvet collar and cuffs, buff waistcoat and breeches, a black stock and a cocked hat.

The East Indiamen, most of them over one thousand tons, anchored for loading and unloading along the length of the Thames from Blackwall Reach to the Pool of London. They picked up passengers at Gravesend or at the deep-sea ports of Portsmouth, Falmouth and Plymouth on the south coast. The captain of an East Indiaman bought his ship from the owner, the 'ship's husband', and was poorly paid by the Company. He made his money by selling on the surplus of food allowed for the voyage, by charging heavily for passengers, sometimes by smuggling. Serious money came from private trading. A large tonnage was allowed to a ship's commander who, if he was shrewd, could make enough by two or three 'double voyages' to retire in comfort – if, that is, he did not get sick and die, and if he and his vessel escaped shipwreck.

Raffles, in his ten years at India House, transcribed millions of words, and retained throughout his life his practised, clear, flowing handwriting and a facility for composing lengthy 'narratives'. His was the time of long everything – long journeys, long speeches, long dinners, long sermons, long poems, long scholarly papers, long book reviews, long personal letters, long reports – and long attention spans. Only death moved swiftly. Whether in Britain or out East, you could dine with a friend one day, and hear of his death from some sudden fever or infection the following afternoon.

Excess of verbiage was matched by excess of privilege. Admirals, generals, and senior administrators were rewarded with titles, treasure and trinkets, and vaunted them. There was a culture of immodesty and a bonus culture of extravagant ritual gifts – subscriptions raised for those moving on or retiring; douceurs in foreign negotiations and trade agreements; cuts, bribes and commissions.

Society was intensely relaxed about people getting filthy rich out East – 'shaking the pagoda tree' as the phrase was – unless they went too far, like Warren Hastings, the first Governor-General in Bengal who, after a trial lasting seven years, was cleared of peculation, bribery, injustice, oppression, cruelty, tyranny and murder in 1795, the year in which Raffles entered India House. Warren Hastings came up against a parallel culture personified by nonconformists, industrialists and 'new men' – a culture of good governance, Enlightenment values, evangelicalism, radicalism – with a groundswell demand for public morality and social reform, plus a semi-lunatic fringe of visionary millenarianism. Most people picked and mixed, Raffles among them. He had Enlightenment values and liberal principles. He also liked to move in the great world and Establishment circles. He liked honours. He was not greedy for money. He wanted fame, and he wanted to do good.

Raffles caught a whiff of the world beyond Walworth at India House, from the documents he copied and the topics and personalities he heard discussed. He was continuing his education on his own in 'stolen moments' before he left for India House in the mornings and after he came home to East Street in the evenings – about three miles' walk each way. 'I contrived to make myself master of the French language, and to prosecute enquiries into some of the branches of literature and science... I shall never forget the mortification I felt when the penury of my family once induced my mother to complain of my extravagance in burning a candle in my room.'

The overworked boy became unwell, was given two weeks off work and, according to his second wife Sophia in her *Memoir*, used the time not to rest but to walk all the way to Wales and back, covering thirty miles a day, whether alone or with a friend we do not know. He 'returned to his desk with restored health.' The story has an apocryphal air. But Raffles' energy and resilience were always extraordinary.

Raffles made a close friend among his fellow clerks in William Brown Ramsay. In July 1800, the month of Raffles' nineteenth birthday, both young men were promoted to the status of Junior Clerk, on £70 a year. What was happening in the Raffles family around that time is a mystery. *The Times*, on 10 May 1800, carried under the heading 'Leasehold Houses' an advertisement for 'A Genteel, substantial Dwelling House, pleasantly situate, No 10 Camden-Street...let to Capt Raffles, tenant at will, at a net rent of £25 per ann., held for 63 years, at a low ground rent.' There is no Captain Raffles on record other than Raffles' father. It sounds as if he were the sitting tenant. Normally, one would assume that the whole family had moved to Camden Street. But knowing how Captain Raffles' life ended, and that Mrs Raffles was frequently 'distressed' over money, it is likely that he had separated from his wife and children. His problem was probably gambling. His son would never attend a race-meeting.

Young Ramsay, Tom Raffles' new best friend, was the son of the Secretary of the Company, also William. He was already working for his father in the Secretary's Department, where Raffles now joined him. The Secretary's House had its own street entrance within the precincts of India House, making it easy for William Brown Ramsay to take Tom Raffles round to meet his parents.

The position of Secretary was central to the Company's operations. All correspondence with the Board of Control passed through the Secretary's Department, as did all the papers connected with the proceedings of the Court of Directors and the Committee of Correspondence. Listening to Mr Ramsay, Raffles learned about the Company's operations and the fortunes lost and won on the other side of the world.

The Ramsay household showed Raffles a way of life and a set of assumptions with more latitude and wider horizons than could be discerned from East Street. His social and imaginative ranges were enlarged. One can pull oneself up by one's own bootstraps only so far. In the life of every obscure person who becomes successful there are one or two mentors or patrons who see a potential, and have the means and the will to activate it. The first of these, for Raffles, was Mr Ramsay, and the opportunity came in 1804.

The Company had three 'Presidencies' in mainland India – Madras, Bombay and Bengal. Of these Bengal, centred on Calcutta (Fort William), was the senior. The Governor-General of India, in 1805 Richard Wellesley, was the Company's representative. The 'Governor-General in Council', whence all communications and directives issued, called the shots.

The Company possessed two settlements on the Strait of Malacca in the eastern Archipelago, on the coast of the Malayan peninsula – Malacca itself, and, 250 miles southwards the island of Penang. On behalf of the East India Company, Captain Francis Light had leased possession of the island from the Sultan of Kedah on the mainland in 1786 and gave it the official name of Prince of Wales Island; he called the settlement Georgetown, after the reigning monarch. The fort at Penang was Fort Cornwallis, after the Governor-General of the time. In 1800 the Company bought a slice of the mainland. This outpost was named Province Wellesley, after the Governor-General. Never did such modest and unprofitable territory sink under such a weight of noble names.

The value of Penang was that it gave the Company a trading post and a harbour towards the south of the Strait of Malacca, a pirate-infested stretch of water on the all-important trade route to China. The British Government, in the face of Dutch and French aggression, wished to develop Penang as a naval dockyard, and the Company agreed to upgrade its establishment and defences; Penang was to become a fourth Presidency, on a par with Bombay and Madras, with its own Governor and Council. This meant that a full establishment of Company civil servants must be sent out to supplement the handful already there.

There were scores of bright young men in India House, though not all of them would have wanted to leave home for the unpredictable East. Tom Raffles did. Mr Ramsay recommended him, writing to Sir Harry Inglis, an elderly and influential Director and former Chairman of the Company, that the loss of this young man in his Department would be like 'the loss of a limb' to him, yet he felt bound to recommend him on account of his 'superior talents and amiable private character.' In March 1805 Raffles was appointed Assistant Secretary for Penang, at the massively improved salary of £1,500 a year.

This spectacular advancement, like his closeness to the Ramsays, did not make him popular. A boy called Robert Ibbetson, in line for a cadetship at Penang, remembered waiting for his father in a room in India House where there was a lighted fire at which clerks took turns to warm themselves. There were two other clerks beside himself in the room. 'One of these was standing by the fire, when the other came and, with a kick, sent him away. The one who was removed from the fire in so undignified a manner was Mr Raffles who became the celebrated Sir Stamford Raffles.'

Captain Thomas Williamson, retired from twenty years in the army in Bengal, wrote for the East India Company a handbook for their young men going out East – *The East India Vade-Mecum*. His other main work was *Wild Sports of the East*. In his *Vade-Mecum* Captain Williamson addressed the question of making settled relationships with indigenous women.

He was for it, with some caveats. 'The attachment of many European gentlemen to their native mistresses is not to be described! An infatuation, beyond all comparison, often prevails.' Most kept women were Muslim, often with Portuguese blood. They expected an allowance, with clothes and service provided. He did not advise Company servants marrying a local mistress. The Court of Directors would not approve. An Indian or Eurasian wife would not be invited to public occasions. There was no objection to common-law wives, living with the children in a different house. This arrangement was usual among even the most senior civil servants and military officers.

It was an arrangement that Raffles himself was not going to make. His appointment as Assistant Secretary of Prince of Wales Island was announced on 8 March 1805. On 14 March, he got married. He was twenty-three. His bride was Olivia Mariamne Fancourt, *née* Devenish. She was thirty-three, tall, dark, good-looking, high-spirited – and he loved her.

They were married in London in St George's Church, Bloomsbury. Their witnesses were Richard Tayler, a lawyer of Gray's Inn who was to look after Raffles' affairs when he was abroad; his uncle Charles Hamond; and two women, Maria Walthen and Mariamne Etherington. The coincidence of the unusual name 'Mariamne' suggests that this last was a relative of Olivia Mariamne's.

⌇

Raffles chose to marry a widow ten years older than himself, and there has been much speculation about Olivia's life before she knew him.

The inscription on her memorial in Java, which Raffles erected, says that she was 'Born 1771 in India'. There was a family belief that she was born in Madras and then sent back to Ireland, and that her mother, who was not married to her father, was Circassian. That would account for her un-British good looks.

To be Circassian is to be from the Northwest Caucasus, but it meant more than that in Olivia's time. The phrase 'Circassian beauty' was a cliché for exotic female desirability. Byron in *Don Juan* wrote of a Circassian slave girl whose loveliness raised the bidding at auction until none but the Sultan could afford her. In the early 1800s cosmetics, lotions and hair-dyes were advertised in the most extravagant terms as containing essences used by Circassian women, the most beautiful women in the world. An opera called *The Circassian Bride* opened at Drury Lane in February 1809. The very word 'Circassian' had erotic overtones.

Raffles' Circassian bride already had a child. No one would ever have known, had not the novelist Charlotte Louisa Hawkins-Dempster, in the first chapter of her memoir *The Manners of My Time* (1920), revealed that her grandmother, the heiress of John Hamilton Dempster of Skibo, was 'his illegitimate daughter, Harriet Milton'; and that Harriet's mother was Olivia Mariamne Devenish of Co Roscommon, 'partly Irish and partly Circassian, and whose beauty finally secured for her, in 1803 [*sic*], a union with Mr Stamford Raffles.'

'Milton' was the surname the Dempsters gave to Olivia's daughter. The rest of the paragraph in which this bombshell was embedded is so riddled with inaccuracies about Olivia and Raffles as to be verbal cobweb; what Mrs Hawkins-Dempster thought she knew had been passed down from generations of family and servants, like Chinese whispers. But she surely knew who her own grandmother and great-grandmother were.

The father of Olivia's daughter, Captain John Hamilton Demp-ster, known as Jack, was the illegitimate younger half-brother of prosperous George Dempster MP, Laird of Dunnichen in Scot-land, and a Director of the East India Company. Captain Jack, aged thirty-five, may have met and bedded the teenaged Olivia Devenish when his ship the *Rose* was detained by Customs in Cork for several months in 1785. Their daughter Harriet, according to the tablet to her memory in Ashburton Church in Devon, was twenty-five when she died in 1810. (Her date of birth was not recorded, but she would have been born in 1786.) Before the birth, in October 1785, Captain Jack had married Jean Fergusson, old George Dempster's god-daughter. Captain Jack was grounded, and Olivia put to one side.

Captain Jack and his wife Jean had a son in 1786, idolised by George Dempster, who added to his properties Skibo, a Highland castle with 18,000 acres, hoping that Captain Jack would settle there with his family. But Jack made a further voyage with the *Rose*, to Madras and Calcutta, in 1792. Olivia Devenish, now twenty-one, sailed with him. In February 1793 they reached Madras, where three months later Olivia was married, to Joseph Cassivelaun Fan-court, Assistant Surgeon in the Company's service.

This is the most likely scenario. However, it has been posited that Olivia and Captain Jack met and had their affair on this 1792 voyage, *after* his marriage. The *Rose* in 1792 called in at the Irish port of Youghal, and Olivia could have joined the ship there. If this version is right, Olivia's Harriet was born shortly before she married Dr Fancourt; and Harriet's age as given on her memorial in Ashburton Church has to be wrong. But who knows – and it doesn't really matter. The swiftness with which Olivia married was normal. Young women risked the voyage out to find husbands among the British bachelors and widowers rattling around in the settlements. These gentlemen, unless they had come to an understanding with a local woman in ways described by Captain Williamson, were equally keen, and there was no point delaying. Everyone understood what the mutual needs and expectations were. Olivia needed to be married. Let's hope she liked Joseph Fancourt.

Olivia's daughter Harriet was not disowned by her father, even though she did not bear his name. According to Mrs Hawkins-Dempster, she was educated in Scotland. Old George Dempster certainly knew her when she was in her teens, finding her 'a virtuous girl with a tender and feeling heart and no small share of good sense.'

Captain Jack's wife died, and he shot off to London to secure a new command – and to see Olivia Fancourt, back in England without her husband after five years' marriage. She was living in lodgings in Golden Square. We know this because in December 1798 she had her servant Mary Goring arrested and sent to trial at the Old Bailey on a charge of stealing 'four muslin neck handkerchiefs, value 3s (shillings), two muslin pocket handkerchiefs, value 12d (pence), and a wooden pen case, value 4d, the property of Jacob Cassivilaun [*sic*] Fancourt Esq.' (A married woman's property belonged legally to her husband.) A petticoat and a pillow-case came into the story. After a query about whether Mrs Fancourt's 'black [i.e.Indian] servant' might have given Mary Goring the articles to wash, and discussion of Mrs Fancourt's dirty linen, the prisoner called in her defence two gentlemen in whose service she had been previously. They gave her 'an excellent character' and the jury brought in a verdict of Not Guilty.

The only conclusions that can be drawn are that Olivia was not wholly indigent, since she kept two servants and Golden Square was a good if bohemian address; and that she had a strong personality, and was not shy.

On 7 January 1800 Captain Jack Dempster, commanding the *Earl Talbot*, sailed for Bombay, taking his and Olivia's daughter Harriet with him. While they were at sea, Olivia's husband Joseph Fancourt died in India. In August, Captain Jack took the *Earl Talbot* on towards China, leaving Harriet in Bombay with his friend Philip

Dundas, Master Attendant (harbour master). Dundas's wife Charlotta sailed with Captain Jack, intending to return to England via the China route. They were caught by a typhoon in the South China Sea, the *Earl Talbot* was broken up on rocks, and all on board were lost.

Before she knew of her father's death Harriet, aged sixteen, married in Bombay William John Soper, Commissioner of Customs at the port of Surat, a friend of Philip Dundas, and twenty-two years older than she. In the same year Captain Jack Dempster's legitimate heir died, and childless George Dempster made over the property at Skibo to Harriet. So she and her new husband left India, and he changed his name to Soper-Dempster. They had a son and four daughters within six years and lived at Skibo Castle.

Olivia's daughter would seem to have fallen on her feet, but Olivia was written out. Her name does not appear in the genealogical reference books, which devised ingenious ways of accounting for Harriet's origins.

In the course of the year 1800 Olivia Fancourt, rising thirty, lost her lover and her husband, and her daughter got married.

She had a new friend in Thomas Moore, the Irish poet. 'Melodious Moore' sang most beguilingly the settings of his poems to his own piano accompaniment. Moore's main patron was the fellow-Irishman, soldier and statesman Lord Moira, whose own patron was the Prince of Wales, to whom Moore in 1800 dedicated *Anacreon*, the volume of verses which made his name. Moore reported to his mother in June 1802 that he had attended with Mrs Fancourt a fancy-dress 'Masquerade' for which tickets cost '*fifteen* guineas each'. 'Mrs Fancourt, as Wowski, was the best dressed and supported character I ever saw. I accompanied her as Trudge.' (Wowski and Trudge are servant characters in a popular comic opera, *Inkle and Yarico*, set in the West Indies.) There could have been several Mrs Fancourts running round London, but Moore's party-partner does sound very like Olivia.

Lord Minto, when Governor-General of Bengal, meeting Olivia Raffles for the first time in 1811, wrote to his wife: 'Mrs Raffles is the great lady, with dark eyes, lively manner, accomplished and clever. She had a former husband in India; and I have heard, but am not sure of the fact that she was one of the beauties to whom Anacreontic Moore addressed many of his amatory elegies.' Olivia liked to suggest that she was the 'Nona' of a birthday poem by Moore published in 1801, even though Nona was a 'lovely mortal child' and Olivia a mature woman. Moore was eight years younger than Olivia, ambitious, gifted, self-made and self-making; small and vital. Tom Raffles, ten years younger than she, had similar attributes, and others more substantial.

Raffles either met Moore through Olivia, or vice versa. As a Company widow she had the right to apply to the East India Company for support from their Compassionate Fund. Raffles, in the Secretary's Office, could have been instrumental in processing the lump sum of twenty-five guineas and pension of one shilling and eightpence a day which she was awarded in 1804. But however the relationship between them began, it led within less than a year to their marriage.

Before the new couple left for the East, six weeks after their wedding, Raffles arranged for some part of his salary to be paid to his mother. His father was out of the picture. In the letter to Cousin Thomas of 14 October 1819, Raffles wrote that when he was at India House the friends who 'widened my prospects in life' – he meant the Ramsays – were 'entirely unknown to my family, at this time suffering in obscurity and distress. My earnings went to their relief, but it was insufficient. Long-standing debts, and a want of the means to prevent still further involvement, caused me many a bitter moment.'

The outcome was that in July 1805, shortly after Raffles' marriage and departure for the East, Captain Benjamin Raffles petitioned the Corporation of Trinity House for 'alms and support', leading to his admission to their almshouse for 'decayed master mariners and pilots and their widows' near St Nicholas's Church in Deptford. There was a printed form to be filled in by the petitioner (Captain Raffles' handwriting in italics):

> That your Petitioner *Benj.ⁿ Raffles* was bred to the Sea, and
> served there as a *Seaman & Commander of several Vessels for
> upwards of Forty years. The last Ship of which he was Commander
> was the Lord Rodney. has a wife & 4 Child.ⁿ all females of the age of
> 20 years or under.*
>
> That your Petitioner is not now able to support *him* self *&
> Family* without the Charity of this CORPORATION, having no
> Pension or Relief from any other Public Charity or Company,
> except [blank]
>
> Your Petitioner therefore most humbly prays that *He* may
> be admitted a Pensioner of this CORPORATION, at the usual
> Allowance.

It could be supposed that Mrs Raffles, Harriet, Maryanne, Leonora and Ann were also going into the almshouse, were it not for the singular '*He*' in the last paragraph.

So Raffles' father was going to be looked after and Raffles, with his increased salary, must now support his mother and sisters.

There was contact between Olivia and her daughter. Before Olivia and Raffles left England, the two women were together in London to have their portraits painted in miniature by Nathaniel Plimer of New Bond Street and set in pearl-bordered frames. Olivia and Harriet are very alike. The dark hair of both is fashionably short and curled round the face, and both are wearing low-cut white dresses with short puff sleeves.

There would be malicious gossip about Raffles' marriage, but he thought his decision needed no explanation. 'When I was about to quit all other ties and affections,' he wrote in the letter of 14 October 1819, 'it was natural that I should secure one bosom friend, one companion on my journey who would soothe the adverse blasts of misfortune and gladden the sunshine of prosperity.' He actually had two companions on his journey, for he and Olivia were taking with them to Penang his third sister Maryanne, the pretty one, aged sixteen.

Olivia and Raffles knew each others' sad secrets. She had made the long voyage before, she had lived in India. There was a lot she could teach Raffles. He, who had never since his birth at sea been abroad, and never further from London than Wales, was sailing in April 1805, with his hopes and his high ambitions, into the blue.

Chapter 2

Great Expectations

Penang 1805–1807

It cost money to go out to East India. Raffles borrowed around £2,000 from the Company's agents and other sources, and paid it back over the next four years. He had to pay the captain of the *Ganges* £150 for himself and Olivia, and £110 for Maryanne, and provide clothes for them both. Fortunately for them, female fashion was well suited to the tropics, where they were going to be living in an equatorial rain-forest climate with temperatures between 29C and 35C and extremely high humidity. Modern young women were wearing light muslin dresses gathered under the bosom in the Empire style, which the Calcutta lawyer William Hickey found 'unbecoming and preposterous', calling it the 'no-waist system', making every girl look as if she were pregnant. But it was simple, practical and pretty.

As for Raffles' own kit, Captain Williamson's *East India Vade-Mecum* recommended for young men travelling East in the Company's service an 'out-fit' of four dozen calico shirts, undershirts which would double as nightshirts, pantaloons, long drawers and 'a substantial great-coat' for wearing on shipboard; three dozen pairs of cotton stockings, four dozen neck-handkerchiefs, two dozen white linen waistcoats. Passengers who were still growing should take clothes a size too big, or they would have grown out of them by the time the ship reached its destination. This would no longer apply to Raffles, in his twenties. The average height of an Englishman was about five feet six inches. Since he was reckoned to be a small man, he was probably no more than five feet four inches tall, and slight in proportion.

Passengers provided their own bed, bedding and mattress, washbasin, ewer and chamber-pot; and their own cutlery. Any furniture for the cabin – a desk, a table, chairs, a bookshelf – you also provided yourself, to be utilised on arrival in a new home more than five thousand nautical miles away. Captain Williamson advised packing clothes and books in brass-clamped wooden boxes, and had a packing-tip useful to travellers at any time, recommending making up 'sets' – in this case of a shirt, undershirt, stockings and neck-handkerchiefs – and rolling up each set tightly in a towel.

The *Ganges* sailed with a fleet, for no East Indiaman risked sailing alone, and the Raffles family joined the ship at Plymouth. The voyage to India could take four months, or it could take ten. On this occasion it took under six, including the final leg from Madras to Penang. During the voyage, the heaving, lurching vessel was the whole world – a wooden world, with constant risk of fire. Smoking was not allowed except on the forecastle. No candles to be lit for reading in bed, and no candles at all after ten p.m. Fresh water, in barrels stacked between the gun emplacements on deck, became unfit to drink after a while, so passengers were advised to bring crates of beer and wine.

The decks were washed twice a week, but still the ship stank. There was no sanitation other than tipping matter overboard. Infections on board spread fast, and two young writers (clerks) died on the *Ganges* on this voyage. To add to the noise and smells, there were live chickens, ducks and turkeys in coops, and sheep, goats, pigs, rabbits and cows living on hay on the poop deck, for slaughtering at sea.

The passenger cabins were temporary constructions, divided by means of thin wood bulwarks or hanging canvas partitions.

Not much privacy there. The best were fitted along the sides of the 'great cabin' in the extreme aft, with great square windows letting in the light. Here a rich man, eating his own provisions and drinking his own wine, could make himself really comfortable. The Raffles trio had no luxuries, though another family party on board doubtless did: among the twenty-six Company officials on board, some with wives, was the new Lieutenant-Governor of Prince of Wales Island, as the Presidency at Penang was officially called. He was the same Philip Dundas with whom Olivia's daughter Harriet had stayed when she went with her father to Madras. Since he and Captain Jack Dempster had been good friends, Dundas knew who Olivia Raffles was. So did the commander of the *Ganges*, Captain Thomas Harrington, who had been fourth officer on the *Rose* when Olivia sailed for Madras with Dempster in 1792.

Dundas was a scion of a powerful Scots family long associated with British Government and the East India Company. He was the nephew of Henry Dundas – from 1802 the first Viscount Melville – a former Lord Advocate of Scotland and Home Secretary of England, First Lord of the Admiralty, and confidential advisor to the young Prime Minister, William Pitt. Henry Dundas had been active in establishing the Board of Control, was one of its first members, and later its President. Philip Dundas, impeccably well-connected, had made serious money for himself in Bombay as Master Attendant, always a coveted job, responsible for receiving port dues and customs duties and overseeing the harbour and its wharves. Allowances, private arrangements and levies raised a Master Attendant's income considerably. The Company salaries were moderate, and corruption, not seen as corruption but as necessary supplements and the perquisites of office, made up the lack.

Dundas was travelling to Penang with his new second wife, daughter of another Scots grandee, and his wife's sister. The meeting between Olivia Raffles and Philip Dundas, if it had undertones of embarrassment, was carried off by them both. Since Dundas must have approved the appointment of Raffles as his Assistant Secretary,

Olivia's history cannot have disturbed him. Raffles always got on well with Dundas, but trouble came from Dundas's wife and sister-in-law. They decided that raffish Mrs Raffles was not someone whom they wanted to know and ostracised her accordingly – very awkward, in the enforced intimacy of the ship. Raffles kept his head down, occupying himself during the voyage by learning Malay.

Our informant for the Dundas ladies' snootiness is another Company passenger to Penang on the *Ganges*, sixteen-year-old Robert Ibbetson. He had picked up a different reason for Olivia being ostracised. He spread a story that William Ramsay, the Secretary of the Company, had a relationship with her, and that Raffles was given his advantageous appointment in exchange for taking her off his hands.

This canard may have been circulating in the grimier corridors of India House at the time of Raffles' promotion and marriage. It first surfaced publicly in 1816, after the deaths of both Olivia Raffles and Mr Ramsay, when Raffles was in England on leave. The supplement to Henry Colburn's *A Biographical Dictionary of the Living Authors of Great Britain and Ireland* alleged that Raffles went to India 'through the interest of Mr Ramsay, secretary to the company; and in consequence of his marrying a lady connected with that gentleman.'

Ibbetson never had anything good to say about Raffles. He lived to be ninety-one, the last survivor of the cohort which sailed to Penang in 1805, and dined out on Raffles anecdotes. If his assertion were true, Raffles would hardly have remained the closest of friends with William Ramsay's son William Brown Ramsay, as he did. Nor would he have referred to Mr Ramsay, in a letter to William B., as 'more to me than a parent'; nor would he have expressed 'the grateful sense I do and ever shall entertain of his friendship and protection – I look upon him as I have often told you, as a father.'

Raffles happened not to see Colburn's *Biographical Dictionary* until 1819, after he remarried. The discovery provoked the long autobiographical letter of 14 October 1819 to his cousin the Rev. Thomas Raffles. He insisted that Olivia was 'in no way connected with Mr Ramsay, they never saw each other, neither could my advancement in life possibly be accelerated by that marriage – it gave me no connections, no wealth, but on the contrary a load of debt, which I had to clear off.' It increased his difficulties, and thus increased his energies; 'it gave me domestic enjoyment and thus contributed to my happiness, but in no way can my advancement in life be accounted owing to that connection.'

He is not gallant in this letter about 'that marriage', but then his devoted second wife, Sophia, encouraged no sentiment about Olivia. She probably thought that Olivia had just been trouble. When in widowhood she came to compile her *Memoir of the Life and Services of Sir Stamford Raffles* she made no reference to her predecessor. The book reads as if she were the one and only wife that Raffles had ever had. On the sole occasion when Sophia absolutely had to refer to Olivia in order to make sense of the text, she did so in a brief, inaccurate footnote. And so for a second time, Olivia was written out of her own history.

For any British coastal settlement in India and the East Indies, all commercial opportunity and all human interest came by sea. Officers on the ramparts of the fort, merchants on the quays, Government aides on long first-floor balconies, the sentry on the Hill, all raked the distant horizon through their telescopes. A Hill always had a capital H, in the East. A Hill meant not only reconnaissance, but a desired place to live, with fresher air, fewer mosquitoes, escape from the miasma of foetid streets and waterways.

The dark specks on the horizon could be the predatory Dutch or, during the long war, the hostile French, who might, this time, pass slowly across the line of sight and disappear. An incoming fleet from home, sailing round the perilous Cape of Good Hope and carried on by the southern monsoon winds, brought in European household goods, wine, crates and bales of commodities for buying and selling, boxes of official documents, precious letters from home, new books and months-old newspapers and journals, news of victories and defeats in the war with the French, gossip from ports of call, old friends, young ladies.

Then, the bay was lovely with the towering sailing ships riding at anchor and small boats ferrying goods and people to the shore, and the settlement alive with excitement and bustle, dealing and partying. At other times of year there were only smaller vessels coming and going in the bay – country traders, Chinese junks and native prows with matting sails. The settlement relapsed into coastal trade, bureaucracy and backbiting, with the knowledge that if you felt bad this evening, you could be dead by tomorrow. Malaria, typhoid, cholera, dysentery. Depression, paranoia, despair.

Raffles, Olivia and Maryanne reached Penang on 25 September 1805. A hundred years later Sir Frank Swettenham, a colonial administrator for over thirty years, recorded how a passenger was still struck, as his ship rounded the northern tip of the island, by 'the extraordinary beauty of the scene to which he is introduced with almost startling suddenness.' The prospect was of steep, deep-green forested hills rising almost from the water's edge to a peak 2,500 feet high – Mount Ophir – and the coast of the mainland, Province Wellesley, a few miles away. On the sandy bays and rocky promontories of the island fishing nets were laid out to dry, and fishing-stakes stood in the shallow water. Drawing nearer, the lighthouse and the town on the shore came into focus. As the ship approached, it seemed to be running right up into Beach Street, the main street of Georgetown.

Swettenham did not mention the long, low-walled Fort Cornwallis on the north-east tip of the island, at an angle to the open sea. Captain Francis Light's Fort had been just a wooden stockade. The year before he died he rebuilt it in plastered brick, with two skins of wall and a moat. Ten years on, when Raffles arrived, it was in disrepair. Bengal never allocated enough money to make it good. It was never going to be effective for defence in spite of the cannon on its broad ramparts.

Francis Light had been dead for a decade. He left a street named after himself and as his main heir his unofficial widow, Martina Rozells, with whom he had five children, and 'who has co-habited with me since the year 1772' as he stated in his Will. She was his *nonya* – Malay for 'lady', the familiar term for the female companions of Europeans.

John Crawfurd, who came to Penang in 1809 as Assistant Surgeon in the hospital, and would have known Martina, said she was 'a mestizo Portuguese of Siam'. Captain Light left her his land and houses, his plantations, pepper-gardens and animals, his bungalow in Georgetown, his furniture and plate. His property included a fine country house, Suffolk House, named after his birthplace in England. Martina and her children should rightly have inherited Suffolk House, but it was acquired from Light's executors in 1805 by William Edward Phillips. (There was some funny business here.) Phillips had been in Penang since 1800, and had at various points been both Secretary to Government and Acting Lieutenant- Governor, as he would be again. Philip Dundas, arriving in Penang, gave Phillips back his former job of Collector of Customs and Land Revenues. Eleven years older than Raffles, Phillips became jealous of him and never liked him.

Old-timers still talked about Light. He had run a country ship between India and the Malay Peninsula, he spoke colloquial Malay and mixed freely and comfortably with all ranks and all races. He believed in the strategic importance of Penang and ran the settlement as if he owned it. If Thomas Raffles were looking for an intriguing role model, though the term did not yet exist, it was Francis Light.

Extending west from Fort Cornwallis was the *padang*, or esplanade, the open space for recreation and riding customary in British Indian settlements. Captain Light's Government House, now the headquarters of Dundas's administration, had a high double-arched entrance facing the town and a long verandah at the back looking on to the ocean. Georgetown was a small and simple place, with Light's grid-pattern of streets stretching no more than half a mile inland. No one had a proper address. Advertisements for houses for sale in the *Prince of Wales Island Gazette* resorted to description, as for example: 'That house, at the top of China Street, lately occupied by W. A. Clubley Esq.' Anyone likely to buy a house would know which was Mr Clubley's. Not until 1810 was it decreed that every house must have a number, displayed 'on a painted board'.

The houses for Europeans were normally single-storey wooden bungalows with slatted shutters to the windows and façades shaded by verandahs. The better houses were described as 'well-raised', with open, arcaded first floors and perhaps two floors above. Some were 'packa' or 'pukka' built i.e. from local bricks. The word just means 'baked'. 'Pukka' was being used in British India to mean anything genuine or permanent – which was ironic, because the bricks crumbled in the heat. If roofs were tiled, it was a selling-point. Ordinarily, the bungalows were topped with *atap* (palm-leaf thatch).

Young bachelors shared rented lodgings. An advertisement in the *Gazette* offered a 'snug little cottage' furnished for four persons with '4 bedsteads, one dining table, one card table, 6 chairs, 5 cooking pots, 6 wine glasses, 6 tumblers, a set of coffee and tea things, a tureen, 5 dishes, 8 flat and 4 soup plates, with a cruet stand, a water jar and buckets.' Quoits and skittles were thrown in. The water jar and buckets were for toilet requirements, performed in a lean-to structure alongside, half-open to the air. To wash or cool yourself, you sluiced your body with water from the big jar with a dipper. Servants prepared food in a detached hut on the other side.

Raffles and Olivia were renting a Government bungalow. The object of bringing Maryanne out to East India – to find a husband – was speedily achieved. Among the new officials who sailed to Penang with them was a young man called Quintin Dick Thompson, appointed to the posts of Sub-Warehousekeeper and Deputy Paymaster. He and Maryanne reached a romantic understanding during the voyage and were married within a week of their arrival in Penang.

Before another month was out, Raffles and Olivia had acquired a new and extraordinary friend. John Leyden, poet and scholar, arrived in Penang with three servants, knowing no one and in bad health. Still cold-shouldered by the Dundas ladies in Georgetown, Olivia and Raffles welcomed a kindred spirit. With Maryanne married, Leyden joined the couple in the bungalow.

Leyden came from Teviotdale in the Scottish border country, as did Lord Minto, the Governor-General of Bengal from 1807 – but Minto came from a great house and Leyden from a shepherd's cottage. This was never to bother Leyden, whose lack of conventional respect for anyone at all could make him come across as cocky and presumptuous. His home-language was 'broad Scots' – a dialect, not just a regional accent. His voice was loud and grating, and he talked non-stop. He had studied divinity at Edinburgh University, and obtained a medical degree from St Andrew's; he collaborated with Walter Scott in collecting ballads, and had edited and contributed to Scots periodicals. He had arrived in Madras in 1803 to take up the post of Assistant Surgeon in the Company's hospital. Meanwhile the volume of verse for which he is known in his own country, *Scenes of Infancy: Descriptive of Teviotdale*, was published in Edinburgh.

Leyden had a phenomenal aptitude for languages. When laid low by his frequent illnesses, he would set himself to learn a new one: Hebrew, Arabic, Sanskrit, Persian, Hindustani – allegedly seventeen in all – with the aid of dictionaries, before he even left Scotland. His idea in coming to Penang was to master Malay while picking up more South Asian languages along the way. He could 'grasp' a new language with rapidity, even if he was unable to speak it fluently. He relied for his studies partly upon *munshis* – native speakers, employed as translators. Lord Minto thought that his facility was 'more like the ancient gift of tongues than the slow acquisitions of ordinary men.' It was not only languages that interested Leyden, but the history and cultures of the peoples who spoke them, and he collected Indian manuscripts. His behaviours and characteristics match those identified by Asperger in 1944.

Leyden's influence on Raffles was enormous. Raffles had come to grips with Malay, but had never met anyone passionately dedicated to linguistic scholarship, or to publishing his researches with an ambition to gain the highest reputation. Leyden held Government posts in order to live, but his own work was much more than a hobby. For Raffles, who had painfully little formal education, Leyden's erudition, his encyclopaedic general knowledge, and his willingness to share it – or his inability to refrain from sharing it – were overwhelmingly stimulating.

Raffles accordingly set his own sights higher. They worked together, Leyden finding Malay 'childishly easy'. The friendship was deeply personal. Raffles later wrote that Leyden was 'my dearest friend, and I may truly say that while I looked up to him with all the admiration and respect which his wonderful talents and glowing virtues were calculated to command from all who knew him, I felt towards him the most brotherly affection.'

Leyden was older than Raffles and younger than Olivia. He fell for her, and she established with him a sentimental, poetical attachment, as with Thomas Moore. Olivia and Leyden, like Moore, were both inclined to emotional extravagance, publically enacted; the intensity of intimacy was thereby diffused, both parties enjoying the display. Raffles understood his wife, and Leyden too. The imagery between the three is steadfastly fraternal. Leyden's long 'Dirge of the Departed Year: to Olivia' appeared in the *Prince of Wales Island Gazette* on 22 March 1806, after he left Penang:

> …Olivia! ah! Forgive the bard
> If sprightly tones alone are dear:
> His notes are sad, for he has heard
> The footsteps of the parting year.

The bard's notes are sad because he is missing the friends of his youth and knows he is 'foredoom'd to seek an early tomb'. He is cheered by the beautiful places he has seen:

...But chief that in this eastern isle,
Girt by the green and glistering wave,
Olivia's kind endearing smile
Seemed to recall me from the grave.
Olivia! I shall think of thee: –
And bless thy steps, departed year!
Each morn or evening spent with thee
Fancy shall mid the wilds restore
In all their charms, and they shall be
Sweet days that shall return no more.
Still mays't thou live in bliss secure,
Beneath that friend's protecting care,
And may his cherished life endure
Long, long thy holy love to share.

The last four lines, of course, are referring to her husband. After three months in Penang, Leyden sailed for Calcutta to pursue his Oriental studies. The surviving letters from Leyden to Olivia are so mannered and facetious that they do not bear much quotation. He wrote on 6 March 1806, having reached Calcutta, hoping that his 'dear quondam patient' had complied with his medical advice. He could not close his letter without telling 'my dear amiable Olivia again how much I *love* her. Don't start now at the term for I repeat it. I love you with a true brotherly affection... Therefore my dear good matronly sister let me hear often from you.'

Leyden's own indispositions, when not 'intermittent fever' i.e. malaria, affected the 'liver and bowels'. Olivia's illnesses were described by Raffles as liver trouble. Hepatitis was common among Europeans in the Indies. Both amoebic dysentery, caught from unclean food and unwashed hands, and malaria, endemic in the tropics, can also affect the liver. Raffles wrote to Leyden in May 1806: 'My dear Olivia I regret to say is far from well – a desperate attack of the liver has reduced her to a *mere* skeleton – in consequence of a fall in dancing she ruptured some of the blood vessels in or near

the liver which occasioned a violent hemorrage [*sic*].' Convalesc-
ing, she wrote poetry. The *Prince of Wales Island Gazette* became the
vehicle for her verses, and on 5 July 1806 her sixteen-quatrain poem
addressed to a departed friend – i.e. Leyden – appeared under the
title 'Forget Me Not!', and signed 'Psyche'.

There was not a lot to do in Georgetown for young Company officials and officers in their spare time. The Prince of Wales Island Club
met monthly at the Commercial Hotel on Bishop Street; Thomas
McQuoid, the Police Magistrate, who was to be a longtime friend
of Raffles, was its first President. 'The whist parties,' reported the
Gazette in October 1806, 'which have lately been formed have tended
much to dissipate the *ennui* which long since has pervaded the settlement.' The following month a subscription dance was held at the
Navy House 'numerously attended and graced by the presence of
all the youth, beauty and elegance of the settlement, enriched by
the new arrivals.'

The most lavish host in town was the rich merchant Syed Hussein,
a contender, with his son, for the throne of Acheen (Aceh), a prosperous and cosmopolitan port of 30,000 inhabitants strategically positioned on the north-west coast of Sumatra at the head of the Malacca
Strait. The actual Sultan since 1802, the insecure and not very bright
Johor Alum, had great respect for the British, which was not properly reciprocated – a bad mistake – even though he offered a base in
Acheen in exchange for military aid against his enemies.

Dundas's predecessor had shilly-shallied over supporting John
Alum, as did Dundas. Hereditary monarchy in the East Indies was
rarely simple. Monarchs had more than one wife and family, plus
children with other women; brothers contested brothers and half-
brothers, nephews contested uncles and vice versa, and blood was
shed.Yet securing a foothold in Acheen was scheduled as an inte-
gral part of a rolling programme complementing the upgrading of
Penang. The succession issue in Acheen mattered, a running sore in
which Raffles became injudiciously involved.

Meanwhile Syed Hussein, on behalf of himself and his son, ingratiated himself with the Penang Government. He gave an 'elegant entertainment' in Georgetown in October 1806 attended by Governor Dundas and his suite, and around sixty ladies and gentlemen of the settlement. Not only his 'extensive premises' on Beach Street but all the streets around were illuminated. The band from HMS *Blenheim* played appropriate airs to accompany each toast at the dinner, which was followed by fireworks, and dancing by 'young and beautiful Nautch Girls', whose style contrasted strongly – we are not told in what way – with the 'females from the Malabar coast' who performed after them. The European ladies being 'inspired' by these demonstrations, the 'sprightly dance' continued until two a.m.

Olivia loved a party, and so did Raffles. But he had no problem with *ennui* in Penang because he did not have leisure as such. He pursued his studies purposefully after Leyden left. Leyden's ambition was to equal the achievement of the polyglot prodigy Sir William Jones – a Company man, a judge of the Supreme Court in Bengal, founder of the Asiatic Society of Bengal – dead in his forties in 1794. Jones' comparative philology challenged the Eurocentric assumption of the primacy of Graeco-Roman language and civilisation, linked Sanskrit, Greek and Latin, and marked the beginning of modern Indology. If Francis Light was an exemplar of an independent adventurer, William Jones was an exemplar of an Oriental scholar.

William Jones was a university-educated intellectual. He had Persian and Arabic before he ever went East. His range and depth serves to put Raffles' achievements in context. Raffles' passion for learning was lifelong and unfeigned, and could be turned to professional advantage. He began employing *munshis*, as Leyden did, to assist him as he began to translate *Undang-undang Melaka*, the 'Malay Laws', from old manuscripts. 'Go on and prosper my dear fellow,' wrote Leyden, 'the work will not only be very desirable in a literary point of view, but will I should conceive do everything possible for your reputation at home.'

Raffles sent a memo to Governor Dundas informing him that he now felt 'competent not only to detect any error or misrepresentation made in translating or transcribing letters from the English into the Malayee' [*sic*], but, when necessary, to translate or transcribe them himself. He was looking for Company funds to pay his four assistants, the *munshis*, in his translation, a work he believed would prove most useful to Government.

Remarking that a Malay Translator to Government had not yet been appointed, he hoped that his name would be borne in mind, since he could also undertake to write 'all letters in the Malayee language that may be deemed of a secret nature in my own hand,' rendering it unnecessary for Government affairs to be 'intrusted in the hands of a native.' The matter of financial assistance was referred by Dundas to the Court of Directors in London with a strong recommendation as to Mr Raffles' application and talent; he got his money, and some fine phrases of approbation from India House. In January 1807 the *Gazette* announced the appointment of 'Mr Thomas Raffles to be Acting Malay Translator to Government.'

Raffles would not have been able, then or ever, to translate literary Malay, or High Malay, without some assistance. Swettenham, echoing Leyden, observed that to learn enough to carry on a simple conversation is 'an easy task'. This was Low Malay, or service Malay as the Dutch called it, or market Malay – a contact language, flexible and forgiving, already in use for administrative and commercial purposes throughout the Archipelago for a century, along with shreds of Portuguese, Dutch, Arabic and Chinese. (Wherever trade was, the Chinese were.) But to speak Malay well, wrote Swettenham, takes 'years of study, and constant intercourse with the most cultivated Malays of the peninsula.' High Malay idioms 'have no counterpart in European tongues,' and discourse is made subtle with riddles, parables and proverbs. But in Raffles' time in Penang, when most of the English civil servants knew at most only a few hortatory phrases, Raffles' level of comfortable fluency and competence, and his resulting ability to make friends with native speakers, was impressive.

Someone whose level of competence was more impressive was William Marsden, Irish-born and in his fifties, former Company civil servant, and the distinguished author of *The History of Sumatra*. He was living in England and devoting himself to Oriental scholarship. He wrote to Governor Dundas with some queries about the system of chronological cycles used by the Malays, and about the Malay words for chess-pieces, and other matters. Dundas knew less than nothing about any of this, and passed the letter straight over to Raffles.

Raffles had to do some research and make some enquiries among his Malay acquaintances; and as he reminded Dundas, he was particularly busy because the Secretary to Government, Henry Shepherd Pearson, was away on sick leave. As Raffles put it to Leyden, 'Pearson, heartily sick of his office, has obtained permission to proceed to Bombay at the first opportunity and remain 6 months on leave – this, of course, is to my advantage although I don't expect to derive much pecuniary benefit, as I can only be Acting Sec.' He reported to the Governor in Council the poor record-keeping he discovered, and undertook to bring everything up to date, for which he was commended.

He consulted Leyden too for help in answering Marsden's letter: 'Were you aware that the Malays ever used a Cycle, in conformity to that of the Indians and Chinese in general? On this, I made such rapid discoveries that I expected to have been enabled to send you their whole Chronology – but it was like the mountains in labour and produced little or nothing.' It was not until July 1806 that he wrote a long letter to Dundas, to be sent on, if approved, to Mr Marsden, addressing all Marsden's points and adding observations of his own. 'Should you deem the replies to Mr Marsden's queries in any way satisfactory, and worthy of communication, I hope you will, at the same time, state them as coming from a young man, who never made Oriental literature his study, and is but lately arrived in the place which furnishes the means of his observations.' This was the start of an epistolary friendship between Marsden and Raffles, and in the end the two would be friends.

Thomas Raffles, Acting Secretary to Government in Penang, was proving indispensable. (The William Clubley whose house had been up for sale was appointed his Assistant Secretary.) The minutiae of administration were not Governor Dundas' forte. Raffles' ten years in India House, and his period in the Secretary's Department, had not been lost time. He had absorbed the Company style and the Company's protocols. He knew their official jargon and their codes. He knew the conventions for denoting approval and disapproval ('unwarranted', 'unworthy'), he knew how to frame a letter, a memo, a narrative, a despatch, an Order in Council, a General Order and a Proclamation. He understood meetings, minutes and reports.

From August 1806 General Orders were being signed by 'T. Raffles, Acting Secretary to Government'. A Governor's official correspondence was conducted in the third person and signed by the Secretary of the moment. Raffles, privy to the sessions of the Governor and his three-man Council drafted, and more often composed, outgoing documents, despatches and letters. Like effective senior civil servants at any period, he armed himself with the documentation and information required at each juncture, contributed opinions and advice, and had some influence over outcomes.

The way he combined his workload with his private studies impressed a young man in the Company's military service, Lieutenant Thomas Otho Travers, who met Raffles when he was posted with his regiment to Prince of Wales Island in 1806. He was a Protestant Irishman from Cork, four years younger than Raffles. When Sophia Raffles was compiling her *Memoir*, Travers obliged her with his memories of her husband from those early days in Penang. Given the circumstances, what he wrote could not but be an encomium. Travers, soon to be one of Raffles' intimates, was always one of his most ardent supporters:

> At that time, which was soon after his arrival, he had acquired
> a perfect knowledge of the Malay language... The details
> of the Government proceedings, as far as related to local

arrangements and regulations, together with the compilation of almost every public document, devolved on Mr Raffles, who possessed great quickness and facility in conducting and arranging the forms of a new Government, as well as in drawing up and keeping the records. The public despatches were also entrusted to him; and in fact he had the entire weight and trouble attendant on the formation of a new Government. This, however, did not prevent his attending closely to improve himself in the Eastern languages; and whilst his mornings were employed in his public office, where at first he had but little assistance, his evenings were devoted to Eastern literature.

Travers, acknowledging difficulties among the 'different characters' in the Penang Government, wrote that Mr Raffles was 'respected and consulted by every member of it,' which may be a tad optimistic. He noted too how Raffles was acquiring 'a general knowledge of the history, Government, and local interests of the neighbouring states, and in this he was greatly aided in doing by conversing freely with the natives, who were constantly visiting Penang at this period, many of whom were found to be sensible, intelligent men, and greatly pleased to find a person holding Mr Raffles' situation able and anxious to converse with them in their own language.'

In parallel with the expensive upgrading of Penang went the downgrading of Malacca, down the coast. It held a strategic position towards the south of the Strait, and had been a useful stopping-off point for Company ships, and for the warehousing and exchanges of cargos. But it exploited no local products to trade from its hinterland and imported most of its food from Madras.

The wars with France determined Company policy. The British had taken Malacca over from the Dutch in 1795 as part of a campaign, endorsed by William V of Orange in exile in England, to stop South-East Asian trading bases from falling into the hands of the French after the French conquered the Netherlands. The Dutch were not expelled; when the British flag was raised alongside the Dutch one, the formulation was that Malacca had been taken into the 'custody and protection' of King George III on behalf of William of Orange. Dutch governance continued, with a British military presence and under British supervision. While restoration to the Dutch at some future time was envisaged, it was decreed that any resistance against the English, right now, would be forcibly suppressed. The arrangement did not work. The Dutch Governor, Abraham Couperus, was soon instructed to leave – after seventeen years, and with a Malay-Portuguese *nonya* and seven children who had never been out of Malacca.

Economically, Malacca stagnated. Captain William Farquhar of the Madras Engineers, the Commandant of the settlement, was not allocated money to dredge the mouth of the river, obstructed by a mud-flat at low tide. East Indiamen had to anchor inconveniently far offshore and so, increasingly, often just sailed on by. Farquhar had reported gloomily to Madras in 1799 on the shocking state of Malacca's defences and the shortage of money and manpower. The reaction of the Madras Government was to recommend to the Supreme Government in Bengal that the fortifications in Malacca should be demolished altogether, in order to render the place useless as a war port, and therefore of no interest to the French. Bengal referred this idea to the Court of Directors in London, who jumped at it, advising that Malacca's defences be 'completely destroyed and demolished', and British personnel transferred to Penang.

Because of the cumbersome nature of decision-making, nothing happened immediately. When Philip Dundas arrived in Penang as Governor in 1805 and reviewed the Malacca situation, he questioned the policy of withdrawal on the grounds that it would facilitate incursions from 'Americans and other neutral flags' and damage British trade. He wrote to Captain Farquhar, Commandant at Malacca, for his expert local opinion.

Farquhar's reply was unambiguous. Local native trade used Malacca regularly, plying round the Archipelago. The British presence was a check to the piracy that threatened all shipping in the Strait, and no French ships could pass Malacca without being spotted from the watchtower on the Hill. To destroy the Fort would just leave an opening for an opportunistic power to move in and build another. It would be more expensive to destroy the Fort and remove the materials than it would be to improve it. No one from Malacca would want to relocate to Penang; Malacca was multinational, and many Chinese, Indian and Portuguese mixed-race families had been there 'since time immemorial'. The fertile territory if properly funded could become self-supporting. As for himself, he declined Governor Dundas's invitation to join him in the new Penang.

Governor Dundas was impressed, and in March 1806 referred the matter back to the Court of Directors, sending them Farquhar's report. Meanwhile the viability of Malacca was systematically eroded by the cutting back of jobs and wages, including Farquhar's. Not for another whole year, until April 1807, did the final decision come from India House. All the fortifications and public buildings in Malacca were to be destroyed, and the building materials thus released shipped to Penang.

Penang had once had a reputation as a health-giving place, 'the Montpelier of India' as William Hickey put it. It seemed no longer to be the case. Mrs Dundas, who had been such a thorn in Olivia's scant flesh, sailed to Calcutta in an attempt to recover her health and died there a few days after she arrived. Governor Dundas himself was ill too. More work was devolving on Raffles. In March 1807 he was promoted from Acting Secretary to full Secretary to Government, as well as being Malay Translator. He did not intend to be exploited. Later he put in for, and received, permission to draw the difference in salary between Secretary and Acting Secretary for the months when Pearson was away and he was doing the Secretary's job. The sick Dundas left Prince of Wales Island on a ship of the Royal Navy on 1 April 1807, with a doctor in attendance. 'A short sea voyage' was the standard treatment for those brought low by infections, fevers and the humid heat.

Governor Dundas died on board a week later, aged forty-four. The ship turned around and brought his body back to Penang, where he was buried with full honours in the Protestant cemetery where Captain Light's tomb also was.

The announcement that Henry Shepherd Pearson by reason of seniority was appointed Acting Governor was signed by 'T.Raffles, Secretary to Government'. Since Mr Pearson was barely able for the task of governorship, Secretary Raffles had even more on his plate, one of the first tasks being to take the necessary steps towards implementing the Company's decision about the destruction of Malacca.

Travers, in Sophia Raffles' *Memoir*, recorded Raffles' sociability as well as his industry. 'Being of a cheerful lively disposition, and very fond of society, it was surprising how he was able to entertain so hospitably as he did, and yet labour as much so he was known to do...' Raffles and Olivia became more than socially acceptable. They were at the forefront of life on Prince of Wales Island. For the ritual celebration of the King's Birthday on 6 June 1807, 'an elegant dinner was given by Mr Raffles' reported the *Gazette*, followed by 'a splendid ball and supper' at Admiralty House. The following month the marriage of a Miss Oliphant was solemnised by Mr Pearson, the Acting Governor, 'in the house of Thomas Raffles Esq.' Not until October was a new Governor, Colonel Norman Macalister, appointed. He had come out to Penang at the same time as Raffles, and there was a long-running row about whether he, or Pearson, should succeed Dundas. The Court of Directors in London finally decided for Macalister, whom Raffles also backed. The disgruntled Pearson reverted to the role of Warehousekeeper and Paymaster. Penang was not a harmonious community.

The State of Massachusetts had abolished slavery back in 1783. It was not until January 1807, after twenty years' campaigning spearheaded by William Wilberforce, and eleven rejected Bills, that the

British Government under Pitt's successor, Lord Grenville, passed an Act of Parliament abolishing the British slave trade. That was not the same as abolishing slavery, which could not be achieved overnight in Britain's overseas possessions; and there were to be complex systems of compensation for slave-owners and those dependent on slave labour, especially in the sugar plantations of the West Indies. Even the banning of the trade took time to put into practice. In 1810 a British ship on the Thames was found to be carrying a cargo of padlocks, handcuffs, shackles and chains.

The Slave Trade Act was however a massive step forward, and the Penang Government was prepared to take it on to the next stage. The *Prince of Wales Island Gazette* carried an article at the beginning of December 1807 stating that no slaves were now being imported into the settlement, and orders would soon be forthcoming for 'total abolition of slavery in this island... Although the system of slavery must, in a few years, have died a natural death, we think Government entitled to praise on having accelerated its dissolution; and their equity in making compensation to the sufferers...we hope to make part of the general system.' (The sufferers to be compensated in this case were the slaves, not the slave-owners.)

The article was unsigned, but the trenchancy of its tone makes it likely that it was written by Secretary Raffles, for whom the abolition of slavery was to be a crusade. He himself was ill and exhausted. According to Sophia's *Memoir*, 'the attack was so severe, that for some time little hopes of his life were entertained.' In convalescence, having applied for a medical certificate from the Chief Surgeon – a sick-note – he was authorised to 'proceed to sea immediately.' In November 1807 he and Olivia sailed up the coast to Malacca, and to another turning point for Raffles.

Chapter 3

Rising on the Thermals

Malacca and Calcutta 1807–1810

⌘⌘⌘⌘⌘

'Far off, on the shallow sea, phantom ships hover and are gone, and on an indefinite horizon a blurred ocean blends with a blurred sky,' wrote the lone, middle-aged English traveller Isabella Bird, visiting Malacca in the 1870s. The ancient town lies on a long bay, clustering round the mouth of a winding river, deep enough at high tide for boats and ferries to come up as far as the bridge and unload cargos from the ships straight into the open ground floors of the godowns, or warehouses.

St Paul's Hill – 'the Hill' – rises from the water's edge, topped by the old Portuguese church, already roofless and in ruins well before Raffles arrived. The Portuguese were in Malacca from 1511. St Francis Xavier preached in that church in the 1540s, and was buried there. The Dutch held Malacca from 1641 until the unsuccessful condominium with the British after 1795. There were still a few hundred Dutch in the town in the early 1800s, and a Chinese and Malay majority, much intermarried, with a strong Portuguese strain in the gene pool.

In the late eighteenth century, as M.C. Ricklefs has written, 'In the midst of corruption, inefficiency and financial crisis, the first Dutch Empire was gently going to sleep.' That had certainly been true of Malacca, and it had not woken up under the British either. Because there was not a lot going on in the way of international trade, Malacca was relaxed – 'very still, hot, tropical, sleepy and dreamy' as Isabella Bird found it.

Raffles went there because Malacca was considered a place to go to recover your health, and it was picturesque. But the local mosquitoes were 'insupportable', the day-time variety inflicting an even worse torment than the nocturnal kind, according to Miss Bird. Their taste for European blood seemed to diminish over time. Lord Minto, in India, was advised to put some young fellow fresh out from England next to him at dinner, to divert the mosquitoes' attention.

Captain William Farquhar, Commandant at Malacca, who spoke fluent Malay, was a popular, respected and familiar figure. He was called 'the Rajah of Malacca' and had a Portuguese-Malay *nonya*, with whom he had six children. A young Malacca-born scholar-translator, a *munshi*, Abdullah bin Abdul Kadir, wrote that it was 'Mr Farquhar's nature to be patient and tolerant of other people's faults, and he treated both rich and poor alike… Whenever he travelled about in his carriage or on horseback the rich and the poor, and the children too, saluted him and he at once returned the compliment. He was ever generous to all the servants of Allah. Truly all these qualities I have related were as cords tying the hearts of the people to him.'

When Raffles and Olivia arrived in November 1807, the destruction of the Portuguese Fort, begun in August, was far advanced. Farquhar had been right when he said the fortifications would be less costly to repair than to demolish. They were built of ironstone, set in strong cement. Some of the walls were sixty feet high and fifteen feet thick. To break these down required explosives. Abdullah reported how when Farquhar lit the fuse 'the gunpowder exploded with a noise like thunder, and pieces of the Fort as large as elephants, and even some as large as houses, were thrown into the air and cascaded into the sea.' Apart from the walls, there were nine bastions with living space and stables underneath, four gates, and three drawbridges. All this destruction, even though it created employment, made the town uneasy, and coolies employed on the work were afraid of the ghosts and devils who lived in the stones.

Farquhar's Residence was the seventeenth-century Dutch Stadhuis, or Government House, which, like the flat-faced Dutch church, and the massive, ornamented southern gate (all still there today), he decided just could not be demolished. The Stadhuis and the church were essential for administrative and community purposes, and the gate was spared because the adjoining guardrooms were still in use. The Stadhuis and the church had been within the walls of the Fort. Now they were surrounded by rubble, freestanding at right angles to one another, flanked by the river bank, the shore, and the Hill.

Raffles was meeting William Farquhar for the first time, and Farquhar had seniority in all ways. From Kincardineshire in Scotland, he was thirty-seven years old, and had joined the Company as a cadet in Madras at seventeen. Raffles was twenty-six, with only two years experience in the East. Farquhar had already held the command of Malacca for twelve years, and had seen action at the capture of Pondicherry in 1793. Farquhar was seasoned as Raffles was not. He was intelligent, competent, confident. Talking with him, Raffles learned a lot.

Raffles would have stayed longer in Malacca, but heard that a vessel was shortly to leave Penang for England, and that the official despatches and reports required by India House had to be on board. In desperation, Governor Macalister sent word that 'we shall not be able to make up any despatches for the Court without your assistance. This is truly hard upon you, under the present circumstances of your delicate state of health, but I trust you will believe that nothing else would induce me to press so hard on you at this time. And with the exception of Mr Phillips, the rest of the board can give but little assistance in making out the general letter: none, however, so little as myself.'

There being no more suitable ship, Raffles was rushed back down the coast to Penang in a 'pleasure-boat', Olivia returning a little later.

A Presidency, such as Penang had become, had statutorily to have a Court of Justice, and in July 1808 Sir Edmond Stanley arrived to be the first Recorder. To celebrate, the rich Achinese merchant Syed Hussein gave yet another 'splendid entertainment'. He had just founded and funded a large mosque for his compatriots. A couple of years later he demonstrated his good citizenship even further, 'to evince his gratitude to the Government under which he has lived for many years', by donating 'a large sum' to liquidate its debts. It was getting progressively harder to consider supporting the friendly, needy, and equally Anglophile current ruler of Acheen.

Before the advent of Sir Edmond, the law had been administered somewhat ineffectively, since 1801, by a John Dickens. He went off to Calcutta in a huff, resenting the fact that he had not been appointed Registrar, and angry because Raffles (who had added Licenser of the Press to his duties) did not allow a farewell address from the merchants of Prince of Wales Island, and his own gracious reply, to be printed in the *Gazette*. Olivia loathed Dickens: 'He is really the most *impudent, ignorant, affected* envious ungrateful old *Jay* I ever heard of.' Added to this unpleasantness, Sir Edmond and Governor Macalister were not getting on. Raffles again came forward and, as he put it, 'voluntarily acted as Regular Clerk to the Crown' i.e. as Registrar; and 'stepping between them judiciously I am confident that I stopped a breach that might never have been healed up.' Sir Edmond expressed his gratitude for this, as also for Mr Raffles' 'cheerful disposition'.

In the letter to John Leyden in which she excoriated Dickens, Olivia told him that her sister-in-law Maryanne – 'pretty Mrs Thompson' as Leyden called her – had 'a beautiful little girl, two months old yesterday, and has been living on the Hill for the past month – did I tell you about *our* Hill?'

Both the Raffleses and the Thompsons had country retreats, *atap*

bungalows about nine kilometres out of Georgetown, not far from
Captain Light's Suffolk House in the lee of Penang Hill. The Raffles
house was at the foot of the smaller Mount Erskine, named for a
long-standing civil servant in the settlement, which they peremp-
torily renamed Mount Olivia. 'I have cleared my Hill,' Raffles wrote
in March 1809, seeking horticultural advice from his local friend
David Brown, 'and intend planting 3,000 coffee plants.'

Maryanne and her husband on Mount St Mary were close by,
and had two more babies in quick succession. A steward of Quintin
Dick Thompson's, Edward Robarts, recorded a party at Mount St
Mary: 'After dinner in rotation tea and coffee were served up and
about ten o'clock the Merry Dance led off, afterwards several songs
were sung. The Boyne Water was sung by Mrs Raffles in high stile,
the Banks of the Dee on the German flute by Captain Phillips and
sung to by Mrs Thompson, the sweetness of her voice would melt
a heart of adamant... The evening was spent in the most agreeable
and pleasant manner.'

Now the Raffleses were to have a new town house, as Olivia
told Leyden. 'Mr R. is building a pretty brick house on the beach,
which I hope will be finished in eight to ten weeks.' Before he had
left Penang for Malacca, Raffles commissioned this house on the
seaward side of a new carriage road along the north beach, outside
Georgetown. They named the house Runnymede.

As the *Prince of Wales Island Gazette* reported in January 1809:
'The North Beach will, ere long, assume a very handsome appearance, when the several elegant villas, now building, are finished.
The new buildings commence with Runnymede, the property of
Mr Raffles, and adjoining are the grounds of Mr Hobson, Mr Robinson, Mr Erskine [whose name had just been erased from a small
mountain], Captain Douglas, Mr Pearson [the former Acting Gov-
ernor], and Mr Laurence, on which houses are erected.' Runnymede was long, low and spacious, brick-built over an open, arcaded
ground floor, with louvred window-shutters and carved balconies.

In November of the same year the *Gazette* noted, under the lightly ironic heading 'The Beau Monde and the Gaieties of Penang', that Mr Robinson had 'a select party of friends to dinner at his mansion on the North Beach,' followed by 'a most elegant fete' given by Mr Clubley, who had also built on the North Beach. 'The dancing began between 8 and 9, and Mr Clubley had the honour of leading Mrs Raffles down the first dance, to the tune of "Off She Goes".' Olivia was now in her late thirties. A midshipman on a vessel anchored in Penang observed Mr Raffles coming aboard 'with a rather elderly lady, dressed rather fantastically, a good and clever creature, and one already celebrated in song – 'Rosa' [he meant Thomas Moore's 'Nona'] of a certain little bard. Ye gods! Well, anything but Rosa! How well your poetic flights thus point to a discrepancy!' The young are cruel.

William Robinson, the civil servant who gave the select dinner party, became Raffles' most 'intimate friend'. When he finally left Penang, he told Leyden that William Robinson was 'the only friend I leave behind... if ever we establish our Eastern Empire he must not be left out – he possesses every local qualification with the best heart and not the worst head in the world.'

This is eavesdropping on the dream of an 'Eastern Empire' which Raffles and Leyden were privately projecting. There was a twitch of the fantasist in both of them. Raffles was to pursue the vision, but Penang was not the right place for a visionary. In spite of the parties and the pretty new houses, the Presidency of Prince of Wales Island was failing in its purpose. Trade was good and fortunes were being made by private traders. But the point of the expansion was to develop the island as a naval arsenal and a regional centre of ship-building, and this was not happening. Skilled labour, and even the timber for ship-building, had not materialised, whether by bad man-agement or a miscalculation of local resources. In 1810, the failure was faced up to, and the ship-building programme transferred to Trincomalee on the east coast of Ceylon.

Pepper prices were falling. There was a bad fire in Georgetown in March 1808, when much of the wooden, *atap*-roofed housing stock was lost. Much property in the town was up for sale, and much sick leave was taken, including by William Clubley, Assistant Secretary to Government and therefore to Secretary Raffles. Penang, with its now pointlessly enlarged establishment, was costing the Company more than it was bringing in. Raffles was among the first to realise that there was not much future for Penang, nor for anyone who got stuck there.

Apart from the satisfaction gained from being indispensable, there was little pleasure or profit in his situation, and Olivia complained to Leyden: 'He has taken the enormous task of Registrar and without *fee* or present reward – Secretary without assistant, or any one who can afford him the least possible assistance – the consequence begins to shew itself very soon – he is ill and quite worn – and I dread another long lingering fit of illness such as he had last, which was brought on by intense labour of mind and body.'

He did become ill again, with jaundice, and again sought permission to take a short sea voyage. He and Olivia went straight back to Malacca, for two and a half months this time, staying with Farquhar in an apartment on the upper floor of Government House. Isabella Bird lodged there all alone in 1879, and left a description of great arched corridors leading to large dim rooms with floors of Dutch red tiles, blue-washed walls, whitewashed rafters, and 'ancient beds of portentous height'. There had been more animation when Raffles stayed there, but nothing much else would have changed.

Government House was built into the lower slopes of the Hill. It was several storeys high on the facade facing the town, but the back was single-storey, with open tiled arcades extending into a garden where Farquhar kept a menagerie of native birds in aviaries and wild animals in cages. According to the *munshi* Abdullah, Farquhar had a leopard, a wild cat, a wild dog, a porcupine, a cassowary, various kinds of monkeys, and a tiger, which he shot dead after it mauled a Chinese carpenter repairing his cage. The tiger was then skinned and stuffed.

Farquhar was interested in all branches of natural history. Many

Malayan flora and fauna were unknown in the West, let alone properly described and classified. Farquhar sent specimens of birds and animals to the Asiatic Society in Calcutta, and plants to the Calcutta Botanic Garden. He had also, ever since his arrival in Malacca, been building up a collection of coloured natural-history drawings commissioned from local Chinese artists. These were exquisite in execution, if not always scientifically satisfactory.

John Leyden had opened Raffles' eyes to the intrinsic interest of the world of linguistic and cultural scholarship and to the added value that published research might lend to a career. Now William Farquhar opened Raffles' eyes to the fascination of zoology and botany – and to a new field for his pursuit of excellence, and of excelling. Natural history was to become his main preoccupation, and collecting a part of his claim to fame. He learned from Farquhar, as he had learned from Leyden.

Raffles and Farquhar also mulled over again the mistake of dismantling the Fort at Malacca, and the good reasons for retaining both the settlement and its defences.

Raffles and Olivia arrived back in Penang on 29 October 1808, and Raffles produced a long report on Malacca only two days later. It must have been written or at least drafted in Malacca, fuelled by discussion with Farquhar. He passed his report to Governor Macalister to be sent on to the Board of Control and the Court of Directors in London.

It was another strong appeal, paralleling Farquhar's previous memo, for the retention of a garrison in Malacca as complementary to Penang. He did not refer in his report to Farquhar's contribution, or acknowledge Farquhar as the main source of the general arguments, which were much the same, though he deferred briefly to Farquhar's specialist expertise: 'It does not fall within my line to submit the actual advantages of Malacca as to its natural defences... They can be professionally pointed out by Captain Farquhar, the Engineer officer now in charge of the Government.' He recommended that Captain Farquhar be authorised to lay out 'a small sum' for the repair of some defensive works, and the erection of others.

Raffles' ideas were not always initially his own; and neither were his discoveries nor even his enthusiasms. But having adopted them, he picked them up and ran, either carrying them forward himself – as others, by temperament or circumstances, would or could not – or enabling those with the necessary qualities. In this, Raffles did what entrepreneurs and managers always do. He did not have a magpie mind, picking up bright bits and pieces. He had a mind like a magnet, drawing in what caught his imagination and taking it further.

In the case of Malacca, Farquhar's views on the Fort were known. His memo was on file in Penang, Calcutta and London, so there could be no question of Raffles' report masquerading as a new view. But with his minimal reference to Captain Farquhar, he seems to be limiting Farquhar's contribution to his engineering expertise at the expense of his informed geopolitical opinions. Raffles was also assuming the seniority of the civil branch over the military which, in the Company hierarchy, was correct, though a constant source of friction. The Secretary to Government in Penang had more clout than the Commandant of Malacca.

Governor Norman Macalister duly forwarded Raffles' report to London. It was a whole year before there was a response – which was highly favourable. 'We have derived much satisfaction from the perusal of Mr Raffles' report, and we desire that you will communicate to that gentleman that we entertain a favourable sense of the talents he has evinced upon that occasion.'

This was a high point in Raffles' standing with those in power at India House. For a short period he was their golden boy. A copy of his Malacca report was sent to the Governor-General Lord Minto in Calcutta in February 1809, with Governor Macalister's endorsement. Minto agreed that it would be 'highly inexpedient' to withdraw the garrison from Malacca. The destruction of the fortifications at Malacca was countermanded, though the damage had already been done.

Damage had also been done to the relationship between Raffles and Farquhar, which escalated into torturous hostility, to the detriment of both their reputations years later in Singapore. When Sophia Raffles published her *Memoir* of her husband in 1830, Farquhar wrote a letter to the *Asiatic Journal* protesting against many of her judgments, among them the statement that it was only when her husband's representations on Malacca were received, that the orders for the destruction of the Fort were countermanded. 'Now I happened to be in command of Malacca at the period alluded to,' wrote Farquhar, and 'the truth was' that he himself had sent a petition to Government against the destruction, 'which petition was recommended by me to the most favourable consideration of Government.' Unfortunately and unfairly, the truth also was that it was Raffles' report and not Farquhar's that had made the difference.

Submitting Raffles' Malacca report to the Court of Directors, Governor Macalister drew their attention to the 'unwearied zeal and assiduity with which he has since the formation of the establishment devoted his talents to the furtherance of the Company's interests.' ('Zeal' was the ultimate praise word, implying commitment, energy, enterprise.) 'The situation of Secretary,' continued Macalister, 'affords facilities for the person holding it of acquiring a better knowledge of your affairs here than any other officer below Council; and I can with truth say, that Mr Raffles' abilities and general conduct give him a right to my recommendation... I understand that he has submitted to his friends an application to be provisionally appointed to the first vacancy, and I shall be happy if my recommendation may weigh with the Honourable Court in his behalf.'

Since Governor Macalister on his own admission found it hard to frame a letter, the likelihood is that this one was drafted by the person to whom it referred. Raffles was looking for a transfer, and promotion. Meanwhile he took on yet another commitment (unpaid), as one of the first three Commissioners of the new Court of Requests for the recovery of small debts. He wrote to William Brown Ramsay in England that he feared his health would not permit him to carry on in this way for long. 'My constitution was always delicate; with care I have no doubt it could last as long here as in England. Without it, I am afraid they will work the willing horse to death.' And again, to William Brown Ramsay: 'A Secretary is, in general the organ, but in some places the very soul.' He felt he was neither. 'You can guess the situation. The arrogance that a temporary exaltation has given to some is scarce to be borne with, except by such a patient body as mine.' He himself was experiencing the kind of 'temporary exaltation' he diagnosed in others. His multiple offices and his 'zeal' did not endear him to all in Penang.

Change for the better came through the Governor-General in Calcutta, Lord Minto. Raffles did not know Minto, but John Leyden did. Leyden talked about his friend, and impressed upon the Governor-General the importance of Raffles' work on Malayan subjects, reinforcing the approving noises about Raffles' talents which emanated from India House. Raffles sent Leyden a paper he wrote on the 'Malayan Nation', with special reference to what he had learned from people he talked with in Malacca – local traders, and tribal people from the dense forests of the interior and from isolated Malay *kampongs*. Leyden showed the paper to Minto 'who was greatly pleased and desired me to say he should be gratified in receiving immediately from yourself any communications respecting the eastern parts of a similar nature.'

The paper was submitted to the Asiatic Society in Calcutta; and Minto praised publicly Raffles' project of translating 'the Malay Laws' in an address to the College of Fort William. Leyden sent Raffles a printed report of the address, which was drafted by Leyden himself, and Olivia replied: 'Who but you could, who but your dear self would have remembered my beloved and *every way worthy husband* in the elegant and honourable manner in which we saw his name. Ah my dear friend I shed many grateful tears on the paper, as did your friend. The little paltry wretches here were astonished and nearly maddened by envy...'

Another lesson Raffles had now learnt was the importance, and the relative ease, of going straight to the top. The price to be paid was the resentment of those less gifted or enterprising.

Maryanne's husband Quintin Dick Thompson died on 9 June 1809 after just three days' illness, aged twenty-six. He joined Francis Light, Philip Dundas and many others in the tree-shaded Protestant cemetery.

Perhaps to comfort her, Maryanne's two elder sisters, Harriet and Leonora Raffles, made the voyage out from England, and the following year joined the household at Runnymede, as probably Maryanne and her three little children did too.

Thompson had been Acting Naval Agent in Penang. Raffles, as his brother-in-law's executor, and with the acquiescence of Governor Macalister and of Rear-Admiral William O'Brien Drury of the Royal Navy in Penang, took the job over. The post was unpaid, but its holder took commission on all transactions. The immediate and only reason why Raffles was authorised to occupy the position was to sign off Thompson's accounts.

But Raffles held on to the job. Henry Pearson, who had disliked Raffles ever since he backed Macalister as Governor in preference to him, lodged a lengthy written complaint to Council on behalf of the naval establishment. Mr Raffles should never have taken a situation 'so entirely incompatible with that of a confidential Secretary to the Government, and in violation of the positive orders of the Honourable the Court of Directors... I did not, for a moment, imagine that he should wish or expect to retain the situation, but that he was merely closing the accounts of his brother-in-law.'

Raffles himself, as Secretary, had to sign the reply on behalf of the Governor and Council, conveying that 'your intimation of Mr Secretary Raffles being in possession of the office of Naval Agent at this Port is the first that has reached them on this subject, and the Board now cannot sufficiently express their regret that such an irregularity has tacitly been permitted to exist for even a single day.' In permitting Mr Raffles to assume 'the temporary charge of the office of Naval Agent,' the Governor was aware that 'such indulgence in no way sanctioned arrangements unconnected with the accounts of his brother-in-law.'

Governor Macalister had been slack. Raffles had been opportunistic. The episode was his first black mark.

Then there was another setback. Council, on account of Raffles' increased workload, had authorised an increase in his salary in 1807, subject to agreement from the Court of Directors at India House. Not a word was heard about this from London until early 1810, when a despatch arrived vehemently disallowing the rise. Mr Raffles was to refund the overpayments – in English money, £1,625.

Raffles appealed, citing the extra offices devolving upon him, his resulting illnesses, and 'the increased demands upon my earnings' in consequence of his having to support his bereaved sister and her three infant children. The appeal was supported by Governor Macalister – and by Henry Pearson, presumably in self-justification as he had been Acting Governor when the rise was approved in Penang. But the Court of Directors was adamant. Their decision had less to do with Raffles personally than with the financial retrenchments considered essential in failing Penang. The debt hung over Raffles until he was back in London on leave in 1817 and managed to get it written off.

Governor Macalister now fell ill, and in March 1810 C.A.Bruce, a brother of Lord Elgin, arrived from Calcutta and took over as Acting Governor in Penang. In mid-August, Macalister departed 'for the recovery of his health' on a short sea voyage in the Company's ship *Ocean* – and never came back. The *Ocean* went missing. (She went down in a storm.)

Raffles was not in Penang at the time. On 7 June 1810 he precipitately took two months leave – which extended to four. He sailed for Calcutta in a dangerously light vessel which was all that was available. He had been offered an opportunity, and a way out of Penang, and could not wait to follow it up. He was going to meet the Governor-General, Lord Minto.

The opportunity was not a dazzling one. In April 1810 the British took the Moluccas – the Spice Islands – from the Dutch almost by default, there being no resistance to a raiding party. Lord Minto was chary of taking on their governance without confirmation from the East India Company, and Rear-Admiral Drury, the Raffleses' family friend, suggested that Raffles should be put in charge there provisionally, based on Amboyna (Ambon), the chief of the Spice Islands, while they awaited a decision from London.

Raffles was keen to demonstrate his availability but, unfortunately, by the time he arrived in Calcutta the Amboyna post had already been disposed of. However, Minto and Raffles were to be engaged in discussions about something far more momentous – the invasion of Java.

Lord Curzon, Viceroy of India 1898–1905, wrote that 'Lord Minto was one of the class of Governors-General who leave no particular mark on history and cease to be remembered either for good or ill.' Raffles would have been aghast at that judgment. Minto was the most benevolently influential figure in his whole life. Mr Ramsay at India House had believed in him and given him a leg up. Lord Minto believed in him, and raised him higher.

Minto became Governor-General by default, the Court of Directors having vetoed the Board of Control's first choice. Land rich and cash poor (relatively), he wanted the money. His wife Anna Maria stayed at home in Scotland. He had inherited a baronetcy; he had practised as a barrister, excelled as a diplomat, been MP for Roxburghshire and Viceroy of Corsica, and Pitt gave him a peerage as Baron Minto of Minto. He was a shareholder in the Company and briefly, in 1806, President of the Board of Control. An unassertive person, he was told by his friend Edmund Burke, 'You *must* be less modest… You must be all that you can be, and you can be everything.'

But Minto was an unassuming man, impossible to dislike, though

Calcutta society felt that he kept too much to himself, surrounded by members of his family. His eldest son stayed at home with Lady Minto and their daughters. His second son, Captain George Elliot, was commander of the ship *Modeste* in which he sailed to India in 1807; his third son John Elliot, a junior civil servant in Madras, joined his father at Fort William as his private secretary, and his youngest, William, was a thirteen-year-old midshipman on the *Modeste*. William Hickey, Clerk to the Chief Justice in Calcutta, found John Elliot 'one of the most pert, assuming, and forward coxcombs I ever saw,' but then Hickey was horrible about most people. George and John both got married in India soon after their father's arrival, and the two young couples lived with him in Government House.

George Elliot was subsequently malicious about Raffles, who 'though a clever man, was neither born nor bred *a gentleman*, and we all know that the nicer feelings and habits of a gentleman are not to be acquired – he was full of trick, and *not so full of truth* as was desirable, and he was the most nervous man I ever knew.' Raffles, wrote George Elliot, looked upon him as a friend, but 'I never could have any real feeling of friendship for the man.'

Of course Raffles was not a 'gentleman' in George Elliot's sense. He had no known family and no property, and was self-educated. George, a few years younger than Raffles, was irritated by his father's partiality for his new protégé and, with the perceptiveness born of hostility, discerned Raffles' eagerness, his insecurity, and his aspirations.

Minto's first three years as Governor-General had been difficult. A combined French and Russian attack on British India, supported by Persia, seemed a strong possibility. He sent a mission to the Rajah of Lahore to persuade him into an alliance and to sign a treaty extending the Company's frontiers. Britain's defences on the northwest frontier were crucial. He sent a mission to Kabul, over wild land never before trodden by Europeans. When news came through of the first British successes in Spain and Portugal, the Napoleonic threat from the north receded and Minto cancelled further operations 'to save Johnny Company's cash' as he put it. There was a mutiny of army officers in Madras, which necessitated a long visit there to resolve the conflict between the insensitive Governor, Sir George Barlow, and an army which was, Minto said, 'not like any other army or set of people that ever was.'

Raffles already had his eye on Java. From 1806 the Royal Navy had been maintaining a blockade of Javan ports, paralysing not only French-Dutch shipping and trade, as intended, but that of Malay coastal vessels as well. This last impacted negatively on Penang's trade, which led Raffles to focus on the strategic importance of Java. He learned that British attacks were planned on the French-held islands Réunion and Mauritius – as indeed took place, successfully, in 1810 and early 1811 – and prepared for Minto a memorandum with all the information on Java that he had, with a view to urging on the Supreme Government the conquest of Java as a crucial step towards furthering Britain's maritime supremacy in the Archipelago.

This wasn't his own idea, nor a new idea, but an old one that had been scotched, twice, by Lord Castlereagh as Secretary of State for War and the Colonies before Minto's time. Before Minto left London for Calcutta, Java had been mentioned again, along with Réunion and Mauritius, as desirable acquisitions from the French who, after they conquered Holland, took possession of Batavia (Jakarta), the Dutch headquarters in the region.

Minto saw the logic of such a move, and had already written to London in March 1810, informing the Government of his proposal to attack Java. It was far too soon for any response to have arrived. What did arrive, in June, was belated permission to take Réunion and Mauritius. Minto received very little feedback from London, partly due to factional intrigues among the Directors at India House, partly because the administration which had appointed him fell from office. Replies to his despatches came even later than was customary – two whole years later, in the case of Company approval of his sanctions against the mutinous officers of Madras.

Minto had no scruples about not waiting for instructions when he was set upon a course of action that he believed to be the correct one. This was the first thing that Raffles learned from him, and it suited Raffles' temperament. In the future, he would disregard, as well as anticipate, instructions received from London. Another of Minto's tenets was the supremacy of civil over military authority: 'A military commander should come out [to India] penetrated with, and well instructed in, the indispensible subordination of the military power to the superintending superiority of the civil Government.' Raffles was to take these two doctrines of Minto's to perilous extremes.

The reduction of Java became urgent as the French prioritised the island, and Batavia as a strategic port. In 1808 Napoleon appointed Herman Willem Daendels as Governor of Java. A Dutchman who fought with and for the French, Daendels' brief was to check the worst of the self-enriching abuses that had grown up under the long Dutch occupation, reduce the power of the Regents – the Javanese rulers – and improve the defences of the island.

In the memo Raffles brought to Calcutta for Minto, he stressed the comparative ease with which the island of Java might be taken. The slack, tyrannous and 'degenerate' Dutch had lost control. The native powers had all but shaken off their authority, and could be brought onside. Java was 'the rice granary of the East', and its coffee, pepper, cotton, tobacco and indigo could be sold so well as to undercut every other settlement. He used the word 'annexation', implying occupation of the whole island, whereas Minto was only envisaging the reduction of Batavia. When instructions finally did come from London, Minto was authorised only to 'destroy the fortifications, to distribute the ordnance, arms and military stores amongst the native chiefs and inhabitants, and then to retire from the country.'

Minto received Raffles and his memo warmly, as later Raffles described to his cousin, the Rev. Thomas Raffles: 'On the mention of Java his Lordship cast a look of such scrutiny, anticipation and kindness upon me, as I shall never forget. "Yes," said he, "Java is an interesting island. I shall be happy to receive any information you can give me concerning it.'" From that moment on, Raffles wrote, 'all my views, all my plans, and all my mind were devoted to create such an interest regarding Java as should lead to its annexation to our Eastern Empire; although I confess that I had never the vanity to expect that, when this object was accomplished, so important an administration would have been intrusted to my individual charge.'

It was all in line with his and Leyden's dream of an 'Eastern Empire'. Raffles paid lip-service to the Company's maxim of 'trade not territory', but his visions were other. He was staying with Leyden while he was in Calcutta, and in August 1810 Leyden wrote:

> Dear Sister Olivia
> He is looking quite famously and the ladies one and all have
> done nothing but take him for a batchelor since his star first
> rose in our quarter of the world. In short he is at least a foot
> higher than he used to be in consequence of being puffed by
> their flattery... However I have the pleasure of informing you
> that he has received the most cordial attentions from Ld Minto
> and that in my opinion everything will tend to the best possible
> issue...and don't you be in the least alarmed about his health, as
> I will not suffer or permit him to be unwell here, but the truth
> is that if it were not for a few recollections of your Ladyship he
> would be a famously gay fellow and beat us all in spirits.

The invasion of Java would take long and detailed planning, carried out in total secrecy lest the French caught wind of it. Raffles offered his services to Lord Minto 'for carrying into effect any arrangements which your Lordship may have in contemplation as regards the Malay countries.' He was offering to prepare the ground, to investigate the practicalities and logistics, to gather intelligence, and to communicate privately with the native rulers in Java, and the other significant rulers in the Archipelago, seeking their co-operation and support, perhaps arming them, and enjoining secrecy. He snowed Minto with memos.

Minto virtually went into partnership with Raffles over the great project, officially appointing him 'Agent to the Governor-General with the Malay States'. Raffles' instructions were drawn up, drafted by himself. He chose Malacca as the headquarters for his communications and investigations, and as the mustering point for the invasion, not only for geographical reasons – it was closer to their objective – but because it would be harder to pursue his secret mission under the jealous watchfulness of Penang.

Before he left Calcutta, he read his paper on the Malayan Nation to the Asiatic Society. He carried back with him to Penang a strictly confidential letter from the Governor-General to Governor Bruce, informing him of the plans and requiring him to allow Mr Raffles to indent for any supplies he needed. He also carried back a letter for Olivia from Leyden, assuring her that Raffles' success was 'in every respect compleat. If he succeeds in his present objects he will have a much finer game to play than he has hitherto had and one to which Amboyna is not in the least to be compared. I have to conjure you now to take care to throw no obstacles in R's way, as I see every moment of the next six or ten months must be precious to him.' Leyden had settled with Raffles 'that the instant he is Governor of Java I am to be his Secretary.'

Raffles got back to Penang on 22 October 1810, in time for his sister Leonora's wedding. Aged twenty-five, she had found a husband within a few months of arriving. On 24 November, at Mount Olivia, she was married to John Billington Loftie, a widowed surgeon on the Madras establishment, now Acting Surgeon in Penang.

Raffles did not want to return to Penang after the invasion of Java. He put Runnymede up for auction – 'that valuable and very eligible Estate on the North Beach, with a most excellent brick-built dwelling house and offices erected thereon,' as the *Gazette* announced. The day after Leonora's wedding, he wrote to Leyden that he would be leaving for Malacca in a couple of days. He had found out that the Navy's blockade of the Javanese ports had officially been lifted, but the ruling had never been implemented. At his request, Governor Bruce gave the order. This would please the all-important Javanese rulers and Malays and so put himself, Raffles, in the 'very best light possible in the Eastward.'

'Mr Bruce has personally behaved most kind, I cannot calculate tho' Mr Bruce as a *political* character,' he told Leyden, since his main preoccupation was the re-allocation of Raffles' various offices and his salary. 'Here they think of nothing but themselves... I shall write you fully from Malacca – here I am full of confusion.' He was taking with him to Malacca 'Mrs R and two sisters – one of them I have got rid of as you may see in the papers – you'll judge I have not been idle – Olivia is too full of trouble and confusion to write to you from hence – you will hear from her often enough from Malacca... I leave Penang with very little regret.'

Olivia and the sisters might well be in confusion. They were to up sticks and leave comfortable Runnymede for they knew not what. Although, as Raffles cheerfully told Leyden, Leonora was 'got rid of', she and her husband also joined the party sailing down to Malacca.

The East India Company was chary of acquiring territory in the East Indies because it meant expense, and could incur armed conflict. Yet it was impossible to establish a trading settlement, if it was to be more than an entrepôt and port of call, without an establishment and territory which, in theory, should support itself by its trade and by the collecting of taxes.

The early Empire, like all protection rackets, worked to the benefit of both sides, with the balance of power on the side of the 'protector'. When it was a case of acquiring territory from a local ruler, the Company agreed by formal treaty to pay the Sultan, Rajah or Chief an annual sum for the occupation and use of some or all of his land and its products, and to provide him with protection, armaments and advisors. The Company exacted loyalty and co-operation, the right to impose laws, rules and regulations in the leased territory, and to raise taxes on everything taxable. The whole point, for the East India Company, was to transfer wealth from the East to Britain.

This did not always happen. What is more, it frequently suited a Sultan, Rajah or Chief to receive money and weapons to reinforce his security and prestige. His concerns were overwhelmingly local and personal, centring on historical chains of events in his own polity, and on relations between himself and the opposition – often members of his own family – and between his own and neighbouring states. The aliens mostly clung to the coasts, swapping islands and ports between themselves by conquest or treaty with every shift in their own wars.

The poor people of the Archipelago were like poor people everywhere. Their rulers, like rulers everywhere, varied between the wise and the moronic, in either case desirous of holding on to power. The principal rulers were subtle and shrewd. Their culture was complex, their thinking at the same time magical and pragmatic, their etiquette sophisticated. They often hedged their bets by keeping in secretly with both the Dutch (or French) and the British. Many European incomers were in comparison blunt instruments. Raffles did not come into that category. In the case of Java, it was crucial to negotiate with local rulers, but only as a preliminary to the main event, which was to be armed conquest.

Chapter 4

'All roads are long that lead to one's heart's desire'

Malacca 1810–1811

The Raffles family arrived in Malacca on 4 December 1810. They moved into a house at Bandar Hill, outside the only Portuguese gate that had escaped demolition. On 18 December, Raffles wrote an unusually agitated letter to John Leyden in Calcutta, asking him to expedite the sending of military stores, because 'from Penang I can get nothing, their narrow minded jealousy and envy has so disgusted [me] ... between ourselves Mr B[ruce] did not act to me as he ought – and I lay the whole to the account of Phillips who has I believe a most rancorous hatred for your humble servant on many accounts.'

He also asked for a dozen pairs of 'good spectacles' for his scribes, and said that Olivia was 'in very bad health and has not left her room these 5 days past.' He was working ten hours a day and had no time to give to his paper on the maritime law of the Malays, which Leyden was keen for him to complete, or to answer linguistic queries from William Marsden, who was about to publish a third edition of his *History of Sumatra*. In it Raffles would read a graceful acknowledgment to himself as 'a gentleman whose intelligence and zeal in the pursuit of knowledge give the strongest hope of his becoming an ornament to oriental literature.'

Raffles was uncertain about his future. It was all very well to be the Governor-General's Agent in the run-up to the invasion of Java, but then what? He wanted Leyden to ascertain from Lord Minto 'what part of the play I am to act hereafter.' Leyden could assure his friend that 'his Lordship was exceedingly well-disposed towards you, desirous of giving you every opportunity of distinguishing yourself, and rewarding you as highly as the imperious nature of the circumstances would permit ... Indeed, Raffles, he has always talked of you to me, with a kindness very uncommon in a Governor-General.' He reported the astonishing news that Lord Minto himself was coming to Malacca, and would accompany the fleet on the invasion of Java – and, crucially, that his Lordship was 'still fluctuating between the two old plans' of holding on to Java, or of making it independent, which was his instruction from London.

Leyden eloquently rehearsed to Raffles their dream of an empire to the Eastward: the Malays 'must be neither independent, nor yet very dependent, but we must have a general Malay league, in which all the Rajahs must be united...under the protection of the Governor of Java.' (It was agreed that this must be Raffles.) Minto had a part to play: Raffles must write to 'all the Rajahs of the Malays, however far, or wherever situated, to come in person, to meet the *Good Maha Rajah of Bengal*' who would 'reign in Malacca, and conquer Java, and drive out all the cruel Dutch, and treacherous French' and bring peace and happiness to the region. 'In short, make a great and mighty noise, for we will compel his Lordship to be a greater man than he would wish to be, if left alone.'

Up to a point, Leyden's vision coincided with Raffles' official brief, which was to activate an intelligence network of native spies to discover the likely movements of the French, and the state and nature of the fortifications of Batavia and its environs. He was to open communication with the Javanese chiefs, and generally prepare the ground for the invasion. He duly made contact by letter with the rulers not only of Java but of the whole Archipelago, reporting back continuously to Minto. It was important for the rulers to treat only with persons of equal rank. The Governor-General was reckoned to be a sort of Rajah, and some of the glory should reflect upon Raffles as his emissary. As he said to Leyden, he did not want 'to appear in the eyes of the natives as a mere *Cat's paw.*'

He made certain that his own eminence was understood by the quality of his letters, enveloped in the traditional yellow silk. Raffles had learned in Penang the Malay tradition of elaborate and decorated diplomatic letters between Eastern rulers, with the royal seal or *chop* of the sender attached. A *chop* was the impression on paper made by blackening a brass seal in the smoke of a candle. Religious letter-headings in Arabic calligraphy were followed by orotund salutations and hyperbolic compliments. The main matter was approached with elaborate circumlocutions.

These letters were both diplomatic tools and works of art. The art-work could be done by hand locally; sometimes the letters were written on papers pre-stamped with gilded floral motifs and borders or spattered with gold and silver drops. Raffles appreciated the art of the Malay letter, and made a collection of those connected with the invasion of Java and, later, the founding of Singapore. He provided his calligraphers with papers ready-stamped with gold and silver motifs, but with an unusual layout: a space for the text on the left side of the paper surrounded by floral trellis with a gilded headpiece, and a cut-away right-hand lower corner. It is a measure of the significance accorded to his missives that Sultans and Rajahs paid the Agent of the Governor-General of India the compliment of replying in the same style – the text-block on the left, and the right-hand bottom corner cut away.

Later, when he was in Singapore, a letter arrived from the King of Siam with the right-hand bottom corner cut away. His *munshi* Abdullah asked why, and according to his recollection Raffles said: 'In his pride and arrogance and stupidity the King of Siam thinks that his own kingdom is the whole world and that other countries are merely the small piece of paper he has torn away.' Since Raffles bought his letter papers with the right-hand corners already cut off, this was a whiff of the 'British sense of humour' which went over good Abdullah's head. 'When I heard Mr. Raffles' words I was filled with utmost astonishment that he should understand such mysteries.'

Raffles was occupied all day long in Malacca. The people among whom the British came to live were often baffled by their continuous activity, for they did not, like normal people, remain at rest until something came up that had to be done. They finished one apparently self-imposed task and immediately turned to another. The *munshi* Abdullah, first employed by Raffles in Malacca, was in 1811 only fourteen years old. He was astonished by the constant activity not only of Raffles but of Olivia. She 'never wasted a moment in idleness'. Malay women married to important men became lazy: 'They just lie down and doze, then dress and arrange their coiffure, or sit and order their slaves about.' But Mrs Raffles was always 'doing one thing after another, after tidying the house she would sew and after sewing she would write letters. May I be blinded if my eye ever saw her retire or compose herself for rest in the middle of the day. She was up and about all the time. Allah alone knows.'

Abdullah was fluent in Arabic, Tamil and Malay; his father had taught Malay to William Marsden. Raffles employed him, along with his friends and relations, as letter-writer, copyist, interpreter and translator, working on literary and historical texts in the Raffles house. 'It was Mr Raffles' nature to study with great enjoyment the history of countries and their ancient customs, and to make enquiries and ask questions about unusual things.'

Abdullah, in the memoir he dictated in the early 1840s, composed a pen-portrait of Raffles: 'He had thick eyebrows, his left eye watered slightly from a cast; his nose was straight and his cheeks slightly hollow. His lips were thin, denoting his skill in speech, his tongue gentle and his mouth wide; his neck tapering; his complexion not very clear [ie not very light]; his chest was full and his waist

slender. He walked with a slight stoop.' As to his character, 'He
was good at paying due respect to people in a friendly manner. He
treated everyone with proper deference, giving to each his proper
title when he spoke.' He was 'tactful at ending a difficult conversation' and he 'spoke in smiles'.

'When he had no work to do other than reading and writing he
liked to retire to a quiet place. When he was occupied in studies
or conversation he was unwilling to meet anyone who came to the
house until he had finished. I saw that he kept rigidly to his timetable of work, not mixing one thing with another. I noticed also a
habit of his in the evening after he had taken tea with his friends.
There was an inkstand and a place for pen and paper on his large
writing-table, and two lighted candles.' He would walk up and down
the room for a while, and then lie flat on his back on the table, close
his eyes, and suddenly jump up and start writing. Then he lay down
on the table again. 'This was his behaviour every night up to eleven
or twelve o'clock when he went to bed.'

First thing in the morning Raffles read over what he had written
the night before, walking up and down the room. 'Out of ten pages
he would take perhaps three or four and give them to a writer to
copy out. The rest he would tear up and throw away.' These nocturnal writings were his reports to Lord Minto. Between February
1811 and June, when the invasion force sailed, he sent Minto hundreds of thousands of words on the peoples of the Archipelago, their
alliances, customs and characteristics. He sent on, too, the English
translation of his 'Proclamation to the People of Java', dated 14
March 1811, disseminated in Dutch on the island by his agents. The
proclamation highlighted the 'blessings of English Government'
and the brutality of the French: 'Are you not at this day subjected to
the grossest military oppression and tyranny?... The English are
at hand...Your future misery or happiness, as well as that of your
families, is in your hands. The English character is not unknown
to you – it is for you to decide.' If the Dutch inhabitants remained
quiet, they could 'rely on the protection of the English.' If they were

to 'make resistance to the British troops, remember that you forfeit that protection.'

He reported opening communications with the Sultan of Mataram in Yogyakarta on Central Java, and with the Sultan of Palembang in Sumatra, 'one of the most important of the Malay states.' Palembang was rich in minerals, and had the monopoly on the products of offshore Banca, an island 'which may be considered as an immense tin mine,' as Raffles told Minto. But the Sultan of Palembang was prevaricating, bound by treaties to the Dutch, who retained a settlement in Palembang. He was under pressure from Marshal Daendels in Batavia, and suspected that Britain would lose the war with France and so lose her possessions to the Eastward. Raffles got nowhere with him. He also had little success in appealing to those chieftains whose younger relatives engaged in piracy, the scourge of the Eastern seas. Consequently, he wrote, 'the maintenance of a marine establishment similar to that of the Dutch will probably be found absolutely necessary.'

Daendels was a harsh man who overstretched his reformist brief. He half bankrupted Java with grandiose projects during his short tenure, and destabilised the economy of the island by issuing large amounts of paper money. Everyone hated him. The British were however to benefit from some of his projects. His field hospitals were excellent, and he constructed – at the cost of thousands of lives – a military road across the island with the result that, as Captain Taylor was to put it, 'you can travel from Batavia to Surabaya in your carriage as well as from Exeter to York.'

Raffles sent Minto detailed reports on the military and naval strength assembled by Daendels, and on the roads, waterways, ports and harbours of Java. He should perhaps have given more prominence in these reports to Lieutenant-Colonel (previously Captain) William Farquhar, but then he was relying equally on another mature and distinguished military engineer and surveyor, Lieutenant-Colonel Colin Mackenzie. Lieutenant-Colonel Farquhar was not part of the invasion force, as Mackenzie was. Farquhar complained later that Raffles 'obtained from me all the information I was able to collect respecting the state of the island of Java...which formed a rather voluminous report, regularly signed by *me*, and transmitted to Lord Minto, together with a general map of the island, *through* Sir Stamford Raffles.'

Farquhar felt sidelined, even though Minto recognised his contributions and corresponded directly with him as well as with Raffles, who when relaying Farquhar's information on the military logistics of the French and Dutch did not claim the intelligence as his own, and when quoting from Farquhar's memos he mentioned him by name. But Farquhar was nettled by what he saw as Raffles' assumption of superior status, and a feeling that his brains were being picked for Raffles' personal advantage.

Of course Raffles was picking everyone's brains. That was his job right now. He was a social animal with lively sympathies and good manners, and in normal dealings with his fellow-humans his sensitivities were pitch-perfect. But when carried away by his own imperatives he tended to forget – as a child does – everything but the absorbing matter in hand, and left his associates standing. What Raffles' letters to Minto chiefly demonstrate is how much more he believed was at stake than just the invasion of Java. He was presenting the conquest invasion as a step towards extending British influence throughout the Archipelago and beyond.

Raffles in Malacca received a letter dated 27 April 1811, delivered by an envoy, from the Sultan of Acheen, complaining about the seizure of one of his ships in Penang, where he was suspected of being in the pay of Daendels and the French. For this very reason Raffles was critical of Penang's action, which might drive the Anglophile Sultan into the arms of the French; and he supported his right to the throne of Acheen against the pretender Syed Hussein in Penang. In his letter, the Sultan conferred upon Raffles the title of 'Sri Paduka Orangkaya Berpedang Emas' – 'His Excellency the Nobleman with the Golden Sword' – the Order of the Golden Sword. This was neither an ancient nor a significant decoration. It took the form of three oval medallions linked by a gold chain, two bearing Arabic characters and one engraved with a wavy-bladed *kris*.

In one of the memos he wrote to Minto before they left for Java, Raffles enclosed the Sultan's letter and, while not referring to the Order of the Golden Sword, observed that 'some marks of attention' would be 'agreeable' to the Sultan. It might, he thought, be a good idea to install a Resident and a couple of hundred sepoys at the Sultan's court. Raffles was alert to Acheen's positional value to an Eastern Empire, and delighted, privately, in his Order of the Golden Sword.

The secretaries read his letter to Minto with the enclosure conferring the Order, and the news spread through Calcutta and Penang. Raffles came in for a bit of mockery behind his back. One who mocked was John Palmer, senior partner of Palmer & Co, Calcutta's most prominent agency house. The half-dozen Indian agency houses were universal providers; Palmer & Co, through subcontractors, was provisioning the fleet for the expedition to Java. Since there were no banks or family solicitors for the thousand-odd Europeans in Calcutta, agency tycoons filled the gap. Palmer, from his office in Old Fort Street, extended credits and loans, managed savings and investments, advised on retirement plans and personal embarrassments, set up trusts, let property, fixed the chartering of vessels. He had valuable connections in the Indian commercial community and among Indian rulers. He was socially intimate with his clients, and hospitable on a lavish scale in his mansion on the Loll Bazaar. He knew everyone, and he knew their secrets. He took an interest in the succession of Acheen, and was an ally of W.E.Phillips in Penang. In his communications with Penang about what he saw as Raffles' ludicrous or damaging machinations, he referred to him sardonically as 'our Knight' or 'Sir Knight' or 'the Golden Sword'.

Raffles in Malacca pursued private passions. When his interest in acquiring works of Malay history and literature became known, people brought manuscripts and books to his house. Some he borrowed and had copied, but bought most for cash. 'I do not remember,' wrote Abdullah, 'how many of these texts there were. Almost, it seemed, the whole of Malay literature of the ages, the property of our forefathers, was sold and which he kept in his own hand, taken away from all over the country.' In retrospect, Abdullah thought this was a tragedy. 'Because these things had money value they were sold and it did not occur to people at the time that this might be unwise, leaving them not a single book to read in their own language. This would not have mattered if the books had been printed, but these were all written in longhand and now copies of them are no longer available.'

Another private activity was the building of a collection of natural history specimens – plants, insects, shells, fishes, birds and animals – employing 'a certain Chinese from Macao who was very expert at drawing life-like pictures of fruits and flowers'. He preserved the bodies of reptiles in spirit. He kept a pair of orang-utan, dressing the male in trousers, coat and hat; it had free range, and his other birds and animals were kept in cages and pens. His collections were a contribution to knowledge and designed to further the prestige of the Company (as well as of himself). But there was a streak of unthinking extravagance in him. One of Abdullah's observations stands out: 'It was Mr Raffles' way to care little for money. If there was anything he wished to buy or any work he wanted undertaken, whatever the cost or fee might be, he paid for it... I know not how much money was paid out daily from his safe to buy things or to pay those who worked for him.'

The female orang-utan died. Her mate mourned her, and died himself within a week. 'If animals can love one another as man and wife, how much more should we human beings do likewise,' wrote Abdullah. He made no overt connection between the union of the apes and that of Raffles and Olivia, but their relationship impressed him, and his memories of Olivia are a corrective to the image of an invalidish and rather stagey woman which emerges elsewhere.

During the first months in Malacca she would have received the news that her daughter Harriet had died of tuberculosis on 16 October 1810. Her husband William Soper-Dempster took her south from Skibo Castle to his home town of Ashburton in Devonshire in the vain hope that the softer climate would prolong her life.

According to Abdullah, Mrs Raffles 'shared her husband's charm, his modesty and prudence in everything that she did. She spoke in a friendly and courteous manner alike to the rich and the poor. She enjoyed making a thorough study of Malay, and used to ask how the Malays say this and that. All the points that she noted she wrote down on paper. And I observed too that whenever Mr Raffles wanted to do something, for instance to make a purchase, he always asked his wife first and if she agreed he acted.' Married couples were not like that in Abdullah's culture. 'For Allah had joined together the pair of them making them of one mind, like a ruler and his minister, like a ring and the jewel set in it, like sugar in milk.' He composed a *pantun*, a Malay form of rhyming quatrains, comparing them to a pair of goldfish in a bowl swimming together, sharing every thought and move.

Lord Minto wrote to the Secret Committee at India House on 22 January 1811, impressing upon them his conviction, contrary to their instructions, that a colonial administration should be established in Java. He was perfectly aware that there was no possibility of his receiving a reply before the invasion. He expressed to his wife his confidence in 'Mr Raffles, a very clever, able, active and judicious man, perfectly versed in the Malay language and manners, and conversant with the interests and affairs of the Eastern states.' Even though he believed it to be nothing more than his duty to 'friskify' off to Java, he confessed that 'I never engaged in any affair with greater interest or with more pleasure.'

Urgent discussions at Fort William in Calcutta between Lord Minto, General Sir Samuel Auchtermuty (a loyalist American, in command of the British troops), Admiral Drury and Raffles, concerned the route that the invasion force should take from

Malacca to Java. With such a large fleet, there would be difficulties in passing through the narrow passages between islands of the Archipelago. Since progress was entirely dependent upon strong currents and the shifting monsoon winds, a straight run was out of the question.

The most direct route was via the narrow straits between Banca and Sumatra, but by mid-June – the earliest the expedition could leave – the wind direction would make this impossible. To choose that way would mean delaying several months for a change of wind. Another idea was to go east from the southern end of the Strait of Malacca, cross open water to the south-west coast of Borneo, then navigate the Carimata (Karimata) Strait, getting the benefit of prevailing breezes, and cross back again towards Batavia. This was considered dangerous and impracticable.

Yet another possibility was to go with the wind all the way round the north coast of Borneo, and work south through the Straits of Macassar, where they would pick up the eastern monsoon to bring them back along the coast of Java. This was very long. They might not make it to Java before the rainy season began in October, and the health of the armed forces, compromised by a long voyage, might not withstand being continuously wet.

Captain George Elliot wrote in his memoirs that Raffles 'knew nothing of winds and monsoons in the Eastern seas, and never pretended to know; nor did he know what route it was proposed to take till he was desired as interpreter at my request to obtain information… as to the winds on the west coast of Borneo at that season, in which he totally failed.' It is true that Raffles did not know much about 'winds and monsoons', nor pretend to, which is precisely why he sent off Captain Greig in the brig *Minto*, to survey the south-west passage through the Carimata Strait and test its practicality.

Greig's report was positive, and Raffles was strongly of the opinion that this was the right way to go. The difficulties, he wrote to Minto, were 'magnified by ignorance', and there was no reasonable doubt that 'the S.W. passage may be effected by the fleet sailing in divisions, in the space of a month or six weeks at farthest.' As his widow wrote in her *Memoir*, 'he did not hesitate to stake his reputation' on the point.

When his despatch reached Calcutta, Minto's Military Secretary, Captain William Taylor, noted how highly Minto rated Raffles' judgment, 'and rightly so, though to my mind he is inclined to be a trifle self-opinionated.' Minto wrote to Raffles in March 1811: 'It is proposed to style you Secretary to the Governor-General when we come together... I hope you do not doubt the *prospective* interest I have always taken, and do not cease to take, in your personal views and welfare. I have not spoken distinctly on that subject, only because it has been from circumstances *impossible* for me to pledge myself to the fulfilment of my own wishes, and, I may add, intentions, if practicable.'

He had a 'very strong desire' upon another point, upon which if he had his way 'the utmost will be done to make the *best attainable situation* worthy of your services, and of the high esteem I profess, with the greatest sincerity, of your person.' This was a vague hint, but Raffles' anxieties may have been assuaged.

Minto was doing everything he could for Raffles. The Council at Calcutta wrote to the Secret Committee in London on 27 April 1811: 'Your Honourable Committee will probably concur in opinion with us that Mr Raffles has manifested a considerable degree of industry, judgment and ability, in carrying into effect the very delicate and important objects of his Mission, and that the information he has acquired...warrants an expectation of the successful issue of the enterprise against the enemy's possessions in the Eastern Islands.'

Minto sailed from Calcutta in the *Modeste*, captained by his son George Elliot, on 9 May, along with his younger son John Elliot as his private secretary. The entourage included Hugh Hope (a Company civil servant, scion of another grand Scots family) as his Deputy Secretary, and Captain William Taylor as his Military

Secretary. Taylor was a cousin of the Mintos, and close to the second of the Mintos' three daughters, Anna Maria. Taylor wrote regularly to Anna Maria Minto, and sent her copies of his journal throughout the Java campaign, which he made on his 'copying machine', using 'carbonic paper', much chuffed by this modern technology.

Archibald Seton, designated as the next Governor of Penang, was also on the *Modeste*. So was John Leyden, who had persuaded Minto to let him accompany the expedition on account of his expertise in Malay. Leyden's garrulity in the narrow confines of the frigate tested even Minto's amused tolerance, and Captain Taylor found unbearable the 'incessant clack kept up by Leyden in the cabin from breakfast to bedtime in the shrillest voice that can well be imagined. If he ceases for an instant, Mr Seton asks a question that sets him off again.' Steps were taken. 'Lord M. having borne with patience for some time the clack I have complained of spoke out at last, the morning is to be quiet now. From dinner till bed time L. may talk as much as he pleases, which [for] him amounts to as much as he can.'

While the *Modeste* was at sea it was learned that Raffles' friend Admiral Drury, sailing on the *Illustrious*, had dropped dead, and Commodore W.R.Broughton had taken over as commander of the naval forces. He was considered inadequate to the task, and before the invasion was replaced by Rear Admiral Sir Robert Stopford, one of Nelson's captains. The *Modeste* reached Penang in the first week of May 1811, and remained for a few days. Archibald Seton was formally signed in as Governor of Penang, though he remained part of the mission to Java. Governor Bruce had died in December 1810, since when W.E. Phillips was Acting Governor in Penang. Raffles had to tell Phillips the secret reason for his sojourn in Malacca, which he had previously, perfectly properly, confided only to Governor Bruce. Phillips was peeved that he had not been informed before.

In Penang Minto and his party added to their stores a load of buffalo meat – the beef of the East Indies – sent as a compliment by the Rajah of Kedah on the mainland. Just as the *Modeste* was preparing to leave for Malacca but still at anchor, reported Captain Taylor, 'a couple of prows passed us, one with a yellow flag at each masthead, and a yellow ensign.' They heard from the shore that this was the Rajah himself paying a courtesy visit to the Governor-General. 'On this hint we got under weigh forthwith and left His Majesty in the lurch.'

Raffles had particularly impressed upon Minto the importance of making an ally of the well-disposed Rajah of Kedah, and of securing from him as much territory as possible on the mainland of the Malayan Peninsula. Minto's failure to take the point provoked the nearest thing to a reproach that Raffles ever addressed to his admired superior: 'From the shortness of your Lordship's stay at Penang, the Rajah was disappointed in procuring the expected interview, which I am informed he regrets, not only as a serious mortification, but as an absolute misfortune.'

On 18 May, Minto and the black-painted *Modeste* appeared in the bay before Malacca, to be welcomed by marching soldiers, thundering cavalry, bands playing, flags flying, and crowds of local inhabitants. Raffles and Farquhar went out to the *Modeste* in a pinnace to escort the Governor-General ashore while all the ships in the roads fired their guns. Young Abdullah was dazzled by all this ceremony, and then amazed by the unpretentiousness of the Governor-General of Bengal when he finally disembarked: 'The man I saw looked like this. He had passed middle age. His body was thin, his manner mild, his face gentle. I should not have supposed him capable of lifting even a twenty-five-pound weight, so fragile was his build. I noticed that he wore a tunic of black cloth, black trousers, and nothing else worthy of mention.' The rows of troops presented arms and Lord Minto mounted the steps into Government House with Raffles at his side – no longer Agent, but Secretary to the Governor-General.

Because of the presence of the Governor-General this small

Presidency was, temporarily, the seat of the Supreme Government of India. Easy-going Malacca was transformed by encampments of troops along the shore, the fleet at anchor out at sea and more ships arriving every day, until the roads were, as the *munshi* Abdullah put it, so full 'that the masts of the vessels looked like the poles of a fence.'

Minto and his entourage were based at Government House, which was blocked off from the sea breezes by the Hill, so 'suffocation is our portion.' But Captain George Elliot had been allocated a one-room bungalow on the airy top of the Hill, and on its verandah 'he and I are at present, writing love-letters to our absent wives.' The remains of the Fort lay around the foot of the Hill, now 'little better than a heap of rubbish'. Minto judged the destruction as 'a most useless piece of gratuitous mischief.'

The Governor-General, with his entourage, paid a breakfast visit to Raffles and his 'pretty numerous family' at home. Reporting to his wife, Minto was positive about Olivia:

> Mrs Raffles, Olivia Mariamne, is a tall and rather showy person, with dark eyes.' Her expression was 'lively and spirituelle, and her conversation deserves the same epithets. Upon the whole, my expectations are more than answered, and I am very happy to see Raffles, who really is a very amiable as well as clever man, so happy in his interior… Raffles has three sisters here, all very fair, one extremely well-looking, and the other two not the contrary. Their manners are sensible and gentlemanlike. The beauty is married to Capt. Flint, a Post Captain in the Navy. Another sister is Mrs Loftie, lately married to a surgeon of that name. The third has not yet made her choice.

The third was Harriet. The 'beauty', the widowed Maryanne, still only twenty-two, had remarried a couple of weeks before Minto's arrival. Her new husband, thirty-year-old Captain Lawrence William Flint of the Royal Navy, commander of HMS *Teignmouth*, was a well-connected Scot – his elder brother was private secretary to the Duke of Wellington – and a plump young man, to judge from his portrait. Raffles always supported Flint – 'as good and as honest a fellow as ever lived' – though he turned out to be a trial owing to his extravagance and his quarrelsome nature.

'After breakfast,' recorded Taylor, Lord Minto accepted gifts – not only a baby orang- utan from the Rajah of Pontianak but '5 slave boys and two girls, none above 6 or 7 years old,' from a Rajah of Bali. The children were emancipated from slavery immediately, which left them with the status of dependant orphans. 'Next day they were all very merry and happy,' wrote Minto. 'George has taken one of the boys to serve him on board ship, and that boy has fallen on his legs. Mr Raffles will take care of one or two, and the rest have fallen to my lot. They will probably grow into very good servants. The girls will puzzle me most. I have some thought of baking them in a pie against the Queen's birthday…' All the children were staying for the time being with Raffles and Olivia, along with the three Raffles sisters, Maryanne's children, and Leonora's husband. Their house must have been rather crowded.

On 7 June 1811, to celebrate the King's birthday, Minto held at Government House a levee in the morning, then a dinner for gentlemen in the evening, followed by a ball. Malacca had never seen anything like it. For Minto, and for Raffles, the most important part of the day had come following the levee. Minto freed the nineteen Government slaves in Malacca – born into slavery to the Dutch East India Company and then to the British, with their children destined to be slaves too. He presented each with a certificate of their freedom and four Spanish dollars to keep them going until they found work, with the option of returning to their former state if they had difficulties.

Earlier Minto had ordered the release of all those imprisoned for debt. Lieutenant-Colonel Farquhar unlocked the gates and the prisoners ran free, praising Allah and Lord Minto. He visited the *terongko galep*, the 'dark dungeon', and ordered it to be destroyed. Finding in the dungeon instruments of torture used by the Dutch, he had all the contraptions made of wood – racks, wheels and gallows – burned at the foot of the Hill, and 'various iron articles for screwing thumbs, wrists, and ankles, and other contrivances of that diabolical sort, were carried out in a boat and sunk in deep water, never to rise or screw poor people's bones and joints again.'

Raffles took possession of a few of these iron torture instruments with their heavy screws. He kept them, and brought them back to England as reminders of abhorred practices.

The invasion fleet, which would inevitably become scattered, agreed to rendezvous off Borneo. On 10 June, with convoys of ships now leaving continuously for Java, Raffles passed to Minto the last of his series of long reports – an overview of his previous memos on the peoples, laws, religions, products and governance of each of the countries of the Archipelago and beyond, including sanguine projections of enhanced contacts with Cochin China, Japan and China.

Raffles had been trained all too well in composing 'narratives' in his years at India House. He laid out in his mega-letters ideas on how populations should be managed, based on assessments of their national characteristics. He always favoured the Malays. It would be important, he wrote, to keep down the Chinese, 'in all ages equally supple, venal and crafty.' (He changed his mind about the Chinese. They were indispensible.) The Arabs of the Archipelago were 'mere drones' and inculcators of religious bigotry. Americans were 'commercial interlopers who will require our vigilant attention.' Americans were 'active and enterprising traders' and wherever they went, 'as fire-arms are in the highest request,' they became arms-dealers.

In his peroration, he unfolded his vision: 'The annexation of Java and the Eastern Isles to our Indian empire, opens to the English nation views of so enlarged a nature as seem equally to demand and justify a bolder policy…' In ancient times the Rajahs and Sultans of Java had authority over their own domains, but there was one great King, the Bitara, above them all. The ancient rulers of Malacca had controlled much of the Malay Peninsula, and much of Sumatra, on the same terms. All the countries and peoples of the Archipelago 'might easily be prevailed upon by suggestions to invest the Governor-General of India with the ancient title of Bitara,' affording 'a general right of superintendence over, and interference with, all the Malay states.'

He signed off by evoking the 'splendid prospect' of 'the total expulsion of the European enemy from the Eastern Seas, and [of] the justice, humanity and moderation of the British Government, as much exemplified in fostering and leading on new races of subjects and allies in the career of improvement, as [in] the undaunted courage and resolution of British soldiers in rescuing them from oppression.'

Raffles' dream is an exposition of British imperialism as it was later to be represented not only to the outside world but to the minds of Englishmen and women.

The fleet comprised about a hundred vessels under sail: four battleships, fourteen frigates, seven sloops, eight Company cruisers, fifty-seven transports and several gunboats. The military strength had numbered 12,000 men, half of them Asian and half European. More than a thousand, most of them Indians, had to be left behind in Malacca because of sickness. John Leyden sailed with the interpreters and writers in Captain Greig's *Minto*.

Last to leave, on 18 June, was the group which included the *Modeste*, carrying Lord Minto, Raffles, and their staff. Raffles wanted to take young Abdullah with him, but when the day came his mother could not bear to let him go. So Raffles gave him a letter of recommendation and thirty dollars, and told him to go and say goodbye to Mrs Raffles – who gave him a piece of leaf-patterned muslin to make a jacket, and another ten dollars. 'I went home feeling very sad, for I was very fond of Mr and Mrs Raffles, who were just like a father and a mother to me.'

Modeste was a fast frigate and overtook most of the scattered fleet, which reassembled on 20 June to pass through the Straits of Singapore – with difficulty, since the weather was stormy. Here Minto and Raffles learned that Napoleon had replaced the rebarbative General Herman Willem Daendels in Java with General J.W. Janssens, another Dutchman in the service of the French. Living on the island of Singapore was the Temenggong, a hereditary ruler from Johore on the mainland, who later told how he watched the passing of this enormous fleet with astonishment, neither he nor Raffles yet knowing of each other's existence.

Having navigated the Singapore Straits, the expedition was in the clear, making directly for Borneo, where the fleet reassembled again at an uninhabited island off Borneo's north-east point and took a week off for rest and recuperation. The *Modeste* was sent as a pilot-fish down the west coast of Borneo, Captain George Elliot being requested by the cautious Commodore Broughton to reconnoitre a safe passage through shoals marked on the charts, 'thinking very properly that I had better drowned than he,' as Minto remarked. The south-west route through the Carimata Straits proved as navigable as Raffles had believed it would. He had predicted against opposition that the voyage could be done in six to ten weeks. He was right. It took seven weeks. On 6 July, at sea, he celebrated his thirtieth birthday.

⌐⌐

In a letter to his cousin the Rev. Thomas Raffles, written much later, Raffles said: 'We had separated from the fleet for a few days, and it was only when we again joined them that we saw all the divisions united, at the close of one of the finest days I ever recollect, and this in sight of the *land of promise.*' Lord Minto, while at Malacca, 'had communicated his intention of appointing me to the governorship, in case of success.' If all went well, Raffles would be Governor of Java. Exalted, he wrote from shipboard to his friend William Brown Ramsay:

> You always said I was a wild strange fellow, insatiable in
> ambition, though meek as a maiden; and perhaps there was

more truth than otherwise in what you said; but withal, I will assure you this, that although from want of self-confidence and from natural shamefacedness (for I will not call it modesty or bashfulness) I am as unhappy at times as any poor wretch need be, I have times in which I am as happy as I think it possible for man to be; and it is one of these life-inspiring moments that I now propose passing with you *à la distance*... Adieu my dear Ramsay, for the present, my paper is out, and dinner is announced, so farewell – I will write to you more fully after we are settled. Conquer we must.

It was a hinge-moment for Raffles. Joseph Conrad, in his novel *The Shadow Line*, one of his tales of the East Indies, wrote that it was the privilege of youth 'to live in advance of its days in all the beautiful continuity of hope.' Time passes, 'till one perceives ahead a shadow line warning one that the region of early youth, too, must be left behind.' Reality takes over from aspiration. Conrad's protagonist crosses his shadow line when he is given his first command of a ship, with the daunting prospect of navigating between the islands of the Archipelago: 'But I felt no apprehension. I was familiar enough with the Archipelago by that time... The road would be long. All roads are long that lead to one's heart's desire. But this road my mind's eye could see on a chart, professionally, with all its complications and difficulties, yet simple enough in a way. One is a seaman or one is not. And I had no doubt of being one.'

With danger and responsibilities ahead, Raffles, at sea, passes over his own shadow line. The fleet anchored in the Bay of Batavia on 4 August 1811.

Chapter 5

The Lieutenant-Governor of Java

1811–1812

T he fleet assembled off the coast of Java 'without the loss of a single spar, or slightest accident, having passed by a route previously almost unknown, and accomplished passage declared to be impracticable,' Raffles wrote to Cousin Thomas eight years later, in the letter of 14 October 1819: 'I will not attempt to say what my feelings were on that occasion.' His arguments for the controversial route were justified. The responsibility had been awful, 'and the relief which I felt was proportionate.'

Troops, ordnance, horses and supplies were landed during the evening of 3 August 1811. Raffles remained on the *Modeste* with Lord Minto and the other non-combatants, receiving despatches from the field. The invasion force disembarked about twelve miles from Batavia. John Leyden was first on shore, prancing through the shallows dressed up as a pirate. He 'bore the brunt of the attack,' recorded the contemptuous Captain Taylor, 'which came from a flock of barn-door fowls headed by an aggressive rooster.'

The advance division under Colonel Gillespie found Batavia almost deserted. Janssens had withdrawn the French army, plus the principal Dutch, to the fortified military post of Meester Cornelis. The British found the store-houses broken open. 'I do not exaggerate,' wrote Captain Taylor, 'when I say that the streets were covered with coffee and pepper as with gravel, and in other places quantities of sugar.' Colonel Gillespie had Batavia under occupation by 9 September, but it was hardly glorious, and the main battle was to come.

The British army marched on south, past the deserted French military Cantonment at Weltesvreden, and encountered serious enemy opposition. Colonel Gillespie attacked 'with spirit and judgment' as General Sir Samuel Auchtermuty, the Commander-in-Chief, reported to Minto, and 'at the point of the bayonet, completely routed their forces' with 'trifling' loss of life. On 14 August Minto and his party came ashore and established themselves in 'a good spacious house' south of the town at Weltesvreden. Raffles and Leyden were nearby in a house belonging to a departed Dutch official on the canal at Molenvliet.

The enemy – the 'E' as Captain Taylor called them – were superior in numbers. As Gillespie and his division moved forward there was close combat ('hard service' was the military term). Sometimes, Taylor said, Colonel Gillespie positioned himself provocatively and seemed 'really disappointed if they will not fire at him.' He collapsed with fatigue, but carried on after a swig of grog.

At dawn on 26 September, as General Auchtermuty reported, 'the assault was made, the principal attack entrusted to that gallant and experienced officer, Colonel Gillespie,' who met the E's advance, 'routed it in an instant, and with a rapidity never surpassed, and under a heavy fire of grape and musketry, possessed himself of the advanced redoubt.' So it continued 'till the whole of the enemy's army was killed, captured, or dispersed.'

The carnage was horrible. 'About 1000 have been buried in the works; multitudes were cut down in the retreat; the rivers are choked up with the dead, and the huts and woods were filled with the wounded, who have since expired.' Five thousand prisoners were taken. General Janssens was thrice invited to surrender by Minto's aide-de-camp Captain William Robison (not to be confused with

William Robinson), who had a Dutch wife so spoke some Dutch. Janssens refused, and retreated to Samarang, where he formally capitulated.

As for Gillespie, 'he was everywhere.' It was conventional for a Commander-in-Chief to single out brave officers for special mention, but Auchtermuty's repeated lauding of the 'gallantry, energy, and judgment' of Colonel Gillespie was more hyperbolic than usual. Robert Rollo Gillespie was a compelling character and inspired adulation in his men. His small, girlish physique was deceptive. He was a testosterone-fuelled dynamo. Already in his mid-forties by 1811, he was known as 'Rollicking Rollo' in his home town in Co. Down in the north of Ireland.

Major William Thorn, who fought beside him, wrote Gillespie's biography – a saga of eloping, duelling, escaping from the law in disguise, being court martialled for financial irregularities, surviving an assassination attempt in Jamaica... Major Thorn's stories about his hero grow tall. Behind his narrative you hear Gillespie in Java, regaling the younger men with extravagant anecdotes about his exploits over multiple bumpers of brandy. But in 1806 Colonel Robert Rollo Gillespie, borderline psychopath, had achieved fame when, in the south Indian town of Vellore, sepoys in the Company's army broke out in violent mutiny.

The sepoys had mutinied against insensitive regulations – Hindu soldiers must not wear caste-marks, Muslims must shave off their beards, and all must wear a hat with a cow-hide cockade. The defeated Tipu Sultan of Mysore, living under house arrest within Vellore Fort, was on the side of the rebels. On the night of 10 July the sepoys in the Fort broke out, and by dawn were in control of the Fort. An officer escaped and rode the sixteen miles to Arcot to raise the alarm. He met Gillespie, Commandant of the garrison, enjoying a dawn ride. Gillespie turned his horse around, alerted a relief force, and then galloped off on his own to Vellore.

Gillespie shinned up the Fort on a rope and led the surviving

British officers in a bayonet charge. When his dragoons arrived, he had them blow up the gates of the Fort, and the cavalry stormed in. He lined up a hundred rebels against a wall and had them shot. John Blakiston, the engineer who blew up the gates, found it hard in retrospect to 'approve the deed'. Equally harsh deeds were done after the mutineers were brought to trial – some were shot out of cannon, others by firing squad, others hanged.

The British officers who had imposed the offensive regulations were eventually disciplined and the orders countermanded. But Gillespie was credited with having saved the Carnatic, the six hundred-mile strip of land on the south-east coast of India. The East India Company voted him 'a handsome present' said to be £2,500. Gillespie himself thought he was insufficiently rewarded. There was an underlying resentment and sense of entitlement in Colonel Gillespie.

The patriotic poet Henry Newbolt, born 1862, wrote a jingling fourteen-stanza ballad about the 'Hero of Vellore', ending:

> They've kept the tale a hundred years,
> They'll keep the tale a hundred more:
> Riding at dawn, riding alone,
> Gillespie came to false Vellore.

Gillespie, like Raffles, became part of the mythology of Empire.

'Colonel Gillespie will be left in command of the troops on the island,' wrote Lord Minto. 'He has been the great hero, and the chief means of our success.' Raffles as Lieutenant-Governor would represent the civil authority, and Gillespie, as Commander of the Forces, the military authority. Maybe foreseeing trouble, Minto underlined the recognised seniority of the civil power, 'strongly recommending' to the Secret Committee of the East India Company that this arrangement 'may not be superseded for the purpose of uniting the Government in the same person with the command of the Army.'

～

John Leyden, the day before the assault on Cornelis, went into the library at Batavia to investigate the Dutch archives, and then into a depository said to contain antiquities. This room had long been closed up, and when Leyden emerged he was shivering and feverish.

When Raffles tried to tell Leyden about the victory at Cornelis, he was too ill to take it in. He died on 28 August, with Raffles at his side, and was buried on the same day in the Tanah Abang burial ground in Batavia, with Raffles and Minto in attendance. Raffles paid the funeral expenses. 'I attended him from the first to the last,' Raffles wrote to Leyden's friend William Erskine in Bombay, asking Erskine to send out a 'handsome and appropriate tombstone or slab engraven on it what you please.'

Leyden's chest-tomb has two engraved slabs on its top, one giving the details of his birth and death, and the other – whether composed by Erskine or Raffles – celebrating his scholarship and his character: 'His principles as a man were pure and spotless – and as a friend he was firm and sincere. Few have passed through this life with fewer vices or with a greater prospect of happiness in the next.'

In a preface to his *History of Java* Raffles was to pay further tribute: 'There was one, dear to me in private friendship and esteem, who, had he lived, was of all men best calculated to have supplied the deficiencies in the very imperfect work now presented to the public…but just as he reached those shores on which he hoped to slake his ardent thirst for knowledge, he fell a victim to excessive exertion, deeply deplored by all, and by none more truly than myself.' Sir Walter Scott, the friend and patron of Leyden back home, published a biographical memoir of him in *The Edinburgh Annual Register*, and a poem:

> Quenched is his lamp of varied lore,
> That loved the light of song to pour;
> A distant and a deadly shore
> Has Leyden's cold remains!

Whether Leyden would have been an able or responsible

right-hand man for Raffles when it came to the nuts and bolts of administration is doubtful. 'He was to have been my private Secretary, and in this capacity, what would he not have done, with the latitude I should have given him?' wrote Raffles to one of the executors. This loss was a personal disaster for Raffles. He was bereaved not only of his 'dearest friend' but of his inspiration, his daemon.

Lord Minto sent a triumphant despatch reporting the conquest of Java to the Secretary for War and the Colonies, Lord Liverpool. He received a congratulatory reply; his communication had been 'laid before His Royal Highness the Prince Regent' and it was his Royal Highness' intention to confer medals on the principal officers 'in conformity to the principle which has of late been adopted with respect to the Campaigns in Spain and Portugal.'

This was gratifying. But the British in 1811 were more concerned about 'the Campaigns in Spain and Portugal' than in the acquisition by the East India Company of an island on the other side of the world. One of the effects of Raffles' initial posting to Penang was that his talents, his ideals and his hopes of fame remained anchored in the Eastern Isles – hence his expansionist vision for the region. In 1811 there was little hope of making Java's strategic importance to the Empire, nor the richness of its cultures, as interesting to the British Government as they were to himself.

The Prince of Wales, aged forty-eight, had become the Prince Regent, owing to the incapacity of his father King George III, a few months previously. He kept himself going on laudanum, alcohol, and the commissioning of improvements to Carlton House and the Brighton Pavilion. His biographer describes how in this very year, 1811, he was observed sitting at a table at Carlton House between his Secretary and his Secretary's assistant, 'the one placing a paper before him for his signature, the other drawing it away,' and the Prince Regent neither knowing nor caring what they were. Lord Liverpool's assurance that Lord Minto's despatch had been 'laid before His Royal Highness' meant exactly that.

⌣

On 11 September Lord Minto drove in state to Government House at Ryswick. The British takeover of Java was proclaimed in Dutch and English, and Raffles was proclaimed Lieutenant-Governor, subordinate to the Supreme Government in Bengal. Those Dutch gentlemen of the civil service who were to continue in their posts were named. Dutch laws were to remain in force provisionally, with modifications which included banning the torture or mutilation of criminals.

Raffles, as Lieutenant-Governor, was empowered to introduce new regulations 'to meet any emergency.' But all new regulations must be 'immediately reported to the Governor-General in Council in Bengal,' disclosing any representations received against the pro-posed measures. Bengal would confirm or disallow the regulations 'with the shortest possible delay.'

Minto, in consultation with Raffles, laid down guidelines for the governance of Java. He was at pains to justify to London his decision, against instructions, to retain and occupy the island. 'This is a much greater country than I believe is generally conceived,' he wrote to the Secret Committee. Java should be made an English colony 'as soon as we can, by the introduction of English colonists, English capital, and therefore of English interests,' although the Dutch, resident over generations, should not be excluded. He flagged up essential changes in the inequitable system of tax-collecting which 'will require considerable preparation.' He had already suppressed the farming of gaming and cockfighting licences, and although the 'monstrous system' of slavery could not be eradicated all at once, he was banning further purchases of slaves.

Minto and Raffles were aware that in the event of a peace with France, Java would almost certainly be returned to the Dutch. 'All I fear is a general peace,' wrote Minto. But this threat (to most Europeans, a hope), should not prevent the administration from 'improving the condition of a people that has become tributary to our authority and tributary to our prosperity. All we are justified in avoiding is the prosecution in this interval of expensive works.'

Reflecting on the uncertainty of England's retention of the island, Lord Minto said: 'While we are here let us do as much good as we can.'

On 3 October 1811 Minto gave a dinner for General Sir Samuel Auchtermuty and the army officers. Auchtermuty proposed a toast which, he said, was never before possible – to Lord Minto, 'Governor-General of *all* India.' As Raffles wrote in triumph on 5 October to William Marsden, apprising him of his appointment as Lieutenant-Governor: 'No man better than yourself can appreciate the value of this new acquisition to the British empire – it is in fact *the other India.*'

Raffles gave a dinner and entertainment for Lord Minto, with fireworks, the day before he sailed for Calcutta. Raffles knew how to give a party. The avenue through the garden was illuminated, a temple at the end bearing the word 'MINTO'. On each side of the avenue Chinese players performed musical burlesques. The dinner itself was distressing, with dissonance between those leaving Java and delighted to be going, and those remaining and less ebullient. Dutch ladies were invited, and Olivia and the Raffles sisters had been shipped over. During Lord Minto's farewell speech, all the ladies present burst into tears. Captain Taylor, longing to see his wife and new baby in Bengal, was 'never in higher spirits in my life…and away we went to our carriages like so many sky rockets.'

Lieutenant-Governor Thomas Stamford Raffles, aged thirty-one, was on his own now, in charge – nominally – of a whole country, a little larger than England, with about the same population. Be careful what you wish for.

Olivia wrote personally to Lord Minto at the end of January 1812. Her handwriting is neat and evenly spaced, as if copied from a draft, but her tone is emotional. 'I am sadly deficient in words, and therefore can only assure you in the simple language of the heart that it throbs with affection as dear and as tender for you as ever a child's did for a Father – you my Lord gave me a right to call you so, when at Malacca you desired me to consider myself as your Daughter, *happy me...*' She hoped to see him once again in '*your Country* – this beautiful Java – everything here is beautiful! sweet enchanting!' The conviction that 'you, and you only have been the cause of our enjoying this sweet happiness adds infinitely to my content.'

'Sweet happiness' hardly described the challenges facing Raffles.

The British had demonised Marshal Daendels. Minto, with uncharacteristic windiness, described him as 'one of the monsters which the worst times of the French Revolution engendered...greedy, corrupt, and rascally in amassing money for himself.' Daendels, by now far away fighting in Napoleon's Russian campaign, was indeed a hard man, and a mean one. Hugh Hope, one of Raffles' civil servants, told Captain Taylor that he had seen 'a receipt of Daendels for the sum which he made Janssens pay for the fish in the pond at Buitenzorg, at so much a fish.'

Yet his legacy was helpful to Raffles, who adopted and carried forward some of his projects. Daendels had, during his short administration, constructed with forced labour not only the excellent new military road, or post road, but other roads, bridges, barracks, hospitals and public buildings, of which Raffles' cash-poor administration got the benefit.

Raffles had the *Java Government Gazette* up and running at the end of February 1812, on the model of the *Prince of Wales Island Gazette*. The first issue announced that 'Advertisements, Articles of Intelligence, Essays and Poetical Pieces' would be accepted. It carried the Lieutenant-Governor's General Orders and Proclamations (in English and Dutch), ship movements, marriages, births and deaths, extracts from the *Calcutta Gazette* and from Westminster debates – a mixture of parish pump and world news, the latter months out of date.

The British Prime Minister, Spencer Perceval, was assassinated in London in May 1812, not to be replaced (by Lord Liverpool) for a year – by which time news of the murder had just about reached

Java. Hostilities had been ongoing for eight months already by the time the *Gazette* reported the outbreak of the 1812 war with America. Raffles did his bit by ordering a blockade on all American vessels.. Since the Americans purchased the preponderance of Javanese coffee, this hurt Java rather more than it hurt the Americans. Social events were reported in the *Gazette* with the customary jocular hyperbole. On 12 March 1812 there was a nocturnal 'Pic-nic' with dancing, attended by 'all the beauty and fashion of the Metropolis of East-Insular India.'

Batavia itself was notoriously unhealthy with, historically, a staggeringly high death rate among Europeans. The shoreline was swampy. The rivers and the Dutch-built canals were foul with sewage. Walls of houses were coated in green slime up to several feet from the ground. Listed illnesses included recurrent fever (malaria), dysentery and diarrhoea, vomiting, hepatitis, rheumatism, venereal, and 'other'.

Daendels had done a lot towards cleaning up Batavia. but Raffles and his family still preferred to be in the fresh air thirty-five miles away at Buitenzorg, the large, shabby neo-classical country house built by a former Dutch governor. Raffles spent two days or so each week at the Residence at Ryswick, just outside Batavia, while conducting much of his business from Buitenzorg. The drive took four hours each way, his carriage drawn by four – and if he was in a hurry, six – local ponies, 'the most beautiful creatures in the world,' as he told William Brown Ramsay. Captain Taylor described the countryside around Buitenzorg as like 'the most beautiful parts of Shropshire or Devonshire.'

Raffles' 'family' at Buitenzorg included Olivia, and from time to time his sisters. The family doctor, Sir Thomas Sevestre, three years younger than Raffles, was part of the household. Raffles' half-dozen aides-de-camp, all a few years younger than he, shared his and Olivia's domestic life and travelled with them. These young men were given additional appointments, which meant extra allowances. Captain Thomas Otho Travers, for example, was Assistant

The Lieutenant-Governor of Java

Secretary to Government in the Military Department, and Town Major of Batavia.

Travers was devoted to Raffles. He was an emotional creature but his literary style was stilted. In his new diary for 1813, he wrote: 'It is now nearly two years since I became intimate with Mr and Mrs Raffles, and during that time, as my intimacy increased in their family, I have had the satisfaction to experience a similar and kind attention towards me.' At Buitenzorg he passed 'the happiest days since I left my own country'. At Christmas 1812 they had 'all kinds of gaiety…the utmost hilarity and good humour prevailed, and continued without interruption from Christmas Day till the 6th of January' – when the party broke up and went back to Batavia to celebrate the Queen's Birthday, 'a very grand and superb fete' with five hundred people to supper. Raffles did not only want fame and to do good. He wanted to showcase British prestige. It all cost money.

Captain William Robison, Minto's former ADC, was appointed Secretary to Government, but this did not work out. Robison, nearly as energetic as Raffles himself, was dissatisfied as Secretary, and resigned. The post was given to Charles Blagrave, whom Raffles had recruited for Java when he called in at Batavia en route for Malacca. This did not work out either. Raffles sacked Blagrave and replaced him with Charles Assey, a young man from Suffolk who proved reliable. Lieutenant-Governor Raffles was not altogether easy to work with. Overwhelmed, he found it hard to keep his small team of civil servants informed of what he required of them.

Raffles was Lieutenant-Governor in Council, and the first three Council members, appointed by Lord Minto before he left, were Colonel Gillespie, Herman Warner Muntinghe and Jacob Willem Cranssen – the last two, Dutchmen friendly to the English, had held office in the previous Government. There were other Dutch families – Engelhards, Van Riemsdijks, Timmerson Thyssens – long-established merchants and former Government officials, who constituted a sort of gentry, supportive of Raffles and his administration.

Two of the ceremonious diplomatic exchanges which Raffles had in Malacca with the rulers of the Archipelago had repercussions early in his administration. Both concerned territories beyond Java.

He had mentioned, in his last mega-letter to Minto before the invasion, the kingdom of Banjarmasin on the south-east coast of Borneo, lately abandoned by the Dutch. The Rajah of Banjarmasin had sent an embassy to the Government of Penang inviting the British to take it over. Any decision, Raffles advised Minto, would be 'premature'.

Sophia Raffles in her *Memoir* wrote that it was Minto, not Raffles, who appointed Alexander Hare as Commissioner and Resident at Banjarmasin soon after the invasion, but who knows on what advice: Raffles had brought his wild friend Hare, whom he had met in Malacca, along with him to Java. Hare was authorised to make a contract with the Rajah on the Company's behalf for a coastal strip. Then Hare acquired, for free, a further 1,400 square miles for himself personally. Raffles as Lieutenant-Governor sanctioned this, even though he had specifically decreed that 'the acceptance of gifts by a Resident will involve immediate dismissal.' Raffles also furnished Hare with a so-called 'working population' from Java, which included a consignment of women, allegedly 'of loose morals', some of them hijacked by force from their villages. Hare had a gruesome sexual appetite. These unsavoury measures became known to historians as the 'Banjarmasin Enormity'.

When Raffles in 1813 revived the dormant Batavian Society of Arts and Science, in his address to the Society he praised Alexander Hare, saying that under his administration Banjarmasin had been 'reduced to order and regulation'. Not so. Banjarmasin was reduced to squalor, poverty, disorder and unprofitability. In *The History of Java*, Raffles wrote about the island of Borneo, but did not even mention Banjarmasin.

In conniving with Hare, Raffles betrayed his values. He was often inconsistent – most people are, but most people are not subjected to scrutiny. What Raffles and Hare had in common was flaring vitality and the same sort of poor-respectable London background. Raffles was sexually disciplined. He aspired to win the approval of the Establishment. There can be a mutual attraction between such a man and a promiscuous, unscrupulous, rule-breaker such as Hare, each responding to suppressed possibilities, paths not taken.

Equally serious in its aftermath was the Palembang affair. Palembang, an ancient jungle kingdom, was a major commercial centre, sixty miles up from the delta of the Musi river off the south-east coast of Sumatra. It had been a dependency of Batavia. In September 1811, shortly after the invasion of Java, the Sultan Mahmud Badaruddin ordered the massacre of the Dutch garrison in Palembang. The men were taken out in a boat down the river to the sea and murdered or drowned. Their women were abused and raped.

Raffles, knowing nothing of this, sent on 3 November a three-man mission (which included Alexander Hare) to Palembang to receive the surrender of the Dutch as part of the capitulation of Java and its dependencies. The Sultan would not treat with the mission, on the grounds that he had broken with the Dutch well before the British invasion, and that Palembang was therefore not a Dutch (or French) dependency, but autonomous.

The massacre, as Raffles understood it, had been perpetrated to conceal a continued Dutch presence. Outraged, at the end of April 1812 he sent Colonel Gillespie with troops and a small fleet to dethrone the murderous Sultan, sign a treaty with his brother Najmuddin, and take possession, in addition, of the adjacent islands of Billiton and tin-rich Banca, which he coveted for commercial and strategic reasons.

When Gillespie and his troops arrived by river at the battlements of Palembang, at night and in a thunderstorm, they found that the inhabitants of the place had gone on the rampage and fired and ransacked the palace. Sultan Badaruddin had fled. Gillespie hoisted the British flag on the bastion, and placed the Sultan's brother Najmuddin on the vacant throne under a ritual yellow canopy in a solemn ceremony.

Raffles wrote to Lord Minto just two days before the departure of Gillespie for Palembang, telling him he was 'aware that I have taken too much responsibility on myself,' but the expedition had to be despatched at once, or wait another whole year because of the winds. This became his pattern. He reported diligently to the Governor-General, but generally after the event.

Raffles appointed Robison, promoted from Captain to Major, as British Resident in Palembang. It was a job suited, perhaps, to his energies, but Robison went too far. Sultan Najmuddin, installed by Gillespie, seemed to Robison ineffective, and what is more he had no money. Part of Robison's job was to make contact with the deposed Sultan Badaruddin, who had all the treasure with him in his jungle exile. Thinking Badaruddin a better bet, Robison re-installed him on the throne on his own authority, taking off him 200,000 Spanish dollars on behalf of the British Government. He brought the cash back to Batavia with a bunch of Palembang princes as diplomatic back-up.

Raffles and Gillespie were appalled by Robison's highhandedness. Raffles decided to annul the treaty Robison had made with Badaruddin, and sent a ship commanded by Captain George Elliot with 400 men to evict Badaruddin once more, in favour of the brother. The accompanying officials took back to Palembang the Spanish dollars, with instructions, according to Travers, to return some to the twice-deposed Sultan, and the remainder to 'the Sultan created by us.' Robison, in retaliation, was to allege that Raffles had kept back half of the money in Batavia.

Robison was officially reprimanded, and his high-handed actions investigated. 'The rumour of the day ran much to the prejudice of Major Robison,' wrote Captain Travers, 'and attributed motives to his conduct which, I trust, will hereafter prove to have never existed.' These motives consisted of Robison having accepted a bribe from Badaruddin. The investigating commission had to report that Colonel Gillespie too had received gifts from the Sultan whom he had installed.

Java had never been completely conquered by any European power.

The ancient empire of Mataram in Central Java had been paramount on the island, first as a Hindu then as an Islamic polity after the Muslim takeover of the island in the fifteenth century. In the mid-eighteenth century Mataram was divided between the Sultanates of Surakarta (also known as Solo, and where the Sultan was called the Susuhunan), and Yogyakarta. Before Lord Minto left the Island, Captain (as he then was) Robison paid a diplomatic visit to the two courts to assure them that their treaties with the Dutch would be respected. Raffles feared that his own plans might be compromised by Robison's injudicious promises, and in November 1811 he replaced the Dutch Resident at Yogyakarta with John Crawfurd.

On 25 April 1812 the *Gazette* reported: 'We understand Mrs Raffles has been requested by the officers of the station to fix a night, upon which to honour them with her presence, at a Ball and Supper, previous to her departure...' For while Gillespie was away in Palembang, Raffles removed himself and his family to Samarang on the coast east of Batavia, well-placed for visiting the kingdoms of Surakarta and Yogyakarta, due south over the mountains. Samarang was a congenial little port with around five hundred European and Eurasian inhabitants. The English established a race-course at nearby Salatiga (never attended by Raffles). Raffles stayed with Nicholas Engelhard, former Governor of Yogyakarta.

On 14 May all 'the beauty and fashion of Samarang' attended a ball and supper, enlivened by 'the bewitching power of Bacchus'. Captain George Elliot and the *Modeste* chanced to put in at Samarang, and the ship's officers gave an 'entertainment' for the English and the 'principal Dutch fashionables'. Captain Elliot was the one who wrote that Raffles was 'neither born and bred a *gentleman*' – to which he added 'he had a low set of people about him [in Java], all of some talent, but unfit for advisers, particularly as to gentlemanly conduct.' He probably meant the gang of young ADCs around Raffles and Olivia, and their convivial, noisy parties.

The purpose of this journey was for Raffles to pay formal visits to the Susuhunan of Surakarta and the Sultan of Yogyakarta, and to counteract any impression of indulgence that Robison had conveyed. He went first to Surakarta, where the Susuhunan agreed to give up the profits from his birds' nests (for soup, much in demand in China and very lucrative) and his teak forests in exchange for a fixed payment. He presented Raffles with a valuable *kris* – the wavy-bladed dagger of the Malays. So far so good.

Colonel Colin Mackenzie accompanied Raffles to Surakarta. He was in the area anyway, engaged on an intractable commission from Raffles – to survey the island of Java from every possible aspect: geographical, social and economic, historical and cultural. It was a mighty task even for Mackenzie, a conscientious and able man, six feet two inches tall, from the Outer Hebrides. Raffles made in Surakarta a new friend – an American physician and naturalist from Pennsylvania, Dr Thomas Horsfield. He had been in Java for more than a decade, retained by the Dutch, and then the French, to research the useful and medicinal plants of the island; these researches expanded into every branch of natural history.

Horsfield and Raffles met at the Susuhunan's official reception where, as Horsfield recorded, Raffles 'came up to me and with an affability and suavity of manner peculiar to himself offered me his acquaintance without the formality of an introduction.' 'Suavity' was a term often used of Raffles. It meant, then, sweetness of manner. Raffles went round to Horsfield's house, and 'devoted several hours to patient examination of the objects of natural history, drawings, maps and illustrations which had been collected and prepared during my excursions through the central and eastern territories of Java.' Raffles signed Horsfield up with the Company, agreeing a salary, and authorising him to enquire into 'all divisions of natural history without limitations or restrictions.' It was to prove a fruitful relationship.

From Surakarta, Raffles sent to Yogyakarta a mission which included W.H. Muntinghe and Colonel Colin Mackenzie to pave the way for a treaty. Sultan Hamengkubuwana II, untruthfully, expressed himself as agreeable to anything, so Raffles set off himself to Yogyakarta, accompanied by light cavalry and his personal staff. There was a stand-off when he was met outside the Sultan's *kraton,* or palace, about whether he should ride in the first or second coach. He appropriated the first, leaving the second for the Sultan. He was making it clear that what was at issue was British supremacy.

The crisis occurred when the Sultan paid a visit to the British Residency in Yogyakarta. There were two golden thrones on a raised dais. One – which Raffles appropriated – was purposefully positioned further forward than the other. The Sultan, who came attended by scores of armed guards, ordered that the thrones should be placed side by side. Raffles refused to allow this. The Sultan's guards each unsheathed his *kris,* the Sultan unsheathed his. Raffles – who had never seen action or fired a shot in his life – drew his sword.

Raffles broke the tension by sheathing his sword. Who knows what was going on in his mind – how to avoid a bloodbath, or just the blankness that shuts down thought in extreme situations. The effect, however, was not of submission, but of a calm assumption of having made his point. John Crawfurd, the Resident, uttered emollient words. The Sultan sat down. The bad moment passed. Raffles and the Sultan proceeded to communicate courteously enough and an agreement was signed (not that the Sultan intended to honour it).

Raffles failed to make the return visit to the Sultan the next day, which etiquette demanded. He and his entourage simply left Yogyakarta. This was a calculated snub and offended the Sultan, who thenceforth began to intrigue against the British. The Dutch Residents at the Central Javanese courts had traditionally acted like ambassadors, not like colonial overseers. Raffles' actions, designed to demonstrate that the British did not accept the autonomy of the Central Javanese courts, amply succeeded. They were also counterproductive, making armed confrontation highly likely.

A Sultan of Yogyakarta had semi-divine status. He was a *bathara* or *bitara,* as Raffles had wished Minto to present himself in the

Eastern Isles. The etiquette of dress, behaviour and precedence at the court were of a complexity which rendered the manners of England's royal drawing rooms rustic in comparison. The interventions, expulsions and substitutions which Raffles made among the rulers in Java and elsewhere would seem breathtaking in their presumption, were it not that the succession, or the continuance of a reign, was frequently disputed, with no input from occupying powers at all. In Yogyakarta, shortly after Captain Robison's earlier diplomatic visit, Hamengkubuwana II ousted from the throne the Crown Prince, reigning as Hamengkubuwana III, who had previously ousted him. Raffles had acknowledged the man he met as the rightful ruler, while protesting, through John Crawfurd, against his revenge killings.

John Crawfurd was a sound appointment as Resident in Yogyakarta. He was from the Isle of Islay off the west coast of Scotland and was, like Colin Mackenzie, a Gaelic speaker. Raffles had known him as a medical officer in Penang, and brought him to Java along with his wife. Like Raffles, Crawfurd collected manuscripts and was interested in antiquities. Though the two were never close friends, Raffles valued him as an administrator, a fellow Orientalist, and a linguist; he was fluent in Malay and became so in Javanese. He was two years younger than Raffles but dour, and did not get on with Hamengkubawana II.

After Raffles' provocative visit, a secret correspondence sprang up between the courts of Yogyakarta and Surakarta, plotting to resist the British. The Sultan of Yogyakarta strengthened the walls around his *kraton*.

Raffles heard of this, and to him the conspiracy was treachery. He was not militaristic and would much rather unseat the Sultan of Yogyakarta by peaceful means – that is, by devious diplomacy. He wrote to Minto on 2 June 1812 that 'the conduct and disposition of the Sultan is so unfavourable and unsafe that his removal becomes necessary... I hope we may be able to effect the change without bloodshed.' But his own actions had made this virtually impossible.

Colonel Gillespie, only back a week from Palembang, was mustering his troops at Samarang in early June 1812.

The *kraton* at Yogyakarta was a compound three miles in circumference, containing the houses of the Sultan, his women and his extended family, guest-houses, open-sided reception halls, offices, barracks, and a water palace – a floating fantasy. John Crawfurd said that in his time as many as 10,000 people lived in the *kraton* – guards, servants, children, retainers, clients and pensioners. An eyewitness account of what happened there between 18 and 20 June 1812 appears in a Javanese tree-bark manuscript – the draft of a historical chronicle, or *babad* – by Bendara Pangeran Arya Panular, uncle and father-in-law of the Crown Prince.

The troops, in their red coats and plumed helmets, clanked out from the Dutch-built Vredeburg Fort in Yogyakarta in the afternoon of 18 June, up the straight ceremonial road called Malioboro to the *kraton*, naked sabres in their hands. They bombarded the *kraton* with shells, 'hard service' raged both inside and outside the walls, and fires were set. Raffles and John Crawfurd remained in the Residency, directly opposite the Vredeburg Fort on the ceremonial road.

Then came the looting. The spoils of war were legitimate perquisites, regulated by 'Prize Agents', who creamed off something for their trouble. But the British sacking of the *kraton* was of an extreme nature, never officially acknowledged. Colonel Gillespie in his report to Lieutenant-Governor Raffles praised his troops' 'steadiness and discipline'; in 'the heat of the storm' the Sultan's person was respected, 'his family was placed in security and protection, and no part of the property was either pillaged or molested.'

The value of the loot was calculated at about 800,000 Spanish dollars. Royal family members were forced to hand over their personal jewels. Panular, while describing the 'unbridled looting, burning and plundering', did emphasise that there was no violation of the palace women. The only officer, Captain Hector Maclean, who attempted to 'carry off' a lady was stabbed by her in the neck and later died. The *kris* was confiscated from each gentlemen of the court. This was humiliating. A man's *kris* was a sacred object, emblematic of his manhood and identity.

Chests and boxes of treasure were carted down the road to the Vredeburg Fort. Precious books and manuscripts were taken to the Residency, where Raffles and Crawfurd pored over them. The Sultan surrendered on 20 June, and the Crown Prince was proclaimed once more Hamengkubuwana III in the throne room of the Residency. John Crawfurd humiliated the losers by making them kneel, forcing their heads down to pay obeisance to Lieutenant-Governor Raffles and the new Sultan – who, unwillingly, had to agree to the annexation of yet more of his lands and privileges.

Considering the cultural treasures which he retained, it was a bit rich of Raffles to complain to Colonel Gillespie, as he did, about the unregulated share-out of prize money among the troops. Gillespie replied that on account of a severe wound in his upper left arm, he had been unable to oversee everything. 'Upon maturely considering the distribution of the prize money, I clearly perceive that the subject should have been referred to your authority, before a measure of so much importance had taken place.' This reply is courteous, if covertly ironic. Gillespie, the hero of Vellore and of Cornelis, did not like being ticked off by an inexperienced civilian.

Raffles wrote to Minto from Samarang on 25 June that 'Gillespie was himself' in the assault, and 'European power is for the first time paramount in Java.' He did not complain publicly about Gillespie's laxness over the prize money. But who would pay the costs of the military operation? The British Government would not want to, nor would the Company, since the attack was not ordered or authorised. Minto conveyed in a private letter – signed off 'most truly and affectionately yours' – his approval of Raffles' actions at both Palembang and Yogyakarta. But he urged Raffles to send him quickly the necessary 'materials' which he needed in order to convey to the East India Company the justification for these operations on grounds of 'justice and expediency', which they would definitely expect.

Captain Thomas Otto Travers recalled how Raffles, in the course of the seventy-two-hour sailing from Samarang back to Batavia, drew up 'the Report on the capture of Djocjocarta, entering into a full and clear account of the circumstances which rendered this measure absolutely necessary for the presence of peace on the Island.' Palembang was another matter; the required materials were never sent. Sophia Raffles in the *Memoir* wrote that 'to this unavoidable omission may be attributed much of the trouble and difficulty in which Mr Raffles was afterwards involved.'

The assault on the *kraton* at Yogyakarta was not an unprecedented outrage. Daendels too had attacked the *kraton* in December 1810 (when Raffles was in Malacca) with more than three thousand men – three times more than were involved in the British assault – and forced Hamengkubuwana II to stand down in favour of his son the Crown Prince. Huge amounts of prize money were carried away on that occasion too.

The British assault was not remembered with any particular bitterness, and not only because the Sultan owed his restored position to Raffles. The Resident, John Crawfurd, was popular. All the references to him in Panular's *babad* are so flattering that it could have been drafted for his eyes, though that is too cynical. Crawfurd was respected for his mastery of the Javanese language and his courtesy to the re-installed Sultan; and admiration for certain European qualities was not uncommon. A study of literary responses to Western culture and values (admittedly in Arabic texts, not Javanese) by Rasheed El-Enany finds a prevailing idealisation of the Western 'other', and a desire to strengthen the home culture by appropriating Western science and technology, and Western courage and prowess. Panular presented the defeat as a moral collapse in the face of the discipline and the bravery of the British.

Politically, Daendels and Raffles between them changed the perspective with an idea of colonialism which did not limit itself to coastal settlements and treaties negotiated with local rulers. Raffles assumed sovereignty – never actually achieved – over the whole island. In a public letter about Gillespie's 'brilliant achievement' in the *Gazette*, he described Yogyakarta as having long been 'the bane of the European authority in Java, maintaining in a state of absolute independence the finest provinces of the Island'. 'Absolute independence' was not to be tolerated.

A private death had taken place on the other side of the world. The burial of 'Captain Raffles, of Trinity Ground' (the almshouse), was registered at the church of St Nicholas, Deptford, on 23 November 1811. There is a constrained note from Raffles to his Uncle William, Cousin Thomas's father, written from Buitenzorg in October 1812, after the news reached him: 'My Mother informs me she is much indebted to you for your kind attention to her in the hour of trouble and at the time of my poor father's death, and I should not do justice to my feelings did I not avail myself of the earliest opportunity to express my acknowledgments.' To this he added a few sentences of family *politesse* and good wishes. There was nothing more to say.

Chapter 6

'Too Sensational'

Java 1812–1814

T he first anniversary of victory in Java was celebrated with 'the best Feast ever on the island,' with Colonel Gillespie 'the Hero of Cornelis' presiding and his health drunk 'in treble bumpers standing'. But in early 1813 Raffles heard that the Board of Control in London was making no decision about the future of Java until 'a more full and satisfactory' report had been received.

Raffles had no job-security and he was, in himself, insecure in the job. He had been a back-office man, albeit a zealous and influential one. He was more than capable of rising to a challenge, and he did not lack bravado. What he lacked was support. In October 1812 he wrote to William Brown Ramsay: 'I am here alone, without any advice, in a new country with a large native population of six or seven millions of people, a great proportion of foreign Europeans and a standing Army of not less than seven thousand men… I can hardly say what change has taken place in me since we parted. I feel I am somewhat older, and, in many points of a worldly nature, I am apt to view men and things in a somewhat different light, but it is my belief that I am intrinsically the same.'

Most people in his uncertain situation would have coasted, doing as much good as they could in the time that they had (to quote Lord

Minto). Raffles did just the opposite. He held fast to his vision. He *would* make his mark, and he *would* convince the British Government of Java's value, just as if the British were to be administering it for the foreseeable future.

His most radical reforms were concerned with the currency crisis and the system of land tenure, and are central to an assessment of his administration – though some may warm to the irony of Miss Prism, the governess in Oscar Wilde's *The Importance of Being Earnest*: 'Cecily, you will read your Political Economy in my absence. The chapter on the Fall of the Rupee you may omit. It is somewhat too sensational.'

Lord Minto was emphatic that land-tenure reform was essential, but only after full investigation, not 'suddenly and ignorantly attempted'. He advised the Secret Committee in London (3 October 1811) that 'the whole system of property is vicious and adverse alike to the interests of Government and people,' but warned Raffles before he left the island not to go too far or too fast.

The system inherited by Raffles was dominated by the principal local chiefs, called 'Regents' by the Dutch. Java was a country of villages, and at the bottom of the economic pyramid were the village cultivators. Goods and services were provided gratis to the Regents through a chain of village headmen, officials and royal relatives, each taking his cut. Neither the Regents nor the Dutch had any direct connection with the cultivators. The Regents supplied the colonial Government by 'forced deliveries' (at fixed prices, under contract, though sometimes not paid for) and 'contingents' (free supplies of rice in exchange for supporting a Regent in his own conflicts). The Regents provided forced labour for roads and public works. The Chinese exercised their own forms of profiteering, hiring whole villages from the Regents.

Raffles determined to improve the lives of the cultivators by contracting for goods and services, not with the Regents but with the cultivators themselves through their village headmen, and

1. No one would guess from this formal portrait by George Francis Joseph (1817), that Sir Thomas Stamford Raffles FRS had recently been recalled by the East India Company from his post as Lieutenant-Governor of Java. Here he is the quintessential statesman and connoisseur, with papers on his knee and at his elbow, and Javanese objects from his collection on the table beside him.

2. Raffles' unfortunate father Captain Benjamin Raffles, around the time that Raffles was born.

3. A drawing of his mother Anne towards the end of her life.

4. The Rev. Thomas Raffles, his first cousin and confidant, and a celebrity preacher.

5. Raffles' much-loved first wife Olivia, ten years older than he and with a child born out of wedlock.

6. India House, the pompous headquarters of the East India Company in Leadenhall Street in the City where, from the age of fourteen, Raffles laboured as a copying-clerk for ten long years.

7/8. Raffles' favourite sister Maryanne, and her second husband Captain William Flint.

9. Their son Charles, 'Charley Boy', aged five. He was brought up by Raffles and his second wife Sophia. They had the drawing done for Maryanne, and Charley Boy's coat, embroidered 'in the Polish fashion', cost them six guineas.

10. Raffles' adoring second wife Sophia, painted shortly after their marriage – note the prominently displayed wedding ring. She was tougher and more resourceful than the fanciful costume suggests, and the mother of his five children.

11. Companion-piece to the portrait of Sophia, depicting Raffles' foxy colouring and light eyes more faithfully than other portraits.

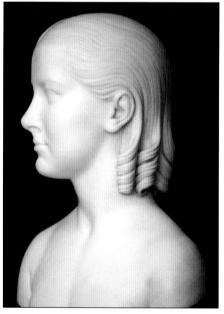

12. Bust of Ella, their only surviving child (until aged nineteen), said to be just like her father.

13. Princess Charlotte, daughter of the Prince Regent, who befriended Raffles and probably engineered his knighthood.

14/15/16/17 (clockwise): William Farquhar, first Resident and Commandant of Singapore, with whom Raffles fell out disastrously. John Palmer, the rich merchant who briefed against Raffles in Calcutta. Lord Minto, Governor-General of India, Raffles' mentor and his collaborator in planning the invasion of Java. He gave this portrait to Raffles. Robert Rollo Gillespie, the military hero who brought charges against Raffles.

18. Borobudur in Central Java, the great Buddhist temple uncovered from the jungle by Raffles' team.

19. Dick the Papuan Boy, whom Raffles brought to London in 1816.

20. A head of Buddha brought home by Raffles from Borobudur.

21. Image of a Javanese shadow puppet from Raffles' collection.

introducing a cash economy. Each village would be charged a fixed land-rent, and cultivators would be free to grow whatever crops they wanted. Revenue would be siphoned directly to Government without passing through the 'grasping hands' of the Regents, and 'the spur given to industry and speculation,' as he told Cousin Elton in October 1813, 'will correct the balance of trade by increasing our exports.'

This was not an original idea. An advocate of the village land-rent system was a liberal Dutchman, Dirk van Hogendorp, in Patna at the turn of the century. He advocated abolition of forced personal services and a cash economy. Raffles did not come to grips with Van Hogendorp's *Berigt* – it was in Dutch – until he came to write his *History of Java*, but its ideas were widely known. Daendels had considered this village land-rent system too, but abandoned it because the Javanese had few needs and didn't have any money anyway. He thought it better to check abuses rather than change the whole system.

Raffles, the 'intrepid innovator' as John Crawfurd described him, determined not to fine-tune the existing system but to transform it. In keeping with Minto's requirement for thorough investigation, in January 1812 he set up a four-man committee, consisting of Lieutenant-Colonel Colin Mackenzie (who already had the general survey of the island on his hands) and three Dutch officials, to collect information and agricultural statistics.

Primarily concerned with the well-being of the people, Raffles instructed his committee that 'Government should consider the inhabitants without reference to bare mercantile profits and to connect the sources of the revenue with the general prosperity of the Colony.' But the relationship between the common good and the profit-making purpose of the Company, answerable to shareholders, was uncomfortable.

His committee duly recommended that 'all kinds of servitude should be abolished.' There should be a capitation tax on all men able to work. Cultivators should grow whatever crops they wanted to. Any loss of revenue would be made good by increased production and savings in central warehousing. Salt-pans, saltpetre works, pearl reefs and bird's nest rocks should remain Government property. Lands might profitably be sold off, preferably to Europeans rather than to the Chinese, who remitted their money back to China.

Raffles had to compensate the Regents with expensive sweeteners; his committee reported that they might be happy to accept a permanent salary and the secure succession of their nearest relative, in lieu of controlling the system. One of his investigators had a worry: 'I am convinced that once the Javanese has land in his possession and is left to himself without any restriction, he will not work for more than is absolutely necessary for himself and his family.'

The creation of new wants would take time and effort. Karl Marx, to illustrate in *Das Kapital* (1867) how simple communities worked, quoted a passage about village continuity from Raffles' *History of Java*: 'The inhabitants give themselves no trouble about the breaking up and division of kingdoms; while the village remains entire, they care not to what power it is transferred or to what sovereign it devolves; its internal economy remains unchanged.'

Muntinghe, on whom Raffles relied heavily, took the view that if the Javanese held property and saw the means of improving their lives, they would 'naturally display the principles and faculties innate in every human being.' While noting Raffles' praiseworthy aim of improving the inhabitants' lives at the expense of 'bare mercantile profit', he observed drily that the 'safest principle' to be adopted was that 'every colony does or ought to exist for the benefit of the motherland.'

Raffles was unresolved on this point. He squared the circle by believing that with more humane practices greater profits would accrue to the Company. He identified one immediate opportunity for the Company to create a market in Java for cheap printed cottons from England. 'I am most sanguine in my expectations of success,' he wrote to Secretary William Ramsay in London, 'provided strict attention is paid to patterns and sizes.' The Company sent out a consignment of cottons, but the experiment failed. Colours in the native batiks and tie-dyes might fade over time, but the dyes of the British goods were not fast, and the colours ran.

Raffles' village collection system was first tried out by John Crawfurd in the Transferred Districts – transferred, that is, from the defeated Sultan of Yogyakarta – where, as Raffles told William Marsden, 'the whole of the uncertain revenues collected by the native princes has been reduced to a fixed land-rent, payable in money half-yearly.' He informed the Secret Committee in London that he intended to extend the system throughout the island, making one compromise in deference to 'popular sentiments and opinion': part of the rent must be paid in money, but part could be paid in rice. That was because, as Daendels had found, the villagers had virtually no money.

He was doggedly optimistic, as anyone had to be in order to force through such a change; though there was just possibly – not probably – some cousinly jocularity in his boast to Elton Hamond that, 'You will thus see, that I have the happiness to release several millions of my fellow creatures from a state of bondage and arbitrary oppression.'

By 1814 Raffles had moved on further, trying out 'detailed settlements': cultivators were to be assessed on their individual holdings and to pay taxes and land-rent individually, not to the village headmen but direct to Government. A cultivator – a *ryot* – was to be secure in his holding so long as he could pay up. He told Minto he was putting in place 'the principles of the *ryotwari* settlement' in India 'without my knowing they had been adopted elsewhere.' But what worked in India would not necessarily work in Java, and since it was almost certain that the island would be returned to the Dutch, the changes could never be seen through properly during Raffles' administration. It was this very feeling that he was working against a deadline that made him over-zealous. If he made a success, whoever came after him would find his admirable system in operation.

On resuming their administration of Java, the Dutch did indeed retain Raffles' village collection system for upwards of fourteen years, correcting some anomalies. There was nothing intrinsically wrong with it. The *ryotwari* system was another matter. It remained incomplete and inconsistent, and in many districts never superseded the village collection system.

The cultivators, unable to pay the taxes and land-rent required in cash, especially in years of drought, had recourse to Chinese moneylenders. They compounded their difficulties by forward-selling their next year's crops. Under the *ryotwari* system the village headmen, most of them illiterate, remained responsible for providing each individual's accounts for the Government collectors. Between the headmen, the cultivators, the collectors, and the native writers called in to set pen to paper, muddle and confusion resulted in insanely creative accounting.

Even the principle of free cultivation was not strictly adhered to. Most villagers, left to themselves, would cultivate almost nothing but rice. In 1814 Raffles acquired from the Sultan of Bantam in West Java his pepper-growing highlands, in return for 10,000 Spanish dollars a year and the annulment of his debts. The cultivators' rent agreements included a demand to plant thousands of new pepper vines for the export market. The teak forests too remained under the control of Government. This was not free cultivation. As John Bastin has written, in Bantam the 'liberal principles' of the *ryotwari* system 'conflicted with reality.'

'Farms', too, were still auctioned by Government during Raffles' time. These farms were not agricultural. They were arrangements by which sums of money were paid to Government by individuals, often Chinese, sometimes Company employees, in exchange for a monopoly of the collection of specified charges. The selling of some ordinary commodities such as fish and tobacco, and the bazaars themselves, were leased or 'farmed'. (Raffles was in favour of farms for arack and opium, thinking the trade was better regulated and controlled thereby.) So the cultivators had to find yet more money that they did not have.

Raffles had to believe that the *ryotwari* system was working, and needed to make the Company believe it. As he wrote to Minto in February 1814, 'in its success or otherwise I am willing to stand or fall.' He never claimed to have brought the whole island into the system, only Bantam, Cheribon and the Eastern Districts – but this entailed, he was to claim in *The History of Java*, 'a population of a million and a half of cultivators,' and this 'not only without disturbance and opposition, but to the satisfaction of all classes of the natives, and to the manifest increase of the public revenue derivable from land.' In his journeys through the island he had been 'a pleased spectator' of the system's beneficial tendency, 'and of the security and satisfaction it universally diffused.'

Java had, in theory, to pay for itself. It could not. Raffles could have made a success of Java if the Company had been behind him, and prepared to invest. There was not nearly enough silver coin in circulation. Daendels in 1810 farmed the right to tax three districts of Eastern Java to a group of Chinese merchants, the exchange being financed by the issue of a whole lot more paper money in the form of bonds known as 'Probolingo paper' after one of the Chinese-run districts.

The Chinese were to pay for their 'tax farms' by buying up, twice a year, a hefty amount of Probolingo paper. Daendels published a general rule that the paper money must be regarded as the equivalent in silver. So when the time came for the Chinese tax-farmers to pay their first dues, they craftily paid not in specie, as expected, but in the paper money – 'toilet paper' as Emily Hahn put it.

When Raffles arrived, Probolingo paper was worth 66 per cent of its face value, and continued to depreciate. The lack of silver currency remained chronic. Raffles, already funded from Bengal, dared not keep drawing on the Supreme Government in Bengal for more money – partly, as he explained to Elton Hamond, because of 'the assurances I had given of the capability of the island to maintain itself.' Yet there was still 'a total want of demand for the produce of the colony' apart from coffee, and the war with America had put a stop to that trade. The coffee was 'literally rotting in the stores.'

Daendels had sold off some public lands to raise hard cash. Raffles did the same on a larger scale in late 1812. He announced in the *Gazette* the outright sale to private persons of choice public lands 'in the Batavian Regency, and around Samarang and Surabaya' for the benefit of Government, by public auction or previous private contract. Payment was to be in silver or 'credit paper'. The increase to the Treasury would hopefully enable him to withdraw Probolingo paper from circulation.

Three commissioners were appointed to determine the value of the lands – Muntinghe, Cranssen and, for the Batavia region, the Resident for Buitenzorg, Thomas McQuoid, the old friend of Raffles from Penang days. He was also Malay Translator to Government, Inspector of Coffee Culture throughout the island, and 'farmer' of some bird's nest rocks. Each of these positions brought with it an allowance. Raffles would later argue that the shortage of civil servants made such pluralities unavoidable. The favouritism afforded to McQuoid did not pass unnoticed.

Offers to purchase by private contract were made to Government through the Secretary to the Lieutenant-Governor, who was at that point C.G.Blagrave. Thus Blagrave was privy to all transactions, which had consequences. Raffles' Council of Three, which included Colonel Gillespie, had agreed with the decision to sell off land – Gillespie only after some demurral. Raffles did not seek permission from Calcutta in advance.

The sales were completed within three months. It was said that the auctions were not well organised, and that certain investors seemed to be given preferential treatment with lots being valued too low, while being too large in acreage to give much chance to small investors. The fine estates thus acquired produced a new class of European landed gentry. Muntinghe, retiring from Council, bought his estate by private contract.

Raffles himself went into partnership with Nicholas Engelhard to buy at public auction four lots, mainly coffee plantations, in the Regency of Cianjur, about fifty miles south-east of Buitenzorg. It was not made public that Raffles was personally involved, but Gillespie knew (and forced up the bidding) and so of course did Secretary Blagrave. Raffles later said that he let himself be persuaded by Engelhard into participating, on the grounds that if the Lieutenant-Governor himself were involved the sales would not be repudiated by the Supreme Government or any future administration.

Another Dutchman, Andries de Wilde was put in charge of managing the Cianjur estates and received one-sixth of a share; McQuoid was allotted another sixth. Raffles put in half the total cost, 58,000 Spanish dollars, all of which he had to borrow from his friend William Robinson. It was recorded that the land sales had raised enough to cover all the paper money in circulation, which was therefore withdrawn for all official transactions.

To make up for the withdrawal of the depreciated paper, Raffles issued Treasury notes at six per cent and authorised the Lombard Bank to issue promissory notes to be accepted as legal tender, payable in nine months on the security of personal property. There was a hopeless confusion of currencies. An attempt was made to pin down the values of Spanish dollars and ducatoons in relation to the 'Java silver rupee', which Raffles wanted to establish as the standard. It was illegal to take Spanish dollars off the island. Stivers, tin doits, and lumps of copper were also legal tender on the island. It was crisis management. The quantity of silver, as Raffles confessed to Elton Hamond just before the land-sales, was 'daily becoming less. Gold has disappeared altogether; and copper is the only metal in general use among the population.'

Raffles assured Elton Hamond that 'our proceedings in this, as well as in every other measure, have met the approbation of the Supreme Government.'

That was an overstatement. Lord Minto was being recalled and leaving India. His letter to Raffles of November 1813 was long, kind, and candid. He asked that what he had to say be accepted as 'the friendly suggestions of the deep and lively interest I can never cease to take in all that concerns your public trust, and your personal reputation and welfare. In this I may be less careful than I might otherwise be, to separate my public from my private sentiments in this letter.'

He acknowledged Raffles' unimpeachable motives for selling off land, given the urgency of the financial situation. 'At the same time…' Then came his list of qualifications. An 'extensive alienation of the public domains' was too important a measure to be taken 'during a provisional Government, the duration of which is more than precarious,' and 'without the sanction of the Supreme Government.' Although he, Minto, was a believer in privatisation ('in the transfer of public territory to the management of individual industry'), such a change should not have been brought about suddenly, since Java contained 'neither capital nor capitalists enough' to establish a fair valuation of the land. Minto would have been inclined to 'small and partial sales of land' on short leases, not in perpetuity.

He warned Raffles that there was disagreement 'at home' on the question of 'permanent settlements' and that he had to expect 'such measures, unsupported by particular exigency, being disapproved, and, indeed, disavowed and annulled by the authorities in England.' Much would depend on the attitude of his successor as Governor-General, Lord Moira.

Raffles could not afford to keep Daendels' roads in repair, so he banned them to heavy wheeled vehicles and buffalo carts, which must trundle on the 'ordinary and long-established cart roads.' He imposed a tax on horses and carriages, and tolls on roads, bridges and ferries. He farmed out licences for vegetable shops, slaughterhouses, candle-manufacture. He set up a lottery to build a new road from Batavia to Cheribon, and another for road improvements between Batavia and Samarang.

Salaries of public officers were reduced. He made cuts in his civil service, commending those 'who have necessarily been removed from official employment' on account of 'the internal resources of the Company (confined as they are by the actual state of exterior commerce at the present moment) and in consideration of the harm done to the Colony if an expenditure were permitted beyond its means.' He hoped 'the exigencies of the public service will be an additional inducement and spur to their exertions.'

Their exertions went towards seeking to augment their incomes by other means. Captain Travers, who was already Town Major, Commandant of Batavia, and one of Raffles' ADCs, was appointed Assistant Commissary General for the drawing of the lotteries. Fewer civil servants meant plurality of offices. Raffles looked after those he thought of as his 'family'.

He did everything else he could think of to save money, reduce waste, and raise cash just to pay for his administration. Duty was levied on imported opium. Port duties had to be collected in cash, not paper. He introduced a capitation tax on the Chinese. He charged the Accountant's Department with 'more regular examination and control of contingent civil charges,' i.e. expenses. Warehouse-keepers and storekeepers must submit accounts to the Commercial Committee, and 'indents for every description of Civil and Marine stores throughout the island, excepting Teak Timber, require in the first instance the signature of the Lieutenant-Governor.' Week after week throughout 1813 the *Gazette* announced new cuts, new taxes, new regulations.

The most severe charges on the treasury came from the Army. Not only did the troops and their officers have to be paid in silver, but the Commander of the Forces, Colonel Gillespie, was insistent about the needs of his men. In October 1812, repairs and alterations to the barracks of the Javanese Corps and the construction of new barracks were authorised – the timber required to be furnished by the Timber Storekeeper, Raffles' brother-in-law William Flint, who made something out of it.

Raffles thought there were too many troops on the island, and wished to drive the establishment down. Gillespie would not tolerate any reduction in the number of his men, nor in their supplies. Under 'General Orders', the *Gazette* for 10 November 1812 announced: 'Difficulties having arisen in the operation of the General Order of the 26th September last, regulating rations to be issued to European troops, the Lieutenant-Governor is pleased to rescind that order, and to direct that the European troops be placed on the full rations as they existed previously.' Captain Travers noted the growing rift between Raffles and Gillespie; it 'must be attended by serious consequences to one or other.'

By December, with army pay and allowances already two months in arrears, Raffles announced 'the necessity of establishing some regular mode of examination of Military Extraordinary Disbursements' and appointed a Committee of Military Accounts. Work on the construction of the arsenal at Surabaya must stop. The Paymaster of the 78th Regiment at Surabaya inserted advertisements in the *Gazette* for 'the sum of £500 sterling for which bills will be issued' – loans, to pay his men, and a reproach to Government. In the same issue a sale of horses of the Horse Artillery and Hussars at the cavalry stables at Ryswick was ordered by the Lieutenant-Governor in Council.

Raffles and Major-General Gillespie – as he became from the end of 1812 – grew more and more infuriated with each other. In every row, both were right and both were wrong. Gillespie's biographer Major William Thorn wrote that Gillespie felt he was 'thwarted and misrepresented' where it was 'reasonable to have expected cordial support and liberal confidence.' His opinions were disregarded. There was no 'congeniality of sentiment'. Improvements to his troops' bad living conditions were 'obstinately rejected'.

He encountered nothing but 'provoking slights' and 'petulant opposition'.

Major-General Gillespie was of the opinion, like military men before and since, that diplomacy only got you so far and that force of arms was the one language everyone understood: 'Whenever the natives shall begin to lose their reverence for English arms, our superiority will quickly sink into contempt.' There was no security for colonists 'without a judicious disposition of military force.'

Raffles had plenty of other priorities. He was a supporter of vaccination against smallpox, and had local people trained to administer the vaccine. A passionate supporter of the abolition of slavery, he had to work within the Act of 1807, which had abolished the trade but not slavery itself, throughout the British Empire. There were more than 27,000 imported slaves in Java when he arrived. He banned the importation of any more and came down hard on transgressors. He banned the cruel punishments to which slaves were legally subject, and emancipated them up to the point of ruling that they were not their masters' personal property. This led to a comically tetchy correspondence in the *Gazette* from gentlemen flabbergasted to find that their domestic slaves were free to leave, causing considerable inconvenience in the home. British law could not extend over the entrenched practices of the Dutch or the Muslims. Even British officers and civil servants – Travers and Gillespie to name but two – had slaves. Raffles did what he could, but within the law the problem was intractable.

There had been a Batavian Society of Arts and Science in Batavia, established by the Dutch in 1778 but long in abeyance. Raffles resurrected it, with himself as President, H.W. Muntinghe as Vice-President, and the 'Arts' component less prominent than the 'Science'.

If there was one product of the Eastern Isles which never failed to fascinate Europeans, including the members of the Batavian Society of Arts and Sciences, it was the Upas Tree (*Antiaris toxicaria*), a tall tree of the mulberry family which grows in isolation. 'Upas' is the Javanese word for poison. The lethal substance is the milky gum that oozes from the bark when pierced. It is applied subcutaneously, administered by a prick from a spear-head, dart or reed dipped in the gum. William Marsden wrote about it, and possessed a sample.

Raffles asked Dr Horsfield for a full report on the Upas Tree, which he submitted to the Society in March 1812. Being, as Marsden tactfully put it, 'at such a distance from the grand marts of scientific information,' Horsfield had nothing very new to report; Continental and British naturalists had recently published responsible experiments and descriptions.

Tall tales of the poison's potency had been around since Raffles' infancy. The fantastical account by N.P. Foersch, a German surgeon in Samarang in the 1770s, was published in the *London Magazine* in 1783 complete with gruesome accounts of the victims' death-throes. It was fatal, he said, to stand to the windward of the Upas Tree, which killed all animal life within fifteen metres. The poet and naturalist Erasmus Darwin claimed to have seen thirteen of the Sultan's concubines in Surakarta, accused of infidelity, drop dead within sixteen minutes after their breasts were pierced by poisoned lancets, and wrote in his extraordinary poem *The Botanic Garden* (1791):

> Fierce in dread silence on the blasted heath
> Fell UPAS sits, the HYDRA-TREE of death.

John Joseph Stockdale reprinted Foersch's account in his *Island of Java*, an opportunistic compilation published in London the year of the invasion. On 24 October 1812, the *Java Government Gazette* carried anonymous 'Stanzas to the Memory of John Leyden':

> A sadder strain a breast should melt
> Far, far beyond Malaya's sea
> The pride of Western Isles has felt
> The foul breath of the Upas Tree.

That last and memorable line is so far-fetched as to be figurative. When Raffles, with Olivia, was again visiting Dr Horsfield in Surakarta in December 1813, they witnessed, as the *Gazette* reported, 'the surprising effects of the Poison extracted from the Oopas Tree, as it operated on a fowl and a dog, the first of which was destroyed in less than two minutes, and the latter in about eight.' The mythology of the Upas Tree outlived Raffles. Mr Rochester in Charlotte Brontë's *Jane Eyre* (1847) makes dark reference to it.

The Harmonie Club was another old Dutch social club, revived by Daendels in a new building in Weltesvreden, which he left unfinished. Raffles agreed to have the project completed, and the result was a 'superb new building' with 'an Arched Ball Room' good for 'the conveyance of musical sounds'. The Harmonie, which Raffles hoped would foster harmony between the British and the Dutch, became a staple of the stuffier end of Batavian social life: ladies were admitted only for periodical dances and suppers. This, like the new premises of the Society for Arts and Science, was funded by non-existent Government money, as was the projected 250-seat Military Bachelors' Theatre at Weltesvreden. To justify the expenditure, Raffles was banking on his impressive success in developing the civilised amenities of Batavia.

He never skimped on gubernatorial entertainments, dinners and balls. Olivia, at least in public, was nice to Gillespie. At a ball on 23 January 1813, reported the *Gazette*, 'Major-General Gillespie opened the dancing with the Lady Governess, who we were happy to observe, appeared to enjoy the dance with her usual grace and spirit.' About four hundred people sat down to supper. 'The bottle circulated with spirit and good humour.' Gillespie proposed toasts to 'the Governor and the Island of Java' and to 'Mrs Raffles and the Ladies of Java.' The Lieutenant-Governor proposed the toasts to 'Major-General Gillespie and the Army of Java,' 'the Land we live in,' and 'the Ladies of Batavia.' As at all such parties, each toast was accompanied by a short loud burst of suitable popular music

from a military band – in this case, 'The British Grenadiers' for
Gillespie, 'Tight Little Island' for Mr Raffles, and 'Off She Goes'
for Mrs Raffles.

Yet in April 1813 Captain Travers noted that 'the unhappy differences between our Chiefs seemed rather to increase than diminish.'
Every day brought 'some new point of contention.' In June, at the
annual ball in celebration of the King's Birthday, the dancing was
again opened by 'our amiable Lady Governess' and Major-General
Gillespie. 'Such a pair were not certainly in the room,' observed
the fascinated Travers. What he called 'the apparent cordiality' –
a subversive attraction? – between the dancing partners had its
effect. Raffles called on Gillespie the next morning 'and everything
seemed settled to keep up appearances better in future.'

The truce did not hold. In February 1813 Gillespie resigned as Commandant of the Forces 'in the heat of passion', and then took offence
that his resignation was so readily accepted. He had assumed that the
Supreme Government would prefer to see Raffles off the island than
himself. Lord Minto's son Captain George Elliot arrived in Java in
the summer, bringing the news that Major-General Gillespie would
be relieved by General Sir Miles Nightingall. Elliot was charged by
his father Lord Minto to bring about a face-saving reconciliation
between Raffles and Gillespie.

In his memoir, written fifty years later, George Elliot made his
derogatory remarks about Raffles, describing him as 'full of trick
and not so full of the truth as was desirable, and he was the most
nervous man I ever knew.' Gillespie, he saw as 'an Irishman, a gentleman in all his feelings, but a very peppery one,' who 'thoroughly
despised the Governor... Gillespie was my friend,' recorded Elliot,
'and I would have done anything for him... Raffles looked to me
as a friend, and his having been appointed Governor by my father,
I was anxious to assist him out of the foolish scrapes he was constantly getting into with Gillespie – for they were usually both in
the wrong.' Gillespie was 'excellent as a second in command, but

unfit for a chief, even as a military man, and still less calculated to take part in a civil Government.'

As for Raffles, he 'was a very able man with his pen, and understood the habits and peculiarities of the Eastern people, but he was unfit to govern and had the fatal misfortune of never inspiring Europeans with respect.' Ironically, Raffles inspired Captain Elliot's father, Lord Minto, not only with respect but with affection.

On the occasion of Minto's recall to England – a blow for Raffles – he was raised from a barony to an earldom, and became Earl of Minto and Viscount Melgund. His replacement, Lord Moira, was the Prince Regent's crony; the Prince had leaned on the Board of Control. Minto was concerned about Raffles' future – 'a subject... deeply and sensibly interesting to my wishes and feelings' – in the event of Java's probable reversal to the Dutch. The Resident of Bencoolen (Bengkulu) in West Sumatra was retiring, and Minto offered to do everything he could to secure the position for Raffles.

Lord Moira was to be arriving in Calcutta prematurely, with Minto still in post, which was humiliating for him as well as 'occasioning a great embarrassment and anxiety about you,' as he wrote to Raffles. Minto feared there might be difficulty keeping the position in Bencoolen on hold until Raffles was forced to leave Java. So while he still could, in June 1813, Minto formally appointed Raffles to the Residency of Fort Marlborough at Bencoolen 'to take effect from your being relieved of your present office or resigning it; the allowance to commence from the time of your departure from Java.'

'I am prepared and ready to meet a change whenever it may come,' Raffles wrote to William Brown Ramsay after receiving this assurance. 'At Bencoolen I am promised the chief authority, if removed hence; at Penang my standing in the service would insure me a seat in Council, but I confess that I should say farewell to Java with a heavy heart.'

Captain Elliot brought with him to Java a portrait of the Earl of

Minto to hang in Government House, done in Calcutta by George Chinnery – full length in full robes, his coronet on a cushion. It was a rather poor painting, and smallish. Before he left India, Minto sent to the Lieutenant-Governor and Council another Chinnery portrait of himself, 'as large as life, and so superior as a work of art, that it may be deemed worthy of the distinguished command under which it has been performed.' As for the smaller one, he requested 'that Mr Raffles will be so good as to accept it as a memorial of our joint labours, and as a token of my personal esteem and affection.'

Raffles took the small portrait with him when he left Java. He presented to Minto a tenth-century stone slab with carved inscriptions on both sides which Lieutenant-Colonel Colin Mackenzie's team of surveyors had came across near Malang in East Java. It weighed between three and four tons and was two metres tall. 'With the consent and by the assistance of the Native Regent from Malang,' Mackenzie had it carted the forty miles to Surabaya, whence it was shipped to Calcutta. Minto, delighted, told Raffles that 'I shall be very much tempted to mount this Javan rock upon our Minto craigs, that it may tell eastern tales of us, long after our heads lie under other stones.'

Captain Elliot did bring about a superficial reconciliation between Raffles and Gillespie, who were briefly allied around this time in monstering Captain Robison over the Palembang fiasco. In late August 1813 Gillespie gave a dinner for Raffles and his staff, 'and to a person unacquainted with preceding events these two characters would have appeared a second Castor and Pollux.' A great deal of wine was drunk, continued Travers in his journal, and 'a most unreserved conversation took place between the two Chiefs, the result of which was reiterated professions of unlimited friendship and goodwill… I fancy few of the number witnessed before so drunken a scene.'

Gillespie embarked for Bengal on the evening of 12 October. Lieutenant-Governor Raffles and the Lady Governess were at Buitenzorg, Colonel Gillespie having expressed a wish to 'go off quietly'.

He did not go off quietly. It was an emotional occasion. 'All the staff accompanied him to the beach where he parted from them in tears.' Captain Travers had said his private farewell earlier, at the departing hero's house where the wine flowed freely yet again. 'He took me by both hands and swore eternal friendship towards me and left me in a flood of tears.' Raffles' close friend William Robinson accompanied Major-General Gillespie on board and had a long talk with him on deck. The worry was, what was Gillespie going to say or do in Calcutta? Robinson told Travers that Gillespie declared his 'attachment' to Raffles and 'his positive determination to support every measure of his administration.'

Three days later Gillespie's replacement, General Nightingall, arrived with his wife on the *Nearchus*. Everyone liked them. There was a whirl of welcoming parties.

Travelling on the *Troubridge* to Bengal with Gillespie was the wife of the sacked Secretary to Government, Charles Blagrave. If Blagrave himself sailed too, his name was not on the passenger list, though he has to be credited, or discredited, along with Gillespie, for what happened after the ship reached India. At some point, they got together and compared notes.

Major William Robison sailed for Calcutta not long afterwards, with despatches for the Supreme Government documenting the charges against him about his activities in Palembang. Robison too was consumed with resentment – against Gillespie for sure, and as much again against Raffles and his administration.

Gillespie reached Calcutta in mid-December 1814, a few days before the Earl of Minto sailed for Madras. From there Minto sailed for England on the *Hussar*, captained by George Elliot, and along with his other son John, his two daughters-in-law, his grandchildren, a couple of the young boys he had freed from slavery in Malacca, a reputed small fortune, and the great stone.

↬

Raffles and Olivia were away from Batavia for nearly two months from mid-November 1813. They sailed up the coast, with William Robinson as Raffles' Secretary and two ADCs, to Samarang, where the Flints were. News reached the *Gazette* of continual 'public breakfasts, dinners, balls and races...and the happy guests only quit one scene of pleasure to become actors in another.' In Batavia, good General Nightingall was left in charge

Raffles, Olivia and their suite went from Samarang in December 1813 back to Surakarta and Yogyakarta. Three miles outside Surakarta, they were met by the civil and military authorities despatched by the Susuhunan, who welcomed them to his *kraton* with public ceremonies, refreshments (handed round by female slaves), compliments and toasts, volleys of musketry, and parades of gun-carriages and ceremonial spearmen. The day ended at the Residency House with all the European civil and military respectables.

Hospitality swung back and forth between *kraton* and Residency throughout the visit. The Lieutenant-Governor, on horseback, inspected his host's troops. The British flag flew over the Fort. The Lady Governess held a drawing-room at which was performed a Javanese comedy 'greatly enjoyed by those with the language to understand the plot and dialogue.' The Susuhunan and his lady – whom the *Gazette* called the Emperor and Empress – came in the evening for a firework display; 'two sets of dancing girls belonging to the Emperor gratified the company with a very excellent specimen of Javanese dancing; and then a conjuring show.' The highlight of the visit was the standard royal entertainment: a fight between a tiger, or tigers, and a buffalo. These contests went on for hours, with intervals for refreshments, and often culminated in massed spearmen putting a cowed and tormented tiger to death.

It was the same at Yogyakarta which, eighteen months on, showed few scars from the sacking. A reception party with an army of spearmen escorted Raffles and his suite up Malioboro to the *kraton*. There were toasts and compliments, gamelan bands, gun salutes, exchanges of gifts and reciprocal hospitalities; they were led through subterranean passages to the Water Palace, and endured another tiger fight. It was reported that the Lieutenant-Governor and the Lady Governess 'supported the fatiguing etiquette of the day with admirable spirit and dignity.' Raffles, describing tiger fights in *The History of Java*, observed that the buffalo almost always won: the Javans 'are accustomed to compare the buffalo to the Javan and the tiger to the European, and it may be readily imagined with what eagerness they look to the success of the former.'

Raffles and Olivia returned to Batavia and to more trouble.

Chapter 7

Theatre of Shadows

Java 1814–1816

On his return Raffles spent an intense fortnight composing a massive Minute for the Supreme Government in Calcutta, dated 11 February 1814, explaining his land-rent reforms and stressing their positive consequences. He was setting out his stall for the new Governor-General, Lord Moira. He did not know Moira: in his mid-fifties, distinctly ugly, born into the Irish Protestant Ascendency and with a distinguished military career behind him.

Moira's main aim in India was to make enough money to clear his debts. A dedicated Freemason, his arrival in Calcutta saw a flurry of resurgent activity in the several Masonic Lodges. Minto too was a Freemason, and before he left Java he initiated Raffles into a small select Lodge, 'Virtutis et Artis Amici' on a coffee estate near Buiten-zorg belonging to the Lodge's Master, Nicholas Engelhard. In July 1813 Raffles was 'raised' to the third degree of Freemasonry in the Lodge of Friendship at Surabaya, and 'perfected' before he left Java in the Rose Croix Chapter in the Lodge 'La Vertueuse' in Batavia. The top Dutch in Batavia were all Masons. The Brotherhood did not mean much to Raffles except in that it was a private 'club' that no public man could ignore.

Lord Moira had no Brotherhood sympathy with Raffles and Java

– a 'drain', as he wrote in his journal for 1 February 1814: 'Instead of the surplus revenue which, for giving importance to the conquest, was asserted to be forthcoming from that possession, it could not be maintained without the Treasury, as well as the troops of Bengal. Just now, in the height of our exigencies, we receive an intimation from the Lieutenant-Governor that he cannot pay his provincial corps unless we allow him 50,000 Spanish dollars monthly in addition to the prodigious sums which we already contribute to his establishment.'

John Palmer, the know-all merchant prince, became very thick with Moira and was briefing against Raffles, writing to the naval commander Sir Home Popham on 10 February: 'What right Lord Minto had to nominate Mr Raffles prospectively, and therefore keep the office [Bencoolen] vacant (already one year) indefinitely, nothing but the calm stoical impudence of his country can determine. Lord Moira must be an ass – as indeed I believe he is – if he does not spurn such presumption.'

William Robinson gave a ball for Olivia's forty-third birthday on 18 February 1814. Just then, news reached Raffles that there was spiteful talk in Calcutta about his participation in the Government land-sales. He spent the whole day of the birthday party writing a Minute setting out the details of his withdrawal from all interest in the properties, in consequence of anonymous 'insinuations' being made 'prejudicial to my public character.'

Worse was to come. A week later a ship from Bengal brought him a blue packet, tied with red tape and sealed. It contained what amounted to the impeachment of Lieutenant-Governor Raffles by Major-General Gillespie, which had been laid before Lord Moira. Gillespie did not act alone. Charles Blagrave abetted him, and gave evidence to the Supreme Council.

Shocked, Raffles called Travers into his office and together they went through the charges of maladministration and corruption. Gillespie questioned the efficacy of the land-rent reforms, of the currency manipulations, and the private motives for the land-sales;

also the impropriety of McQuoid's plurality of appointments, and the profits to individuals of coffee plantations – previously a Government monopoly – on the sold lands.

Raffles had committed no crime. There was no rule against a Company official acquiring property. But it was bad practice for the Government authority who was selling the land, and laid down the system of valuations and auctions, and drew up the conditions of sale, to become himself an investor – and secretly. It was, as his superiors informed him, 'a grave indiscretion.' Gillespie implied that by means of private contracts and low valuations, Raffles enriched his friends. The well-heeled Dutch were in fact the only people, apart from some Chinese, who could afford to buy (and though not prohibited, the Chinese were not encouraged); and the whole purpose of the land-sales was to raise enough cash for the Government to dispense with the 'toilet paper' money.

Raffles spent the early part of March 1814 putting together his answers to Gillespie's charges. They were as good as the case allowed. He made one self-cheapening gesture, throwing in a gratuitous mention of Gillespie's having procured a girl from the orphan school in Samarang. True or false, the accusation was backed by no evidence.

There was always a party at Buitenzorg in March for Raffles' and Olivia's wedding anniversary, and that year there were eighty people round the dinner table, followed by a play, and dancing. 'Mr Raffles was but little amongst us being so much engaged with his despatches,' recorded Travers. This party, like her birthday party, cannot have been much fun for Olivia.

It was agreed in Council that Charles Assey, as Secretary to Government, should travel to Bengal to deliver Raffles' defence to the Supreme Government in person; and that Captain Travers should sail for England to deliver the same to the Court of Directors 'in order to make them acquainted with a true and fair statement of the case, as well as to meet any representations that might have been privately sent by Gillespie.' Raffles, on saying goodbye to Travers, 'took me by the hand with tears in his eyes…"You have my life, my honour in your hands."' Travers' ship put in briefly at Samarang, where he found Alexander Hare from whom he learned 'what I had always suspected, that he was anything but Mr Raffles' friend.' Hare asked Travers to make the case with the Court of Directors for the retention of his position in Banjarmasin in Borneo, in the event of the reversal of Java to the Dutch. The Court of Directors would prove supremely uninterested in the issue.

Major Robison too was in Calcutta, facing the investigation into what Raffles called his 'disobedience of orders and dereliction of duty' in Palembang. Robison knocked out a paper entitled 'Some Account of the General Manner of Proceeding of the Government of Java' and presented it to the Supreme Council, whence a copy found its way to Raffles' desk. It was a splenetic attack on Raffles himself – his extravagance and self-promotion; the 'pomp and parade' of the Lieutenant-Governor and the Lady Governess; her exigent requirements and spoilt behaviour; the opulence of their 'palaces'; the fifth-rate adventurers they kept around them and rewarded with prime jobs. The tone was so intemperate as to be a little mad.

Raffles' ripostes were almost as intemperate, and entirely contemptuous. As he wrote to the Supreme Government, the Lieutenant-Governor could not appear as a pauper. But however crazed Robison's outpourings, given Java's financial straits an accusation of profligacy was the last thing Raffles needed. Everything was forwarded to the Court of Directors in London. Throughout the autumn of 1814 Raffles grappled with 'the extraordinary representations of Major-General Gillespie and Major Robison.' He was prepared to consign Major Robison's rant to oblivion as evidence of 'a disordered mind and unsound heart' but not Gillespie's. Even John Palmer said that 'Gillespie's violence renders his testimony as suspicious as Mr R's integrity.'

Gillespie's charges included complaints about Raffles' attitude to the size and maintenance of the military establishment. General

Nightingall, on the other hand, was recommending the abolition of the Gun Carriage Manufactory and the demolition of 'old and useless barracks.' The Light Cavalry and the heavy artillery, the most expensive items, were 'perfectly useless' since they could go nowhere except on the Military Road. Nightingall recommended the retention only of infantry equipped with light field pieces, and 150 Cavalry and Hussars on 'ponies of the country' for escort duty with the Lieutenant-Governor. By September 1814 the reductions were so extreme that Nightingall judged no more could be done without incurring 'positive detriment'.

Major Robison was in due course acquitted of the charges made against him. Charles Blagrave was appointed Collector of Rungpore, an opium-producing area of Bengal.

While Raffles was fighting to save his reputation, one of his most significant projects in Java, the uncovering and recording of ancient temples and antiquities, was going forward under his direction. Raffles had first heard of Borobudur when visiting Engelhard in Samarang; his garden was full of ancient stones. Maimed and headless statues lay half-buried on the roadsides and in the ditches of Central Java. Lieutenant-Colonel Mackenzie and his main collaborator Captain George Baker had surveyed and sketched the temples at Prambanan in 1812; Dr Horsfield too knew Prambanan and Borobudur. In 1814 Mackenzie, Baker, and a Dutch engineer, H.C.Cornelius, undertook a major investigation.

Around the year 800 AD, Borobudur, a great hill, was entirely enveloped in stone, forming a stepped pyramid with rising terraces carved with vigorous reliefs and topped by a divine cluster of Buddhas. It is one of the largest Buddhist monuments ever known. After Islam was imposed on Java by the end of the sixteenth century, Borobudur was abandoned. Its carvings were cracked by earthquakes and blurred by volcanic ash. Local people carried away stones for their own use. Under Mackenzie, two hundred coolies worked for six weeks, carting away tons of accumulated earth and clearing the fierce jungle vegetation growing around and through the vast high rock.

Many of the 500 heavy stone heads of the Buddha had fallen off, and two of these, plus a stone harpy and many other fragments, were taken away for or by Raffles. They were the jewels of his collection. But during the time of the monumental investigations he was under stress, and this bad time leaked into *The History of Java*. While passionately alive to the significance of the great architectural vestiges, he did not find effective ways of writing about them. Captain Baker's report on the ruined temples was eloquent and poetic, and Raffles transcribed into *The History of Java* Baker's account of how the devastation caused the visitor to reflect 'that while these noble monuments of the ancient splendour of religion and the arts are submitting, with sullen slowness, to the destructive hand of time and nature, the art which raised them has perished before them, and the faith which they were to honour now has no other honour in the land.'

Shelley's 'Ozymandias' was written in 1817 and, throughout Raffles' lifetime, toppled images elicited meditations on the transitory nature of power. Those uncovered in Java quickly became tourist attractions. The *Gazette* in August 1814 carried an anonymous rhapsody about a cluster of dilapidated temples in East Java, evidence of 'former grandeur and magnificence.' This party brought a picnic: 'An immense slab of granite served us for a table, and limbs of mutilated Gods and Goddesses were our chairs.'

Ethnologists and students of world music also owe a debt to Raffles. All the time he was in Java he was amassing objects and artefacts, from the ceremonial to the everyday.

A gamelan orchestra is an ensemble of wood and metal instruments – gongs, cymbals, drums, one-octave xylophones, bamboo flutes, a fiddle. Raffles acquired two complete sets, the frames decorated with carved snakes and birds painted red, black and gold. He also had a small model set made. Dr Joseph Arnold, a Royal Navy surgeon in Java from 1815, recorded that gamelan music accompanied life at Buitenzorg, playing 'almost the whole day beginning before day light and playing till ten at night. Eight or ten persons are employed in it. It sounds at a distance something like bells.'

Raffles also collected hundreds of used puppets from the theatre of shadows, a pre-Islamic entertainment which still survives. All the puppet characters are manipulated by a single person with the aid of attached sticks. Sitting cross-legged, he improvises the story, does the voices, sings, and directs the accompanying gamelan in night-long performances of legendary conflicts between good and evil – versions of the Mahabharata and the Ramayana.

With their exaggeratedly stylised outlines, the *wayang kulit* ('leather shadows') which Raffles collected are works of art, made from buffalo hide stretched to translucency, gilded and painted – even though only their silhouettes, projected on to white cloth from a lamp behind the puppeteer, were normally seen. Raffles also collected *wayang klitik* puppets, crafted from thin flat sheets of wood; and brightly painted wooden doll-puppets (*wayang golek*). He did not want the puppets or the gamelan ensembles – or the hundreds of other artefacts that he amassed – for himself, nor for gain. He collected for cultural propaganda to prove back in England that Java had been, and could be again, a great and civilised country.

Raffles floated the idea of establishing a British presence all over the Archipelago and as far as the Philippines – 'altogether chimerical and impracticable' in the opinion of William Petrie, the current Governor of Penang. Lord Moira was equally dismissive: 'How can it be just or expedient?' Raffles' main target beyond the Archipelago was Japan. He made up his mind that, unlike the Chinese, the Japanese were 'just like us,' telling the Batavian Society of Arts and Sciences: 'They are represented to be a nervous, vigorous people, whose bodily and mental powers assimilate much nearer to those of Europe than what is attributed to Asiatics in general.'

He was guided by the report of Dr Donald Ainslie, Chief Surgeon in Batavia, whom he sent in summer 1813 on a mission to Naga-saki with two vessels, accompanied by Willem Wardenaar, a former factor at the long-established Dutch factory at Nagasaki. The Dutch and their warehouses were strictly confined to Deshima, a man-made, walled, offshore island. Raffles' reasoning was that, since the British controlled Java and the Dutch factory on Deshima island traded in and out of Java, Deshima was one of Java's dependencies.

He instructed Ainslie to 'take possession of the Dutch factory' and negotiate a trade agreement with the Japanese. The vessels sailed under Dutch flags so as to deceive the Japanese. Then Raffles' letter was produced, demanding that the Director hand over the factory to Wardenaar in the name of the British Lieutenant-Governor of Java. These isolated Dutch had never even heard of Raffles. The demand was flatly refused.

Raffles had furnished Ainslie with presents for the Emperor of Japan – including plants, sheep, birds, wine decanters, a clock, ground-up Egyptian mummy and a live white elephant from Siam. The gifts were accepted – all except the clock, which was engraved with barbaric symbols – and the elephant. She could not be lowered on to a boat, and in any case she would have sunk it. The Japanese came out to stare at her and draw her, but she never disembarked. She was the original 'white elephant'.

Raffles was not giving up. In his Minute to Bengal of 11 February 1814, he wrote that the expedition had 'paved the way to further and more decisive attempts, with every prospect of success.' Although Dr Ainslie had not been made welcome, 'an unusual favour on the part of the Emperor' was his acceptance of the presents, apart from the elephant. The Japanese character 'has been misrepresented...they are a race of people remarkable for frankness of manner and disposition, for intelligent enquiry and freedom from prejudice,' in a climate where 'European manufactures are almost a necessary comfort...the consumption of woollens and hardware might be rendered almost unlimited.' The Company could supplant the commerce between China and Japan, and keep the Dutch out.

'If the attempt be not made while we have possession of Java the opportunity lost may never be regained.'

'My idea', he wrote, was for Dr Ainslie to go again to Japan, taking a letter to the Emperor from the Prince Regent; he helpfully enclosed a draft. Equally helpfully, he enclosed a long list of 'suitable' presents for the Emperor, enough to stock a sizeable warehouse. 'My idea' got nowhere. No goods were sent from London, and Moira poured icy water on the project.

The upper echelons of the Dutch in Batavia, clannish and interrelated, allied themselves conspicuously with the Lieutenant-Governor and his wife. Piet Couperus, from one of the eminent Dutch families, christened his son Jacob Thomas Raffles; one of his sisters, Jacobina Maria Tulloch, called her son Stamford William Raffles; another sister, Gesina, called her daughter Olivia. Raffles and Olivia were godparents to all three babies. Gesina was Mrs Timmerman Thyssen, and there were great celebrations when one of Timmerman Thyssen's ships, the *Pekin*, was renamed the *Governor Raffles*. Mrs Raffles was not at the Timmerman Thyssen's ball that evening. The *Gazette* regretted that 'indisposition continues to deprive us of her presence at Batavia, and that some time will yet elapse before we can have the happiness of her fascinating company.'

Raffles in July 1814 hosted a dinner for Vice-Admiral Sir Samuel Hood on the last night of his tour of Java. The Admiral's party included Captain Basil Hall, who got on particularly well with Raffles. They never knew each other well, but kept in respectful touch. Raffles' dinner was followed by a ball and supper given, again, by the Timmerman Thyssens. 'We were sorry to hear that the Lady Governess was unable to favour the company with her presence from indisposition.'

On 14 October 1814 Olivia was well enough to go to an entertainment with dancing given specifically for her by the Nightingalls. That was her last public appearance. On 21 November Raffles wrote to a friend in England: 'Olivia is far from well but in good spirits.'

The new Military Bachelors' Theatre opened on Friday 25 November with George Colman's 1802 comedy *The Poor Gentleman*. The Lieutenant-Governor and the Lady Governess were not present.

The next day, Saturday 26 November 1814, at Buitenzorg, Olivia died.

Olivia's body was taken to Batavia and buried in the Tanah Abang cemetery close to John Leyden. The *Gazette* noted 'the numerous assemblage of persons of both sexes' who attended, and how their 'unaffected grief' reflected the respect and affection in which she was held.

A sour note was struck by Caroline Currie, wife of an army Assistant Surgeon, in a letter to her sister in Scotland retailing the second-hand gossip of the Cantonment. Mrs Currie did not go to the funeral, 'and I am very glad I did not, as I am told they all made themselves ridiculous by weeping aloud when the Corpse was taken from the Government House and when it was put into the grave and all this for a woman whom some of them had only seen once or twice. I had seen her two or three times, she called here and I returned her visit but I never was in her house except at a ball when she was not present... People who knew her seemed to like her very much and said she was a very good hearted woman but she had one great failing and that was being too fond of a glass of Brandy and when she had taken too much of it and got her Aid De Camps [*sic*] around her, I am told that no modest woman could sit in her company.'

Olivia, 'my Olivia' as Raffles called her, was the kind of woman whom the prim and proper always disapprove of. Raffles loved her and her infinite variety. He had a large chest-tomb erected over her grave, inscribed with lines from her own poem 'Forget-me-Not':

> Oh thou who ne'er my constant heart
> One moment hath forgot
> Tho' fate severe hath bid us part

Yet still forget me not.

She wrote this for John Leyden. Whether Raffles intended the inscription to reflect the union of the three cannot be known. He did not have Maryanne with him for comfort. She and Flint had sailed for England the previous autumn. Even Travers was away. Raffles had a graceful classical temple built in Olivia's memory in the grounds of Buitenzorg, visible from the house across the lake.

Olivia Raffles left her mark in Batavia. There were few British wives in Batavia, but almost no Dutch ones. The Dutch had over many decades consorted with concubines and slaves, resulting in a swelling population of Eurasians. The wives spoke Malay with interminglings of Portuguese, and they were not educated. The necessity for schooling for girls was a regular topic in the *Gazette*.

The British officer class accepted the customs of the indigenous population, but from their Dutch colleagues they expected similar domestic conventions to their own. They criticised in the columns of the *Gazette* the airless rooms of the long-established Dutch, their perpetual smoking, their maltreatment of slaves, and above all the segregation of their women. Olivia and Raffles would not accept the traditional seclusion of Eurasian wives. As Jean Gilman Taylor wrote, they 'trampled notions of propriety in the relations between men and women that were fundamental to Mestizo society.'

Olivia never offered betel to visiting ladies at her drawing-rooms, which was seen as uncivil, and she banned spittoons in Government House. She required the ladies to sit on chairs, and to eat with a knife and fork. In sarong and *kebaya*, they looked to the condescending British as if they had come out in their underwear. Minto, when in Java, only discerned their high status by standing behind them 'for at the back of the head a little circle of hair is gathered into a small crown, and on this are deposited diamonds, rubies, and precious stones often of very great value.'

The unfortunate ladies made an effort. As the *Gazette*

sanctimoniously noticed on 2 May 1812: 'At the entertainments recently given at Batavia, it was remarked how great an improvement in respect to the attire of the Dutch ladies, since the British authority has been established. The *Cabya* appears more generally disused and the more elegant English costume adopted. We congratulate our friends on the amelioration of the public taste, because we see in it the dawn of still greater and more important improvements.'

There is no evidence that Raffles gave a damn about the dress code, but he and Olivia were an equal partnership. It was remarkable that she was at his side on the ceremonious visits to Surakarta and Yogyakarta in 1813, so that not only the Susuhunan but his Empress too had to meet and greet them. At the ball that evening, Olivia had danced a few steps with the Susuhunan and Raffles with the Empress. They both visited an interior room to meet their daughters and female relations. It was the same at Yogyakarta. Raffles on his own would never have been invited into the women's quarters, and the Empress could never before have danced with an unrelated man, and in public.

It was all unprecedented. Raffles and Olivia were not in Java long enough to effect permanent changes, for good or ill. Those that did last were trivial. After the British left, the regulation that bare feet were unacceptable on public occasions remained in force; and Olivia's fashion of wearing white muslin gowns with short puffed sleeves prevailed well after it was abandoned in Europe.

Less than three months after the death of Olivia, the *Gazette* confirmed a report that Lord Minto had died.

He suffered chronically from stranguary, a painful bladder condition. When he was in India and longing for home, he used to lie in bed travelling in his imagination from London, from landmark to familiar landmark, starting with the Red Lion at Barnet, all the way north to Minto. Now that the moment had come, he got as far as Barnet, but twenty miles on up the Great North Road, at Stevenage, during the night of 21 June 1814, he died.

This was another personal loss for Raffles, and a professional one as well. He had been relying on Minto to justify his policies with the Court of Directors. William Ramsay, the Secretary of the Company and his first mentor, had died in January 1814; Raffles had lost his two strongest supporters and father-figures. To add to these sorrows, his great friend William Robinson unexpectedly died too. And he fell ill himself and was unable to attend the Harmonie Society Ball on 18 January 1815. The *Gazette* expressed the hope that 'his health will soon be sufficiently re-established to admit of his presiding, where his example has always acted as a spur to happiness and conviviality.'

Conviviality was the last thing he was capable of. Mercifully, news of yet another unexpected death came as a ray of light. Major-General Gillespie was dead.

In the ongoing war between the Gurkhas and the British authority, Gillespie led an attack on the Nepalese hill fort of Kalunga. In late October 1814 his column, the guns mounted on elephants, stormed the Fort twice and was beaten off. Gillespie rode up to the head of his troops and impetuously urged them forward for a third time – and was shot through the heart from the Fort on 24 October, a month before the death of Olivia.

His body was 'laid in spirits' like Raffles' animal specimens, and taken to Meerut for burial. Lord Moira announced the erection of a cenotaph to his memory in Calcutta. In London, both Houses of Parliament voted a public monument to him. A young lady in India composed an ode:

> Gillespie's gone! – yet still shall fame
> Immortalise the warrior's name.

Gillespie's gone! Raffles was probably the only European on the planet to feel glad. Lord Moira shelved the problem of the charges against Raffles.

Rather as he walked from London to Wales as a boy in order to

make himself well, so in February 1815, accompanied by Dr Horsfield, Raffles climbed the 7,000-foot Gunong Gede, which reared up
behind Buitenzorg. They took barometers to ascertain the height,
and Raffles arranged for a memorial to Lord Minto to be placed on
the summit.

On 10 April the 9,000-foot Mount Tambora on the island of
Sumbawa, east of Bali, exploded in the biggest volcanic eruption
in recorded history. Seventy-two thousand people are said to have
been killed by flying rocks and debris, the firestorm, and the subsequent whirlwind and tsunami. The ash cloud drifted across the
globe, occluding the sun. The summer of 1815 in England was
'the summer that never was'. Raffles was sufficiently revived by
the phenomenon to send a vivid report, compiled from eye-witness
accounts, to William Marsden and the Royal Society.

He needed distraction, and went on a long tour of the whole island
of Java. In a discourse to the Batavian Literary Society in September he told how he obtained on this tour 'a more perfect acquaintance' with the ruins of Prambanan and Borobodur, and showed the
meeting drawings of Borobodur (probably Captain Baker's) and
'some detached pieces of sculpture' which he had carried back. His
party, which included Captain Baker, travelled rough, on horseback
and in boats up the rivers, covering hundreds of miles. After seeing
the volcanic Mount Bromo in east Java, they took ship along the
coast for Banyuwangi on Java's easternmost tip, but landed up by
mistake on Bali's north coast, in the Regency of Bliling (Bululeng).

Raffles was predisposed in favour of Bali because it retained the
Hindu religion and culture which in Java was suppressed by Islam.
'My stay was too short to obtain any very detailed information...
further than a collection of their different manuscripts.' Though the
Portuguese and the Dutch had hovered, Bali had never been colo-
nised, and as a result the Balinese were undeferential. Raffles wrote
about them in an appendix to *The History of Java:* 'What they are
now it is probable that the Javans once were, in national independence, as well as in religious and political institutions... On Java we

find Hinduism only amid the ruins of temples, images and inscriptions; on Bali, in the laws, ideas and worship of the people.'

Travers was back from England the day after Raffles returned from his tour in July. He had seen the President of the Board of Control, now the Earl of Buckinghamshire. His Lordship refused to give an opinion on Gillespie's charges. He had seen the Chairman of the Court of Directors, and other Directors, 'but they seem equally disinclined to listen to anything respecting Java.' So far as the Company was concerned, Java was trouble. Raffles was trouble. Gillespie was trouble. Travers was tiresome. They wished it would all go away.

The whole tragedy of the British administration of Java is that Raffles was trying, against a ticking clock, to make a first-class country out of a bankrupt one, with neither support nor investment from the Company. It was reckless of Minto to have forwarded the idea. Raffles' personal tragedy arose from his unquenchable drive and optimism. He would not see that it was impossible; he would never give up.

Batavia only learned in August 1814 that the British and their Allies had taken Paris. Napoleon abdicated and was exiled to the island of Elba. Raffles was pleased when he escaped. 'The reappearance of Buonaparte,' he wrote to William Brown Ramsay on 5 August 1815, 'has, for all its horrors, shed one consoling ray on the sacred Isle; and Java may yet be permanently English. In this hope I have addressed Lord Buckinghamshire with a general account of the leading measures of my government which appeared to have excited displeasure.'

He was hoping, from Buckinghamshire, for the engaged response he never got from India House: 'I am told that so little interest is taken in Leadenhall-street, that the Directors will not even read dispatches from Java.' It was an appeal to the President of the Board of Control to take on board the commercial and cultural potential not only of Java but of the Moluccas, Banca, and 'the great island of

Borneo… These islands, my Lord, are doubtless the real Taprobane of the ancients – the sacred isles of the Hindus!'

Stressing – indeed over-stressing – the 'perfected' survey of the island of Java and reform of the revenue system, Raffles said he had 'no narrow views of personal interest' in an extended administration over the Archipelago. 'It will require a person of high rank, either noble or military; and I have had too much experience already of the injuries which accrue from the want of that high rank.' (This is the only time that he referred openly to his social disadvantages.)

He therefore declared his intention of stepping down as Lieutenant-Governor. 'Like an anxious pilot I have anticipated with delight the hour when I may deliver [Java] over to her duly appointed Commander. In October, 1816, I shall have been Governor of these Colonies for five years, the usual period for which such a post is held. My health is delicate, and having completed twenty years' service in anxiety, fatigue, and constant application, I would indulge the hope of some relaxation in the honourable retreat which has, with a view to such an event, been kept open for me at Bencoolen.'

In autumn 1815 he withdrew to a house at Ciceroa on property bought in the land-sales by Cranssen and Engelhard. Dr Joseph Arnold, on a visit, recorded that there were always eight or ten people round Raffles' table at dinner – his ADCs Captains Travers, Watson and Methven, his Secretary Charles Assey, Mr Saleh, his Javanese interpreter, and three or four other 'learned natives'. 'The Governor speaks Javanese very well; and is collecting facts for a publication of the history of the island.' Raffles described this project to William Marsden. He did not imagine that he could actually write the book. He 'would rather see the materials worked up by an abler hand than incur the risk and responsibility of undertaking the task myself.'

In September 1815, while they were at Ciceroa, Travers heard from William Brown Ramsay, Raffles' friend and now also his, that the Court of Directors had decided Raffles was to be 'superseded' in Java – that is, dismissed, a whole year before he had elected to resign. (Not that his letter to Buckinghamshire would have yet reached London.) Ramsay's letter was dated 17 May 1815. The crucial despatch from the Court of Directors to Calcutta was dated 5 May in response to one from the Governor-General, not exactly requiring Raffles' removal but highly critical of his every measure, and expressing 'embarrassment' over Gillespie's charges.

India House was only interested in the bottom line. The despatch expressed regret that Lord Moira's critical overview of the economy of Java 'was not directed to the prevention of acts which have rendered the occupation of Java a source of financial embarrassment to the British Government. With reference to these considerations, whatever the result of the investigations of the charges preferred against Mr Raffles, we are of the opinion that his continuance on the Government of Java would be highly inexpedient.'

Raffles did not see this, but Ramsay's letter told the group at Ciceroa what he needed to know. 'The only person in the party who bore it with calmness was Mr Raffles himself.' Confident that he could prove the injustice of his dismissal, he wanted to sail for Calcutta immediately. No one else thought this was a good idea. General Nightingall travelled six hundred miles in four days out of pure friendship to persuade him not to go.

So he wrote letters instead – to Moira, to Charles Grant, Chairman of the Court of Directors, and again to the Earl of Buckinghamshire. He wrote to William Brown Ramsay, saying he would take some leave in England before taking up the post in Bencoolen: 'My character – my future happiness – require my presence in England…for here I am "a lonely man, like one that has long since been dead."' He needed to see his old friends. Another letter to Ramsay told how 'the manner in which my removal from Java was effected' had flattened him. 'The shock was too severe, my health had been undermined, and this injustice threw me on my back. It was the opinion of the [medical] faculty that remaining longer in India was dangerous.'

Then, on 3 November, the news arrived of Wellington's victory at

Waterloo in June. The war with France really was over. By the same vessel came a copy of the treaty by which Java and its dependencies were irrevocably given back to the Dutch. A week later Raffles lost good General Nightingall, now appointed Commander- in-Chief for Bombay. He was replaced by Colonel Nathaniel Burslem, whose son was christened Rollo Gillespie Burslem, so it is easy to see where his sympathies lay.

Raffles in early December 1815 had to deal with one last crisis. The three sepoy battalions stationed in Java were fearful that, with the change of administration, they would be compelled to join the Dutch army instead of going home to India. Sepoy activists conspired to join up with local rulers to form an enclave independent of all Europeans. The conspirators were betrayed and Colonel Burslem took strong action against the ringleaders. But intelligence came that rogue elements in the royal families of Surakarta and Yogyakarta were implicated in the plot.

The situation shocked the British, naively convinced of the sepoys' 'fidelity and attachment', to quote Travers. It was agreed in Council that Raffles himself should go to Surakarta to make his presence felt. On 2 January 1816 he sailed along the coast to Samarang, taking Captain Travers, Herman Muntinghe and a military escort.

The Susuhunan, apprehensive, saw to it that Raffles and his entourage were welcomed with even more than the customary gun salutes, homages, drum-beatings and processions. But the real business was done when the Susuhunan, informal in slippers and sarong, visited the British Residency. He and Raffles retired to a private room, and Raffles reported the conversation to Colonel Burslem. He assured the Susuhunan that he placed no confidence in the adverse reports, and was only speaking of them to point out the danger to his Highness's dignity of having allegedly 'put himself upon a level with inferior officers and private soldiers.' The Susuhunan explained that any action taken had been from fear of what the returning Dutch might do. Raffles undertook to intercede with the Dutch, and the Susuhunan said he wanted nothing more than the continuance of the terms of the treaty made with Raffles in 1812. Then they rejoined the rest of the group and all sat down to a game of cards – 'and we played high,' wrote Travers. The episode exemplifies Raffles with his qualities of head and heart working together. His exercise of authority was couched in terms that contrived to be flattering to his interlocutor. He got what he wanted, and sent his royal guest off in high humour.

He and his companions went on to pay a strategic visit to Yogyakarta, where they enjoyed – or not – equally magnificent ceremonies, and sat through two tiger fights. There was a touching moment in the hall of audience in the *kraton*, when the new teenage Sultan's granny came up to the Lieutenant-Governor, 'threw herself upon his neck and wept.' Other women of the family pressed forward to greet him. Olivia's taboo-breaking visit, and the Lieutenant-Governor's loss, were not forgotten in Yogyakarta.

After this mission, there was only humiliation for Raffles in Java. The party returned to Batavia by land, and at Pekalongan they were met by a ship's captain with despatches for Raffles from Bengal 'of the most unpleasant nature,' as Travers wrote. They finalised his removal from Java, but confirmed him in the Residency of Bencoolen. Lord Moira's comment on that to the Court of Directors was that 'there is no reason why he should not be employed in a situation of minor responsibility and of more strictly defined duties, of which the Residency of Bencoolen may be considered.'

His replacement as Lieutenant-Governor was John Fendall – twenty years older, and a lifelong Company man. He arrived with his family on 11 March 1816. Raffles, according to the *Memoir*, was 'alarmingly reduced at this time by the joint action of illness, and of the violent remedies [mercury] which had been applied.' Travers recorded how Raffles got out of bed to receive the Fendalls at Government House. 'Scarcely able to stand without support, he politely received Mr Fendall and introduced every person present to him, after which we breakfasted and Mr Fendall took the necessary oaths and Mr Raffles retired.' On 16 March he gave a dinner at Government House, inviting a 'select party' to meet the new incumbent, after which Lieutenant-Governor Fendall, his wife and daughters drove off to take possession of Buitenzorg.

Raffles, homeless, went to stay with Jacob Cranssens. From then on it was a matter of receiving sincere if orotund farewell addresses from public bodies, societies, clubs and the different communities – and writing equally sincere if orotund replies. He was to sail on the *Ganges*. Travers booked two-thirds of the roundhouse – the best place on the ship – for Raffles for £650. Freight would be charged at £20 a ton. The *Ganges* was loaded up with about two hundred chests and boxes containing everything Raffles had collected since he had been in the Eastern Isles.

The day before Raffles left Java, Lieutenant-Governor Fendall gave a party for him at Government House, and 'we were glad to observe,' wrote the *Gazette*'s reporter, 'that Mr Raffles appeared to be in good spirits, though much reduced and weakened by his late illness.' He went on to dine with his intimates and ADCs, and the toast was 'May the Ganges run into the Thames.' A gift of plate was voted for him by the principal inhabitants of Batavia, which Travers was deputed to buy in London.

He was to embark shortly after sunrise on 25 March 1816. At six o'clock in the morning troops were drawn up outside Cranssens' house to escort Raffles to the wharf, where a crowd had gathered. Accompanying him on the *Ganges* were Captains Travers and Garnham, his doctor Sir Thomas Sevestre, his Malay writer Siami, his longtime Malaccan servant Lewis, the Radin Rana Dipura, a young Javanese noble, and Dick, a little Papuan slave-boy whom he liberated and adopted in Bali. The decks were piled with gifts of fruit and flowers.

On the third day out, Travers brought to Raffles in his cabin the farewell address from his ADCs, his immediate staff, and Thomas

McQuoid: 'Whatever may be our future destination, and however it may be our chance to be scattered, when we return to our different fixed stations in life, we can never forget the time we have passed in Java.' Mr Raffles' 'spotless integrity and amiable qualities' in their shared private life 'are imprinted in our hearts too strongly to be ever erased.'

Raffles was overwhelmed by emotion. His friends had not referred to Olivia, but she was uppermost in his own mind in his reply: 'You have struck chords which vibrate too powerfully…You have been with me in the days of happiness and joy – in the hours that were beguiled away under the enchanting spell of one, of whom the recollection awakens feelings which I cannot express. You have supported and comforted me under the affliction of her loss… You have seen and felt what the envious and disappointed have done to supplant me in the public opinion…and now you come forward to say that as children of one family, you will hold to me through life.'

After rounding the Cape, the *Ganges* put in for water at St Helena in the small hours of 18 May, where the finally defeated Napoleon had been living in detention since the previous October. The illustrious prisoner lived in comfort at Longwood, a country estate of 15,000 acres, with a group of courtier-companions who included the Count and Countess Bertrand with their several children, and the Count and Countess Montholon with theirs. Both Countesses gave birth at Longwood, the paternity of one being possibly imperial. Longwood was a royal court in miniature, where Napoleon was still the 'Emperor'.

The Governor of St Helena, Sir Hudson Lowe ('a reserved and sour looking man' according to Raffles), negotiated Napoleon's reception of visitors. It was the burning desire of everyone who disembarked at St Helena to gain an introduction to him. Raffles was no exception. Like many Englishmen, he had a fascinated admiration for Napoleon, and he only had thirty-six hours to broker an interview before the *Ganges* continued her voyage.

Afterwards, datelined 'Off St Helena 20th May 1816', he wrote a twenty-five-page letter to, of all people, Alexander Hare, most of it about the time hanging about *not* seeing Napoleon, being lackadaisically entertained by officials. Count Bertrand finally gave them a pass into the grounds of Longwood, as the Emperor might be walking in the garden in the late afternoon, and had agreed to an introduction.

Raffles' first sight of Napoleon across the lawn was a disappointment: 'A heavy, clumsy-looking man, moving with a very awkward gait, and reminding us of a citizen lounging in the tea-gardens about London on a Sunday afternoon.' He was wearing a cocked hat, a dark green coat with a star on his breast, white breeches and white silk stockings. One of his suite peeled off and beckoned to Raffles. Napoleon stopped, took off his hat, put it under his left arm, and rapped out a string of questions. He asked Raffles how he pronounced his name. 'Where are you from? What country? You are from Java; did you accompany the expedition against it? Have the Dutch taken possession? Is the Java coffee better than the Bourbon?'

Raffles introduced his companions, who were likewise subjected to brusque, rapid questioning. Then Napoleon 'making an inclination to move, we mutually bowed, put on our hats, and turning back to back, withdrew from each other.' That was it. Count Bertrand followed them back to the lodge and 'invited us to partake of refreshments, which we had the honour of receiving off the Imperial silver.'

Napoleon's manner was 'abrupt, rude and authoritative, and the most ungentlemanly that I ever witnessed.' Raffles was disillusioned. Napoleon did not really know or care who or what Raffles was, but he was unequivocal about who and what Napoleon was: 'Believe me, Hare, this man is a monster, who has none of those feelings of the heart which constitute the real man... I saw in him a man determined and vindictive, without one spark of soul, but possessing a capacity and talent calculated to enslave mankind. I saw in him that all this capacity, all this talent, was devoted to himself and his own supremacy. It seems as if the despotism of Europe…were concentrated in him. He is the head of the great monster Despotism, but has no connexion with the heart… We are now prosecuting our voyage to England where we hope to arrive the first week in July.'

They were still at sea on his thirty-fifth birthday, 6 July, and had a party. But Raffles was sick and sad, writing to William Brown Ramsay, while 'looking out for the English coast,' that, though much recovered, 'I yet remain wretchedly thin and sallow, with a jaundiced eye and shapeless leg.' His letter 'comes from one who, although he brings back with him from India but a sorry carcase, and wants the blazonments of power, returns with a heart and soul as purely and devotedly attached as it was on the day of parting.'

Chapter 8

'She is devotedly attached to me'
England 1816–1817

◦◦◦◦◦

On 11 July 1816, a clear sunny day, the *Ganges* anchored off Falmouth on the Cornish coast. It was Raffles' first sight of England for more than eleven years.

He left on board the wooden crates containing his books and manuscripts, his animal and plant specimens and drawings, and his Javanese artefacts – thirty tons in weight – for the *Ganges* to carry on to the London docks. They contained around 450 puppets, 135 masks; twenty *kris*es; the torture implements from Malacca; his sets of gamelan instruments; bronze and wooden figures, the two great heads of Buddha and other pieces from Borobudur, plus quantities of weapons, bowls, pots, boxes, coins, textiles, charms, paddles, hats and ornaments.

The new arrivals had to be examined for infection or disease by custom-house officials, apprehensive that they might be suspect on account of their 'pale and emaciated' looks. Having passed the medical examination, they went straight to the inn and, as Travers recorded, 'ordered the best dinner procurable at the place, to be got ready as soon as possible, and passed a most joyous, enjoyable evening.'

Simply being back in England revived Raffles. He snatched the opportunity while in Cornwall of seeing a copper mine, in order to compare it with the mines he knew in Banca. The whole party visited the productive Wheal Busy mine near Chacewater and were greatly impressed by its working; 'and the wonderful power of the steam-engine was no less a novelty.' James Watt's steam-engine had been in operation at Wheal Busy since 1778, but Raffles' only experience of mining had been in the East, with manual labour and basic tools. He insisted on going down the mine, but Travers did not risk it, impressed that Raffles 'made himself quite master of the whole routine, and did not suffer in the least.'

The journey from Cornwall to London was punctuated by sightseeing – the carpet manufactory at Axminster, Salisbury Cathedral, and the new Royal Military College at Sandhurst Park. Travers went ahead to London. He found a house for Raffles and his entourage to rent at 23 Berners Street, and lodgings for himself at number 52 over the road. (Travers was proving indispensable.) Berners Street, just north of Soho over Oxford Street, was favoured by artistic and literary people: Samuel Taylor Coleridge was lodging at number 71 in 1816. Raffles wanted to be placed advantageously, and this was a good, central address, a world away from Walworth.

The rest of the party reached London on 16 July, and next morning Raffles presented himself at India House, confident that he would be vindicated once the Court of Directors knew all the facts of the Gillespie affair. Mercifully, the repayment of his disallowed salary raise while at Penang was swiftly waived. He had to wait longer for a response to Gillespie's charges, and longer still for any judgment on his Javan administration.

He reconnected with his family. Cousin Thomas called at Berners Street towards the end of July 1816, soon after some of the treasures from Java had arrived from the docks. He found Raffles out, and the house 'full of oriental matters…many things curious and magnificent, and multitudes of people waiting to see him – together with servants and others in partially oriental costumes, presenting to my eyes a novel and somewhat amusing spectacle.' Those in 'partially oriental costumes' included Raffles' servant Lewis, the Raden Rana Dipura, and ten-year-old Dick, the Papuan boy.

When Raffles came through the front door, Cousin Thomas was standing at the top of the stairs. He had been a boy when they last met, and was now 'married and settled in life, the Minister of a large Church and occupying a laborious and influential position.' Small wonder that they stared. 'He did not know me, nor did I, for a moment, recognise him,' Cousin Thomas wrote to his wife. 'But when I had leisure to survey his countenance, I perceived that he had lost nothing of himself but his colour and his flesh… My cousin was astonished at my appearance, and so was I at his – he, that I looked so well, and I, that he looked so ill.' They embraced, and 'were immediately at home together.' He was amazed by Raffles' 'unbounded flow of spirits; I fear too much for his strength.'

Raffles took his household to hear Cousin Thomas preaching in Paddington – it was his third hour-and-a-half-long sermon in London that day – and the celebrated preacher expressed to his wife an ardent desire that 'my poor efforts should be blessed to the promotion of the everlasting interests' of so distinguished a relative. Back home, the ex-Lieutenant-Governor of Java was a star, and he expanded in the glow.

Mrs Raffles had moved with Harriet and Ann to St Anne's Cottage in Hampstead, north of London. Cousin Thomas' parents, Raffles' Uncle William and Aunt Rachel, were still at 14 Princes Street in Spitalfields. Cousin Thomas recalled his mother telling him how Raffles went to see her, arriving on foot, having discreetly left his private carriage round the corner so as not to attract attention in that modest neighbourhood. He walked straight into 'the sort of parlour kitchen where my Mother was, busied as usual about her household affairs,' knowing that he would find her there.

Settled in the armchair by the fire where he used to sit in the old days, he was 'affectionate and playful' with her, 'quite unconscious of the elevation to which he had attained since he had last sat there.'

The Rev. Thomas, dazzled by the distinction of his older cousin, could never be entirely unconscious of that elevation. Aunt Rachel was a match for Raffles, as Cousin Thomas recollected:

' "Aunt," he said, "you know I used to tell you when a boy, that I would be a Duke before I die." "Ah," she replied, "and I used to say it would be Duke of *Puddle Dock*" – which was a proverb in London at that time referring to a wretched locality in Wapping: and with which aspiring lads, who had great notions of the greatness they should hereafter attain, were twitted.'

It is a good story, and would be a better one had Cousin Thomas remembered from his London childhood that the small wharf called Puddle Dock was not downriver at Wapping, but at Blackfriars, where Raffles' unfortunate father had been born.

Raffles wrote on 23 July 1816 to Cousin Thomas in Liverpool that 'the Medical Gentlemen' advised him to try the waters of Cheltenham to restore his health, 'and I have resolved upon the trip the moment my more urgent visits to the Great Men of the Town are completed.'

The Great Men of the Town with whom he got in touch were scholars, naturalists and natural philosophers. Some of them he had corresponded with already. Their power bases were the overlapping circles of learned societies, institutions and clubs, within which the scientific, the political and the social formed further intersecting circles. They proved to be very interested in charming, enthusiastic Raffles and his impressive collections. Number 23 Berners Street was always full of curious guests.

He finally met William Marsden, now in his sixties, the oriental scholar, numismatist, and author of *The History of Sumatra*. He was a Fellow of the Society of Antiquaries, a Fellow of the Royal Society (and a former Treasurer and Vice-President), and a core member of its sociable offshoot, the Royal Society Club, dominated by Sir Joseph Banks. Marsden's house was Edge Grove, in the Hertfordshire village of Aldenham, where Raffles visited him and his wife, taking as gifts fifteen square-holed bronze coins – not cash coins, but magic amulets.

Marsden, currently working on a translation of the travels of Marco Polo, was never an ivory-tower scholar. He had held high office in the Admiralty in the early years of the century, and had known the eminent naturalist Sir Joseph Banks, President of the Royal Society, since the 1780s, and been his protégé. Banks was a legendary figure, but now becoming ossified. Meetings of the Royal Society at Somerset House were formal. Papers were read, with no discussion or questions afterwards.

The discussions took place at Banks' London house, 32 Soho Square, where he displayed his natural history and ethnological collections, and held Sunday salons for scholars, naturalists and men of letters. 'We are all delighted with the acquaintance of Governor Raffles,' Banks wrote to Dr Horsfield. 'He is certainly among the best informed of men, and possesses a larger stock of useful talent than any other individual of my acquaintance.' In his introduction to *The History of Java*, Raffles thanked Sir Joseph Banks, 'the venerable President of the Royal Society,' for his 'kindness and encouragement.'

Banks made his name before Raffles was born. Only in his twenties, he travelled – paying his own way – as scientific observer on the *Niger* to Newfoundland and Labrador. He graduated from being a rich young gentleman and collector to a serious Linnean naturalist. At twenty-six he was the official botanist on Captain James Cook's second voyage on the *Endeavour* (1768–71) to the South Seas, financing his own team of natural historians.

The months that the *Endeavour* spent at Tahiti were for the purpose of astronomical observation. At ground level, Banks took advantage of the island's sexual freedoms. He thus entered intimately into Tahitian society, and the collection which he brought home embraced far more than the botanical. The famous *Endeavour* expedition, and his collection, brought Banks to the admiring notice of learned society, and of King George III – only five years older than himself – whose friend and ally he became; he was put in charge of the Royal Botanic Gardens at Kew.

Banks became a Fellow of the Royal Society the year after he returned from Tahiti, and its President in 1778, at the age of thirty-five – a position he contrived to hang on to until 1820 by means of loading the fellowship with his supporters. After he married a rich wife, and became a baronet, he morphed into a public man. He sat on councils, committees and governing bodies connected with science, trade, colonial policy, exploration, 'improvement' in agriculture, industry, elementary education, and imperial issues, becoming an overbearing and not altogether attractive figure. He is to be credited however with introducing and popularising 'useful' scientific knowledge and the practice of scientific methods.

Some Fellows of the Royal Society disapproved of Banks' snobbery: he favoured election to the Society of men who were well-born, socially agreeable and conservative in their politics. He discouraged radicals and dissenters, being of the generation whose Enlightenment values were skewed by the alarming upheavals of the French Revolution and fear of revolutionary contagion in England. This kind of double vision was common. Many men who campaigned for the abolition of the slave trade and religious emancipation were at the same time violently opposed to enlargement of the suffrage and the reform of Parliament.

A large, and largely passive, Royal Society membership supported by their subscriptions the work of active scientists. Some of the aristocrats elected to the Royal Society had serious intellectual interests. One such was the Duke of Somerset; he was probably the person who first presented Raffles to the Prince Regent. The Duke and Raffles liked and respected each other, and his first Duchess (Charlotte, a daughter of the Duke of Hamilton) became Raffles' special friend. The Somersets were a handsome couple, somewhat older than Raffles. She was apparently known for being close with money, but was generous to Raffles, giving him a fine porcelain tea or chocolate set – large shallow cups with handles, plus jug and sugar-bowl, decorated in apricot and gold, intact and in use to this day by a descendant of Maryanne's. She was a lively conversationalist, though delicate health forced her to receive her visitors while reclining on a sofa in her drawing room at number 1 Park Lane. She knew Byron, and corresponded with Metternich. Some of Raffles' best and most informal letters were written to this attractive, intelligent Duchess.

The Duke was a lifelong student of science and mathematics, and would, after Raffles' time, become President of the Royal Institution and of the Linnean Society. He was already in 1816 President of the Royal Literary Fund and a Fellow of the Society of Antiquaries. The Duke's younger brother, Lord Webb Seymour, when he heard from Captain Basil Hall an account of the Raffles-Gillespie affair – entirely in Raffles' favour – wrote to the Duke with a gossipy version of the quarrel as he understood it: 'Gillespie appears to have been a man of infamous character.' The Duke of Somerset's own character is exemplified by his reply: 'I have not looked into the question respecting the charges… Indeed I feel very averse to enter upon enquiries of that kind, unless I am particularly called upon to do so; because there are so many obstacles in the way of coming to a right opinion.' Raffles' *History of Java* however, 'bears many marks of an active benevolence of disposition.'

The Duke of Somerset took Raffles as he found him, and was interested in his ethnological and natural history collections. He was less sympathetic to his geopolitical visions. 'I cannot approve of the interference of one nation in the internal Government of another,' he wrote later in life, 'either in spiritual or temporal terms.'

The Duke's brother Lord Webb Seymour was an accumulator of facts about every branch of knowledge, which led to nothing because – in an earnest parody of the prevailing intellectual culture – he lacked the mental equipment to draw any conclusions. He lived in

Edinburgh, making friends among the professors at the University.

Writing to the Duke while visiting London in October 1816, Webb Seymour provides a glimpse of the changing city which Raffles was encountering: 'The other day I walked to look at the new Vauxhall Bridge. It makes a fine appearance from a distance, but the railing, and all the details of the work, are in a style far too plain... I have not yet been upon the Strand Bridge' – this was Waterloo Bridge, not open to traffic until the following summer – 'which I am told is far more worthy of admiration ...You mention Brunel as a member of the Royal Society Club; that is a name I am not acquainted with. Who is he?'

Byron's *Childe Harold's Pilgrimage*, Lord Webb Seymour reported, was causing a stir. He did not mention the publication of Jane Austen's *Emma*, or Coleridge's 'Kubla Khan'.

Raffles' short period in England was at a wretched time. The years 1816 and 1817 were years of post-war recession and unemployment. The previous summer had been cold and sunless, owing to the ash-cloud from the Tambora eruption. Crops failed, potatoes rotted, prices soared. In 1816 the crops again failed. There was excruciating rural poverty and typhoid epidemics in the filthy alleys and courts of the cities. Home-workers (weavers and lace-makers) were breaking into factories and smashing the new machinery which took away their livelihoods. Labourers marched on the industrial towns and rioted. In March 1817 the law of *habeas corpus* was suspended, enabling law officers to detain persons at will, without trial.

Cousin Thomas was properly aware of distress in Liverpool, since his own congregation and community were affected, as were 'connexions' of his own, in his wife's family. None of this wretchedness impinged on Raffles, circulating like a small new planet around the centres of scholarship and privilege in the politer parts of the capital. Going straight to the top, he met the great and the good of the scientific world incrementally. Sir Humphry Davy, just three years older than Raffles, was a key contact.

Davy was elected a Fellow of the Royal Society when only twenty-four, but became more closely connected with the Royal Institution where, from 1802 to 1812, he was the Professor of Chemistry. (The Royal Society did not have its own laboratories, but funded experimental science.) The Royal Institution, in which Sir Joseph Banks was inevitably involved, was founded in 1799 to introduce new technologies and scientific discoveries to the general public. Support, membership (and subscriptions) came originally from landowners, keen to find more productive farming methods. The Royal Institution held popular lectures and demonstrations at its premises at 21 Albemarle Street, with fierce competition for tickets. As with celebrity preachers, celebrity lecturers such as Davy provided spectacle, like the theatre.

Davy was a poor boy from Cornwall who aspired to be a second Newton. Through a chain of lucky circumstances and his own talent, he came to work with experimental scientists and to know the Romantic poets. Culture was unitary; there was little separation between experimental science and the arts, or even between experimental science and mysticism. Davy's first influential monograph was on the various oxides of nitrogen; he moved on to electrochemistry. He would take on anything, learning about tanning in order to give a lecture on the subject, and investigating fertilisers, insecticides, and soil analysis.

There was in Edinburgh a spirited and wealthy Scottish widow, Jane Apreece, who had met Madame de Staël in Geneva, and declared herself to be an incarnation of the eponymous heroine of de Staël's novel of 1807, *Corinne* – that is, gifted, passionate, idealistic, and doomed to suffer. Jane Apreece was a recognisable sort of intelligent, provocative woman who loves to crack the shells and break the hearts of sober intellectuals, and she exercised her charms on Edinburgh University professors. But it was Sir Humphry Davy who married her in April 1811, three days after he was knighted by the Prince Regent. (It was not a happy marriage.)

Sir Humphry Davy had his last major success in the year Raffles returned to London, having put his mind to the problem of deaths from fire-damp and choke-damp in coal-mines. A naked flame would reveal the gas, but precipitated lethal explosions. Davy went down the mines, made experiments, tried out various prototypes, and came up with the Safety Lamp. The appearance of the flame alerted the miners to the presence of gas, while a mesh of iron-wire gauze prevented the flame from passing through. George Stephenson was working on the same idea at the same time, but the Davy Lamp won the day.

When Raffles met Sir Humphry and Lady Davy in 1816, they were living at 23 Grosvenor Street in London's Mayfair. After his marriage, like Sir Joseph Banks after his, Sir Humphry became grand. His rise from humble beginnings is an example of how science was now a career ladder, like the church or the law – or the East India Company.

Medicine was another career ladder. Sir Everard Home (created a baronet in 1813) was a physician and comparative anatomist from Hull whose brother-in-law was the distinguished surgeon John Hunter, on the back of whose fame Home rose like a balloon. He was an executor of Hunter's will, the custodian of Hunter's papers and, while Raffles was in London, became the curator of Hunter's collection of anatomical specimens and published a volume of his own lectures. He had a large medical practice, and read scores of research papers to the Royal Society.

Sir Everard was interested in Dick, the Papuan boy, contributing a paragraph about the particularities of Dick's physique to Raffles' *History of Java*, and he dissected and described some of Raffles' animal specimens and skeletons. Later it transpired that he had been lifting for his own publications material from Hunter's research papers, which he held on to on the grounds that he was cataloguing them. Plagiarism was not yet suspected when Raffles knew him.

Raffles spent time with all these intellectual entrepreneurs and more. When in March 1817 he himself was elected a Fellow of the Royal Society, his chief sponsors were William Marsden and Sir

Everard Home. It was intoxicatingly exciting. As his widow Sophia put it in the *Memoir*, he 'enjoyed the pleasures of society with a zest that can be imagined, when the vigour of his mind and the variety of his tastes are considered. He left England, indeed, at an age when he had no opportunity of judging of the attractions of its best society…and he returned to England with talents ripened, and with a taste formed for all the intellectual enjoyments of life.'

But he had to get his health back.

It was the fashion, as William Hickey put it, 'for all those recently returned from the East Indies to take an early trip to Cheltenham with a view to getting quit of all lurking bile and correcting the debility supposed to arise from living in so sultry a climate, by the efficacious springs of the place.' One sip of the water was more than enough for Hickey. Raffles took the water each morning. The Wells had been exploited for a century as the cure for any number of ailments, but the change came when the King visited in 1788. What was in 1801 a town of 3,000 inhabitants was expanding fast.

In 1816 there was still no sewage system, but the uniform streets and terraces springing up were paved and lit. There were the Assembly Rooms for balls and concerts, where, as at the Wells, it was easy to make acquaintances and gain introductions to the friends of one's friends. The Promenade would not be laid out for another couple of years, but the Royal Crescent was completed, and Raffles, his sister Maryanne, Captain Thomas Travers and William Brown Ramsay were renting number three.

Maryanne's husband, Captain William Flint, was away fulfilling his obligations to the Admiralty, but she had with her in Cheltenham their first child, William Charles Raffles (known as Charles, or 'Charley Boy'). Her son Stamford, by her first husband, died three months before Raffles reached home, and her two elder children were in Ireland with an aunt and uncle. Maryanne was an enchanting person whose domestic life was never entirely happy or stable.

A Mr and Mrs Hull, with a selection of their unmarried sons

and daughters, had recently moved into 349 The High Street in Cheltenham. The Hulls met the interesting group staying in the Crescent, and Sophia Hull struck up a warm friendship with Mary-anne Flint. Sophia, rising thirty, and the elder of the two by three years, sent Maryanne the kind of extravagantly affectionate notes then customary between female friends: 'You know dearest Puss how much I love you.'

There is no way of knowing how much Maryanne's brother and Sophia saw each other at this time, nor the extent to which Sophia's devotion to Maryanne was designed to further her romantic inter-est, or his. But something was afoot, and Maryanne knew about it. 'I did not expect to see Somebody this day,' Sophia wrote to her, 'and yet because I have not done so my heart is very heavy.' The two families only coincided in Cheltenham for about six weeks – for one of which Raffles was away in London, negotiating the release of more boxes from the Customs.

In September Captain Travers left for Ireland and his family home, Leemount, just outside Cork city. Raffles and Maryanne, with the young physician Sir Thomas Sevestre, returned to London and Berners Street. Raffles had begun to use his second given name, 'Stamford', in preference to 'Thomas'; Sophia Hull kept up her contact with Maryanne in letters addressed to 'Mrs Flint, c/o Stamford Raffles Esq' at 23 Berners Street. 'But when shall I see you again?'

Mrs Raffles and Harriet visited Cheltenham after Raffles and Maryanne had left, maybe finishing up the lease on 3 The Crescent, and spent an evening with the Hulls. Sophia Hull complained to Maryanne about the exchange of family members: 'They are I am sure very amiable and good but they are not like you…I can't bear to lose sight of you, for you are quite identified with us as one of the family.' She thanked Maryanne and 'your Brother' for being good to her own brother, Lieutenant William Hollamby Hull, who was in London.

⤛

Raffles, in the autumn of 1816, finally succeeded in 'getting the whole of my baggage freed from the Custom House' with no duty payable except on the wines, and 'our back drawing-room is now quite a Museum,' as he told Cousin Thomas in October, adding the good news that his sister Harriet, having found no husband to her liking out East, had now found one in Thomas Brown of Hampstead – 'he seems a very steady good kind of man and likely to make her happy – he is a widower with one child and has an office in Somerset House.'

Raffles was working flat out on his *History of Java*, having decided to write it himself after all, but was still not well. He was suffering from heavy colds, and was taking mercury for a pain in his side. This toxic treatment, to which he was so frequently subjected, was familiarly known as 'salivation', on account of one of its effects, allegedly proof that the treatment was working. By November, having been 'dreadfully ill', he was feeling better, 'the saliva now flowing from my mouth in a copious stream.' (Other manifestations of mercury poisoning are sore gums, loose teeth, metallic halitosis, and discoloured stool.)

Travers was so alarmed by the news of Raffles' illness that he returned from Ireland, where he was courting Mary Leslie, his future wife. In December Raffles was 'nearly killed' by a mercury overdose, as he reported to Cousin Thomas, but was well enough to entertain a large party of 'all my family that are within reach' to dinner at Berners Street on Christmas Day 1816.

By then his book was almost done. In the New Year of 1817, he was sending sheets to the printer each morning and correcting the proofs late the same evening. He was also moving in the highest circles. He went to see the opening of Parliament by the Prince Regent (whose carriage was stoned on the way), and attended the Prince's levee at Carlton House. where he was introduced to George Canning, the new President of the Board of Control.

Raffles was not over-confident about the book. More than ever he was missing John Leyden's encyclopaedic scholarship. He had worked on his materials during the voyage home, and even got Cousin Thomas involved. Cousin Thomas, as hyperactive and driven as Raffles had, in addition to his itinerant schedule of celebrity preaching, already published the *Memoirs of the Life and Ministry of the Late Reverend Thomas Spencer of Liverpool*; he had translated Klopstock's *The Messiah* from the German, and edited, with annotations, John Brown's *Self-Interpreting Bible*.

Raffles had brought home a partial and literal translation he had done – with assistance – of the *Serat Bratayuda*, which he called the 'Brata Yudha', Java's 'great national poem' written in Kawi, the sacred Sanskrit-soaked language of the Javanese. He was anxious o include it in his book 'to prove that the Javanese are not savages.' Cousin Thomas was press-ganged into rendering the long epic into verse. He heroically produced two versions – one in the style of McPherson's *Ossian*, the other in blank verse. Only fourteen stanzas of it could be fitted into *The History of Java*.

In spite of illness, Raffles produced his two volumes with amazing speed, partly because to a large extent the book was a compilation. The data for the economic and demographic statistical tables derived from Lieutenant-Colonel Colin Mackenzie's surveys. For reliable observations on natural history he relied largely, with warm acknowledgment, on the work of Dr Thomas Horsfield. The plans and drawings of Javanese temples and antiquities were provided by Major H.C. Cornelis, Captain George Baker and others. For the history and nature of the Dutch administration of Java he was indebted to his former Dutch colleagues H.W. Muntinghe and J.W. Cranssen.

His model was Marsden's *History of Sumatra*. Far more than a history, even though it was full of history, Marsden's work started with the climate and ended with the ceremonial cannibalism of the Battas, covering in between – and among other topics – descriptions of people and of their languages, foods, tools, weapons, entertainments, ceremonies, endemic illnesses and sexual arrangements; the wild animals, crops, spices, birds' nests, and the Upas Tree. Raffles' book covered the same ground for Java in even more detail. A 'History' at this time was not necessarily a chronological narrative.

It was natural that readers would compare the two, as did the reviewer for *The Asiatic Journal* for August 1817. Raffles need not 'shrink from the comparison.' But the 'first place' was assigned to 'the elegant author of *The History of Sumatra*' – in spite of the 'vastly greater scope' of *The History of Java*, and 'that degree of zeal tinted a little with enthusiasm in favour of his subject, without which local history, if ever undertaken, is tamely executed.' 'Local history', suggesting as it does the study of an English shire, was an awkward term to use for what was even then called 'historical sociology'.

The Edinburgh Review published two review articles on *The History of Java*. The first, in the issue for December 1818–March 1819, gave a full summary and found something to praise: the 'happiness and fidelity' of the descriptions of the island, the 'correct and beautiful' plates; and the map, 'the best ever compiled.' The anonymous reviewer found the author's provision of 'too ample details' on the civil history of Java 'among the greatest blemishes of the work.'

'The book is hastily written, and not very well arranged. It is a great deal too bulky, and too expensive, to be popular... The style is fluent, but diffuse, and a little careless.' The reviewer guessed that the author 'composes with too much facility, and blots too little.' The best sections were on the character, habits, manners and customs of the Javanese, and the accounts of religion and history 'by far the worst.'

The reviewer was dour John Crawfurd, and the article manages to encapsulate his ambivalence about Raffles' way of being, as well as his scholarship. The second notice of *The History of Java* in the same journal appeared in December 1819, and was a tacit corrective. 'The date of this work precedes that of our journal, but we are anxious, on several counts, to look back to it... We are too sensible of the worth and merits of its excellent author not to step a little out of our way to testify our esteem.' Again, a full summary was given, and a special commendation for the 'spirited manner' in which Sir Stamford condemned the slave trade. The one pull-back was that 'the whole is too little digested into a regular and connected narrative.'

This was written by someone who saw Raffles in London (probably Captain Basil Hall), since the reviewer describes hearing the Radin 'who accompanied the late governor to England' playing on one of the gamelan instruments 'before an eminent composer, several of his national melodies, all of which were found to have a striking resemblance to the oldest music in Scotland.' Whether Raffles himself had a hand in fixing this second notice is an open question.

Raffles' 'zeal' in *The History of Java* was political. 'The English came to Java as friends,' he wrote – an assertion which, made about an invading power, may well raise an eyebrow. It makes sense in that the book is geared towards emphasising the abuses of the 'capricious and semi-barbarous Government of the Dutch,' contrasted with the amelioration achieved during his own administration. Underlying all is his conviction that the British Government made a frightful mistake in handing back to the Dutch such a promising, potentially profitable and strategically important country.

It is an uneven book. The thematic shifts are too sudden, there are repetitions, and long extracts introduced by quotation marks which never close. The meat is in the first volume. The second 'subsidiary' volume is scrappier, containing more history, an account of Batavia, an inadequate description of the antiquities, the sections on Bali and on the Japan trade, and other appendices. The second of the *Edinburgh* reviewers was right when he said that the lasting value of *The History of Java* might be as source material for future historians.

Yet the work remains compelling. Raffles loved Java – especially the central provinces with their fertile, black volcanic soil and abundant water: 'Nothing can be conceived more beautiful to the eye, or more gratifying to the imagination, than the prospect of the rich variety of hill and dale, of rich plantations and fruit trees or forests, of natural streams and artificial currents… The whole country, as seen from mountains of considerable elevation, appears a rich, diversified, and well watered garden, animated with villages, interspersed with the most luxuriant fields, and covered with the freshest verdure.'

Much had been said, he wrote, about the 'indolence' of the Javans. That was wrong. 'If they do not labour during the whole day, it is because such persevering toil is unnecessary, or would bring them no additional enjoyments.' The villagers worked in the morning, rested in the heat of the day, and at six returned home to spend the hours till bedtime 'in little parties for amusement or conversation… I have always found them either pleased and satisfied with their lot when engaged at their work, or social and festive in their hours of pleasure.'

Those, on the other hand, who lived in cities or at the princely courts, or who were in public service 'are frequently profligate and corrupt, exhibiting many of the vices of civilisation without its refinement, and the ignorance and deficiency of a rude state without its simplicity.' The truth was that 'the further they are removed from European influence and foreign intercourse, the better are their morals and the happier are the people.'

He drew no conclusions from these insights, which undermined his every theory about economic colonial expansion.

Sophia Hull travelled from Cheltenham to London sometime in the New Year of 1817, and Travers recorded that both he and Ramsay knew, 'long before' the event, that she and Raffles were to be married. On 4 December, in an emotional letter to Maryanne, 'my dear little Puss', Sophia had confessed that 'it is the charm of my existence to cherish those I *do* love with all my heart and soul, but I am too humble to expect the same in return unless I would deserve it.' Her letter collapses into vague haverings about the ways it is possible 'to love a Husband.' Sophia had already met Raffles' mother, in Cheltenham. This was a rapid but not a runaway romance.

Raffles gave to Sophia, as an engagement present, an oval gold box decorated with whorls of repoussé filigree, and the initials 'SR to SH' engraved on the bottom. On 20 February he and Travers escorted the two famously pretty daughters of Sir Everard Home to the Queen's Drawing-Room, and on 22 February he married Sophia. He slipped out of the house before breakfast, taking neither Travers nor Ramsay with him. Sir Thomas Sevestre, living in the house, knew nothing about it.

The marriage was solemnised at the still unfinished St Marylebone parish church, ten minutes walk from Berners Street. The witnesses were not recorded. Big weddings were not in the culture for people like the Raffleses and the Hulls. There could, too, be personal reasons why Raffles did not make a celebration of the occasion. Olivia had been a great love, to whom he now had to say goodbye. Marrying Sophia Hull was not something that would greatly interest his new London acquaintances. He had a full diary, and a book to get through the press. His marriage was a private matter.

The new couple went off for two nights' honeymoon to Henley-on-Thames – no doubt to the famous Red Lion Inn, where the great Duke of Marlborough had furnished a room for himself, left untouched since his death, to break the journey between London and Blenheim Palace. Boswell and Johnson had stayed at the Red Lion, and it was frequented by royalty.

From Henley, on 23 February 1817, Raffles wrote to Cousin Thomas: 'You will I doubt not approve of the change I have made in my condition in again taking to myself a Wife; and when I apprize you that neither rank, fortune nor beauty have had weight on the occasion, I think I may fairly anticipate your approval of my selection – the lady, whose name is Sophia, is turned of thirty, she is devotedly attached to me, and possesses every quality of the heart and mind calculated to render me happy – more I need not say.'

This is ungracious. It is his bride's devotion to him, and not his to her, that he chooses to mention, and he does not even tell his cousin her last name. The tone is explicable if one surmises that the Rev.

Thomas had warned Raffles not to marry the first pretty face he fell
for, or someone too young for him, or for worldly reasons. In the
same letter he told Cousin Thomas that he had received from the
Company 'the most full and satisfactory conclusion' to the affair of
Gillespie's charges against him, that the post in Bencoolen was open
to him, and 'as there seems an inclination to extend my political
authority there, I think it almost certain I shall go out in the course
of the year.' Outlining immediate plans, he wrote 'I' not 'we'. Raffles
always was the hero of his own story.

Gillespie's charges were thrown out. The significant despatch to
Lord Moira in Calcutta was dated 13 February 1817, but Raffles
would have known its contents in advance. After long examination of the evidence, the Court of Directors decided that 'we think
it due to Mr Raffles, in the interests of our service, and to the
cause of truth, explicitly to declare our decided conviction that the
charges, in so far as they went to implicate the moral character of
that gentleman, have not only been made good, but that they have
been disproved to an extent which is seldom practicable in a case
of defence.'

There was a bit of a pull-back in the Directors' remark that the
'expediency' of Raffles' measures in Java could not be assessed fully
without further information. His purchase of lands at public auction
was 'unquestionably indiscreet' but without 'any selfish or sordid
taint'. His policies might be questionable – they could not yet pro-
nounce on that – but not his integrity or his honour. It was a neat
solution. It is unlikely that the Court of Directors had ever come to
grips with the contents of Raffles' justifications and explanations of
all his Javan policies, or that they ever would.

The author Thomas Love Peacock entered into service at India
House in 1818 at the age of thirty-four; the Department of the
Examiner of Indian Correspondence was in need of some mature
brain power. As an entrance test, Peacock had to write a paper on
'Ryotwar and Zemindiary Settlements' from material supplied.
Maybe the Directors thought a summary of this knotty subject

would come in handy. The official comment on Peacock's paper was, 'Nothing superfluous, nothing wanting.'

Raffles' confirmed return to the East precipitated his marriage to Sophia, as his appointment to Penang had precipitated his marriage to Olivia. Sophia needed a husband. He needed a wife. Neither could have chosen better. Sophia, on the cusp of spinsterhood, embarked on a more exciting life than she could have dreamed of, or than many women would have had the courage to sustain. If Raffles was the hero of his own story, he was the hero of hers as well. She gave him unconditional love, became his confidante, his best supporter and, after his death, the creator and curator of his fame and the keeper of the shrine.

Travers described Sophia as 'amiable, affectionate, sensible, personable, tho' not very handsome, with a good figure, and extremely well brought up and possessing many amiable qualities, both of head and heart.' She was fluent on paper, a good pianist, an opera-lover, and in Cheltenham had begun learning to play the harp. Her background was very suitable. The brother whom Raffles had welcomed in London, William Hollamby Hull, was in the Royal Navy. An uncle, William Hollamby, had been Quartermaster of HMS *Discovery* on Captain James Cook's third voyage to the Pacific. Her father, James Watson Hull – from Lisburn in County Down, in the north of Ireland – had joined the East India Company as a writer at the age of nineteen, and married Sophia Hollamby in Bombay.

Raffles' Sophia was the second of their fifteen children. Mrs Hull was herself the youngest of twenty-one. These were fertile people. Sophia did the one great thing for Raffles that Olivia, for whatever reason, could not: she gave him children.

Sophia's father made money by private trading in Bombay, and in the year that she was born he brought his family home to Ireland. Then, he upped sticks and moved to England where, in 1815, one of Sophia's younger sisters, Mary Jane, married Peter Auber, later Assistant Secretary to the East India Company – a connection which was to be useful to Raffles. In 1816 the Hull family moved to Cheltenham, precisely coinciding with the arrival of Raffles and his party. Another of Sophia's sisters, Alice, married a young military man, Richard Zacharias Mudge, a few months after Sophia married Raffles. If the Hulls' move to England was made with the idea of finding husbands for daughters, it proved effective.

Chapter 9

Sir Stamford Raffles

England 1816–1817

 consin Thomas was slightly acquainted with two dissolute royal
Dukes, and was elated by such encounters: 'I can scarcely realise
my present situation.' Raffles trumped his cousin by becoming the
friend of Princess Charlotte, the only child of the Prince Regent, and
the presumptive heir after him to the throne of England, Ireland,
Scotland and Wales.

In May 1816, aged twenty, she was married to Prince Leopold
of Saxe-Coburg-Gotha. Raffles sent her six Javanese ponies and
some of the tables and chairs which he had made in London from
Amboyna burr timber from Java. Charlotte was delighted with the
furniture, which she put in her new home – Claremont House in
Surrey. A friendship developed between Raffles and the young royal
couple.

Princess Charlotte had been the problem child of dysfunctional
parents. Her father, the Prince Regent, hated her mother, Princess
Caroline of Brunswick. The pair separated after one year. He lived
at Carlton House, she had her own establishment. Charlotte, shut-
tled between them, became a troubled teenager, loud-mouthed and
gauche. She was, like both her parents, overweight, and profligate
with money she did not have. She had a fling with a young Hussar,

whom she met secretly at her mother's house – with her mother's connivance.

At seventeen she was given her own establishment, Warwick House, tucked away across a courtyard from Carlton House. A strategic marriage was arranged with Prince William of Orange, son of William I of the Netherlands, but she refused to marry him. Another fling, with the King of Prussia's nineteen-year-old nephew Prince Frederick, resulted in the Prince Regent crossing the court-yard to Warwick House in a rage and pronouncing she must live out of London in seclusion. Charlotte ran away down the back stairs of Warwick House and into a hackney cab. The unhappy girl was pursued, and immured at Cranbourne Lodge in Windsor Great Park. Her only permitted outings were to see her grandmother Queen Charlotte, wife of the demented George III.

Among the European princelings hovering hopefully around the next-but-one heir to the British throne was Prince Leopold of Saxe-Coburg-Gotha, the younger son of a minor dukedom in Thuringia. He made himself agreeable to the Prince Regent. He was not very royal, as European royalty went, and he had no money. He was lodging over a grocer's shop in Marylebone High Street. But Char-lotte made up her mind to marry him. It is said that when the Prince repeated the vow 'With all my worldly wealth I thee endow', the Princess laughed.

Parliament voted the couple an ample income, plus a lump sum for setting up Camelford House on the corner of Oxford Street and Park Lane in London, and Claremont in Surrey. It was a popular marriage. Charlotte was cheered by the crowd whenever she drove out. People knew all about her misfortunes. Raffles, far away in Java, had known; the *Java Government Gazette* had reprinted scandalous articles from the London papers, and a special supplement, 'The Princess Charlotte of Wales: The Dramatic Escape from Warwick House.'

Nevertheless, the aspirational related to the royal family as if they were exemplars of integrity and the source of all blessings. Royal approval or disapproval could make or break a career. Raffles was well aware that his friendship with Princess Charlotte and Prince Leopold, pleasant in itself, could be nothing but beneficial for his fame and prospects.

On his visits to Claremont he found a happy couple – an animated young woman, and a well-informed young man with whom he could discuss politics. Visiting them at Claremont for the first time on 27 April 1817, he wrote from there to Cousin Thomas – knowing how much he would appreciate the letterhead – urging him to join him, Sophia and Maryanne on a continental holiday they were planning for the following month.

Raffles was a success with the royals, striking the right note of respectful familiarity, not overstepping the mark. Queen Charlotte admired her granddaughter's exotic furniture, and proposed paying Raffles a visit. He judged it more fitting to call upon her, and they met at the house of the Countess of Harcourt. He walked in the Countess' park with the Queen of England on his arm, and she brought up the subject of the furniture. Raffles obliged by imme-diately diverting in her direction a pair of tables which had been earmarked for Sir Joseph Banks.

A further instance of royal cupidity treasured by Cousin Thomas was when he, Raffles and Sophia were breakfasting at Berners Street and an equerry appeared, sent by the Prince Regent to taste the arrack from Java, which the Prince had heard was remarkably good. Raffles responded by taking all the arrack he had in the house round to Carlton House there and then. He told the Prince that he would supply him with arrack 'as long as he lived to drink it' – adding to Cousin Thomas, 'If he drinks plentifully of it, as he is sure to do, it will not be long, for it is the strongest spirit in the world.'

The Prince Regent had given Raffles gracious permission to dedi-cate *The History of Java* to him. Publication was scheduled for 10 May 1817, after which Raffles' family party was due to leave for their tour of continental Europe. The group comprised Sophia's best friend Ella Torriano, Sophia's brother William Hull (who married Ella Torriano's sister Jane), as well as Sophia, Maryanne, and Cousin Thomas. Both publication and tour were postponed when Raffles was commanded to attend a levee at Carlton House on 29 May.

What happened there was probably thanks to Princess Charlotte. Cousin Thomas reported to his wife that the Prince Regent 'marked [Raffles] out at the *levee*, entered into conversation with him, told him he had read a great part of the book, and most sincerely thanked him for the instruction and pleasure he had derived.' The Prince also expressed 'the high sense he entertained of the eminent services he had rendered to his country in the Government of Java,' which, given the Company's grudging attitude, can only have been music to Raffles' ears.

Raffles was invited to kneel. The Prince Regent then knighted him. 'Why, Charlotte,' said Prince Leopold in Raffles' hearing, 'they have made him a *knight*!'

Tom Raffles was now Sir Stamford Raffles. But a mere knighthood was a disappointment. A baronetcy had been expected. 'The honour of knighthood could not be very highly esteemed by him,' opined Cousin Thomas, 'when he had in his own establishment, a man of equal rank as his Body Physician.' (Sevestre had been knighted for his services as surgeon at the capture of Cayenne in 1809.) Some thought that Raffles became 'Sir Stamford' and not 'Sir Thomas' in order to differentiate himself from Sir Thomas Sevestre. But he began using 'Stamford' even before moving from Cheltenham to London. It did sound more distinguished, but never caught on with his intimates. Sophia and the family always called him 'Tom'.

Three days after receiving his knighthood Raffles dined again at Claremont with Princess Charlotte and Prince Leopold. When he was taking his leave next morning, Prince Leopold and Princess Charlotte – happily advanced in pregnancy – gave him a diamond ring. That is Cousin Thomas' version. Sophia remembered the ring being presented on the day before they left London to sail back to the East. It doesn't matter; the diamond was a fine one.

Raffles had long dreamed of some ennoblement. Back in February 1809, in Penang, he wrote to Uncle William Raffles seeking information about an illustrious forebear, Sir Benjamin Raffles, who 'about the time of James 1st or 2nd' was created 'Knight Banneret'. 'Now as Knights Banneret were next to Barons in dignity as appears by Statute made in the fifth year of Richard II, Stat 2 Chap 4…and their *heirs male* are entitled to precedence and therefore the Title, it is of some importance to me to trace this more particularly – not that I am anxious at the moment to obtain the title, but I have reason to think that hereafter it may be of consequence.'

The last time the mediaeval title 'Knight Banneret' was properly used was at the Battle of Edgehill in 1642. From the records, Raffles' idea seems to be pure fantasy. The one significant Raffles from the past was John Raffles, in 1582 the mayor of Beverley in Yorkshire, where there are Raffleses recorded from earlier in the same century; in the mid-seventeenth century, there was a 'Benjamin Raffels' in Berwick-on-Tweed. None were knights, or knights banneret. Raffles wanted Uncle William to go to the 'Herald's Office' and find out what he could 'respecting the family of my grandfather and back from him to the date in which the glorious Knight Banneret Sir Benjamin strutted his hour.' We do not know what Uncle William did about this, if anything.

Sir Stamford Raffles, when he 'strutted his hour', put in for a coat of arms, through the normal channels. His petition to the Earl Marshall, the Duke of Norfolk, requested that the arms would bear 'some allusion' to services rendered 'in the reduction and subsequent Government of Java.' The letters patent, granting the arms, were issued on 2 October 1817.

Raffles had further requirements. The design includes, awkwardly, two small oval medallions on a chain, one bearing Arabic characters and the other a *kris* – representing, as the official description has it, 'a personal decoration (called the Order of the Golden Sword)', conferred 'by the Chief or King of Atcheen [*sic*] (a State in the Island of Sumatia [*sic*] in the Indian Ocean) as a mark of the

High Regard of the said King and in testimony of the good understanding which had happily been established between that Prince
and the British Government.'

Raffles had his coat of arms, or its griffin crest, engraved in versions from large to minuscule on everything – on his book-plate,
his forks and spoons, on gold and tortoiseshell boxes, on his chessboard and each of the chessmen, and on every single piece in a set of
intricately carved Chinese ivory boxes containing mother-of-pearl
and ivory counters for games. A fan of Sophia's, with leaves of ivory
tracery, opening into a full circle, has a tiny griffin on a central leaf;
as does a fan of Maryanne's, its tortoiseshell leaves so fine as to be
transparent.

He chose as the motto for his coat of arms 'Auspicium Melioris
Aevi', which may be translated as 'The hope (or token, or augury) of
a better age'. Whether he knew it or not, the same motto was about
to become that of the Order of St Michael and St George, an Order
of Chivalry founded by the Prince Regent to celebrate the British
acquisition of Malta. The coincidence is curious.

The seven-week European tour began on 5 June 1817. They crossed
the Channel from Brighton to Dieppe. The ladies had berths, and
the gentlemen slept where they could, Raffles wrapped in a blanket
on the cabin floor. At Dieppe they had to go the police office to
obtain passports. Only Sir Stamford Raffles was examined, and
every detail of his appearance noted down.

They took in France, Savoy, Switzerland, Germany and Holland.
Raffles rated punctuality highly among the virtues. Once, at Berners
Street, Maryanne's maid called out that her mistress was not ready
when it was time to leave for dinner. Raffles, at the door, called back
that she would have to come on by herself. On the tour Raffles, as
team leader, made a ruling that 'we should never keep the carriage
waiting, but having fixed the hour of starting over night, should
keep it exactly in the morning.'

As he reported to William Marsden, they travelled through

'Rouen, Paris, and Dijon, to Geneva; passed through the valley of Chamouni, along the foot of the Alps, and returned by Lausanne and Berne to Basle and down the Rhine to Cologne, whence we traversed the Low Countries to Brussels and Ostend.' They stayed as long as a week only in Paris and Brussels.

In Brussels, Raffles was presented at Court and met King William I (since 1815, the first King of the Netherlands), dining with him and his ministers, including G.K. van Hogendorp, and the Colonial Minister, Anton Falck. He wrote to Falck two days later appealing against injustice done to his good friend Jacob Cranssen, who was being 'slighted' by the new Dutch commissioners in Java. Cranssen was 'advanced in life, and he cannot live in disgrace.' A 'more true Hollander' never existed. Cranssen never considered, in joining the British administration, that he was acting against the interests of his own country. 'England had been no enemy to Holland; she had gone to Java as a protecting power…'

Both in print and in private, Raffles was vituperative about the Dutch in the Indies as inhumane colonial administrators and arch-rivals for market share. Individual Dutchmen, his former colleagues, were another matter. The view from London had corrected his tunnel vision. In the European scheme of things they were England's crucial allies. 'They were very communicative regarding their eastern colonies,' Raffles told Marsden, 'but I regret to say that, notwithstanding the King himself, and his leading minister, seem to mean well, they have too great a hankering after profit, and *immediate* profit, for any liberal system to thrive under them.'

Raffles' talent was never for making '*immediate* profit'. The King of the Netherlands assured Raffles that his system of cultivation would be continued, but stressed that 'it was essential to confine the trade, and to make such regulations as would secure it and its profits exclusively to the mother-country.' Raffles felt he had expressed his own opinions 'very freely' and, as they seemed to be taken in good part, 'I am in hopes they may have had some weight.'

Cousin Thomas made a book out of the travelogue letters he had sent home, which he published the following year with a dedication to 'Sir Thomas Stamford Raffles Knt'. Cousin Thomas, on the evidence of his book, was not an open-minded traveller. He was shocked to the core by the streetwalkers soliciting in broad daylight in Paris and Brussels, and declined to visit any place connected with the 'pestilential' and 'diabolical' Voltaire, or the 'blasphemous' and 'depraved' Rousseau.

Raffles kept no journal and did not even write, as he had promised, to the Duchess of Somerset until he was in Brussels on the way home. He felt there was nothing he could tell that was new to her – 'what can you expect from one who knows so little of the European world, and is scarce in one place before he flies to another.' The Duchess had been everywhere. To attempt descriptions of the Rhine or of Belgium 'would be like giving you an account of the banks of the Thames or the fields of England.'

Much of what Raffles made of Europe therefore remains opaque. What he did think worth writing to the Duchess about was French farming. Against all current theories of agriculture, which favoured large enclosures and fewer proprietors, he liked 'the smallness of the properties, and the inclusion of the fruit-trees in the grain and hay-fields':

> Now when I see every man cultivating his own field, I cannot but think him happier far than when he is cultivating the field of another... Throw the people out of these little properties and they lose their independence of character, their pride, and when only accustomed to daily wages are soon fitted for the army, the manufactory, or the poorhouse... I like to see fruit-trees growing among the corn, because it not only affords a refreshing and beautiful scenery, but because it reminds me of those patriarchal times, those days of simplicity, when the son and the grandson, and even the great-grandson, honoured the trees that their father planted.

Subsistence farming is backbreaking and chancy, and Raffles' evocation of 'those days of simplicity' is romantic and aesthetic; the Raffleses were within living memory townspeople. But he is consistent here. His pastoral vision of every man working his own land and having control over its products relates to what he had wanted for the Javanese.

The best moment for the tourists was their first sight of Mont Blanc. Cousin Thomas was moved to write a poem. Raffles was eloquent on the subject to the Duchess: 'That troubled sea which seems to have been in a moment stayed and fettered by an icy hand, still shines in all its majesty; nor has all the vice or all the blood which has stained the lower world, cast one spot to sully the heavenly purity of Mont Blanc.'

Switzerland had been annexed by revolutionary France, a desecration to which Raffles is obliquely referring. Mont Blanc, as the 'stupendous Mountain', was the focus of Coleridge's 1802 poem 'Hymn before Sunrise, in the Vale of Chamouni'. (Coleridge never actually went there.) Shelley and Mary Godwin, with Clair Clairmont, had made an almost identical journey to Raffles' across Europe the previous summer. The Shelleys subsequently published a *History of a Six Week Tour*, the climax of which was Shelley's 'Lines Written in the Vale of Chamouni':

> Mont Blanc yet gleams on high – the power is there
> The still and solemn power of many sights,
> And many sounds, and much of life and death.

Raffles' conception of the 'heavenly purity of Mont Blanc' post-dated Shelley's poem, but he could not have read it when he wrote to the Duchess in July 1817, since it was not published until that November. Nor could he have read Byron's *Don Juan*, in which Mont Blanc is 'the monarch of mountains', as it was not yet written; nor yet the sixth book of Wordsworth's *The Prelude*, already written but not published until long afterwards:

> That very day
> From a bare ridge we also first beheld
> Unveiled the summit of Mont Blanc...

Mont Blanc as 'idea' was iconic to the Romantics. With this small synchronicity, which has everything to do with the opening up of European travel after 1815, Raffles' sensibility chimed with theirs. In another life he could, like his cousin Elton Hamond, have lived among the poets. Sophia recalled that 'a flower would call forth a burst of favourite poetry' and, on the voyage back to the East, he read poetry to Sophia in the evenings.

Raffles chose not to go with Cousin Thomas and Sophia's brother William Hull when they climbed the Montanvert glacier. He stayed behind with 'the ladies', as he did when the two younger men visited the field of Waterloo, already covered with standing corn. Sophia was in the early stages of pregnancy. On the precipitous track down from Chamonix she was carried in a chair borne by relays of guards, while the rest of the party clung to the back of mules, which the ladies rode side-saddle. Cousin Thomas wrote that he twice saw Maryanne 'when the descent was steep and rugged, completely lose her seat on the animal, and only regain it, and save herself from pitching over the precipice, by grasping the hair of the guide.'

On 25 July 1817, the day they got back to London, Raffles was one of a party which included the Duke of Wellington and Government ministers at a dinner given at the City of London Tavern by the East India Company for George Canning, the new President of the Board of Control, whom Raffles had already met at Carlton House. His inclusion in such a top-level gathering suggests that Sir Stamford was now regarded as an ornament to the Company rather than a liability.

Further proof came when, as he was just about to sail, it was decided by the Court of Directors that his appointment at Bencoolen was to be not as Resident but as Lieutenant-Governor, 'as a peculiar mark of the favourable sentiments which the Court entertains of that gentleman's merits and service.' The designation was personal to him 'and not to devolve upon his successor at Bencoolen.' The brand new Company ship in which they were to travel back East was named *The Lady Raffles*. The world being as it is, the Court of Directors' attitude to him was changed by his knighthood, the publication of his book, and the respectful welcome he and his collections received from 'the Great Men of the Town'.

Thus Raffles – Sir Stamford Raffles FRS – was rebranded and relaunched. He had a formal portrait painted in oils by George Francis Joseph (now in the National Portrait Gallery), with the fashionable haircut favoured by the Prince Regent and Lord Byron, his short locks curled forward round his forehead and temples. His right hand is holding papers, and his right elbow rests on a table on which are more papers and Javanese figures from his collection. It is a portrait of the Lieutenant-Governor as author and collector. Another and more informal portrait – now in the Royal Zoological Society – was painted by James Lonsdale, for which he wore a velvet jacket with a wide white collar; his hair is more approximate to its natural colour, with a marked thinning around the temples.

He had one more project to float before he left England. When they were in Paris, staying at the Hotel Mirabeau in the newly-named rue de la Paix, the party visited the Louvre, the palaces and the monuments; they saw the guillotine which had decapitated Louis XVI; they glimpsed his younger brother, the restored Bourbon King Louis XVIII, at Mass in the chapel of the Tuileries. But what impressed Raffles most was the Jardin des Plantes. Knowing little of the work of French botanists, he was amazed to see specimens from Java and the Eastern Isles which he had believed to be unknown in Europe.

Even more interesting to Raffles was the discovery that the Jardin des Plantes incorporated a small zoo. This was established in the revolutionary 1790s, stocked from the royal menagerie and from collections of exotic beasts in private ownership, and subsequently augmented by accessions from the French colonies. It was the first public collection in the world, and the first open to all, free of charge. The animals were kept in conditions as close to their natural environment as possible, and their behaviour studied and recorded. England, thought Raffles, should have something like this, and spoke to his naturalist friends in London about it. But the idea was on hold until his final return.

Between August 1817 and their departure in October there was a flurry of visits. Old Queen Charlotte invited Raffles to spend an evening with her at Frogmore, in the Home Park of Windsor Castle. There he met Lord Amherst, only just back from an abortive trip as Ambassador Extraordinary to the Emperor of China in Peking, with the aim of establishing better commercial relations between Britain and China. The mission failed because Amherst declined to consent to the 'kowtow' ceremony, and so was not admitted into the Emperor's presence.

Amherst's party took the opportunity to explore, sailing along the coast of Korea and to islands south of Japan. At least five members of the mission, including Raffles' friend Captain Basil Hall, subsequently published books about their adventures. On the return voyage the *Alceste*, with Amherst on board, broke up on rocks off Java, everyone escaping in lifeboats to Batavia. At Frogmore, Amherst and Raffles, having so much in common, talked all evening – which saved Raffles a thousand pounds, he said, because otherwise he would have had to play cards with Her Majesty, who played for fiercely high stakes 'and we should have played at least 20 games, and I should have lost them all.'

Cousin Thomas knew William Wilberforce through their shared preoccupation with liberal causes and foreign missions. He took Raffles to meet the evangelical parliamentarian and veteran hero of abolition legislation at his home: Gore House, Kensington Gore, with its ten bedrooms and three acres of garden (where the Albert

Hall now stands). Raffles and Wilberforce established a friendship, though Wilberforce's health was beginning to fail, and he was one of those people in whom compassion and liberal instincts went hand in hand with a horror of public protest and radical uprisings.

Raffles went with Sophia and Maryanne to Liverpool to see Cousin Thomas at home with his wife and baby, allowing two days to get there – 'We have not yet looked at the Book of Roads therefore cannot say decidedly what time we shall arrive.' He left his 'ladies' with the family in Liverpool while he took a side-trip to visit and dine with the Duke of Hamilton, father of the Duchess of Somerset, at Ashton Hall near Lancaster.

Then, with the ladies, across to Ireland to see relatives of Sophia's, and to visit Maryanne's children by her first husband, Quintin Dick Thompson. Quintin's sister Charlotte, the children's aunt, was married to Baron James McLelland, who had built himself a fine house, Annaverna, outside Dundalk in Co. Louth. The McLellands had no children, and took on Charlotte Raffles Drury Thompson and Acheson Quintin Dick Thompson when Maryanne married William Flint.

It was usual for British children to be sent from the East to family at home by the age of four or five because, once they were running around, they were at risk from infection; they were over-indulged by their attendants, and became spoilt brats; they must go to school, and acquire the manners of their tribe. Maryanne never reclaimed Charlotte and Acheson. They became to all intents and purposes the McLellands' children. Baron McLelland was a notori-ously harsh judge, punishing nationalist uprisings and 'outrages' with brutal public floggings and hangings. He may, for all we know, have been as mild as milk at home with his wife and the two children at Annaverna.

Returning to England via Holyhead, Raffles went, without his wife and sister, 'to the Dukes' – the Somersets – at one of their country estates, Maiden Bradley on the Somerset-Wiltshire borders; then to stay for two days with Sir Hugh Inglis, the former Deputy

Chairman of the Company who had approved his first appointment to Penang. Then there was a 'famous dinner' at the Albion tavern. 'Sir Stamford took the chair,' Travers wrote in his journal, 'and Garnham and I were his supporters. We had some good singing, and a number of bumper toasts. On the Island [of Java] being given, Mr Ellis arose and, in a most elegant and appropriate speech, paid Sir Stamford's administration a very high compliment.' (Henry Ellis had been with Basil Hall on Lord Amherst's mission to Peking.)

Sophia and Cousin Thomas had become close during the European tour. 'How much *my* Heart is to *your* Heart, as *yours* to *mine*,' she wrote to him in early October. 'We are still in the midst of bustle and confusion and both much fatigued by the exertions we have been obliged to make.'

Clearing out 23 Berners Street was a nightmare. (Travers was not there to help. He had rushed back to Ireland to get married, returning with his bride just in time to sail to Bencoolen with Raffles.) Writing in his turn to Cousin Thomas from Portsmouth on 21 October 1817, while waiting for their ship to appear on the horizon, Raffles said he had sent to his Aunt Rachel and Uncle William in Princes Street 'a great many boxes of books and some odds and ends; not so many of the latter as I intended, in consequence of my people who, in their anxiety to clear the house, sent off more rubbish than was intended to the Duke' – the Somersets had offered space at 1 Park Lane as a repository for his collections and possessions.

The plethora of important collections arriving in London was posing a storage problem. Live animals shipped back from the East and, increasingly, from the Arctic regions, were generally shot and stuffed. Some of Raffles' material went to the Company's museum in India House. The British Museum, opened in 1759 in the remodelled seventeenth-century Montagu House, was a disgrace. A governor of the Museum, Sir William Scott, wrote to the Duchess of Somerset in 1818, that 'The building is in a most crazy condition;

the floors have sunk; and have given ample notice of danger to our collections there, and to the crowds who come to see them; and all the apartments are so chuck [*sic*] full, that there is no room for any new addition in any department. What is to be done under this want of space and safety? I hope you will approve of our applying to Parliament for a new spacious and solid building.'

Not until 1823 was the demolition of the old mansion, and a long-drawn-out building programme, set in train. Not until the 1880s were the natural history collections moved to South Kensington. Meanwhile, in 1817 while Raffles was in London, the sagging Museum accepted the Elgin Marbles. A Select Committee of the House of Commons questioned the legality of Lord Elgin's action. The ethics of stripping the Marbles from their position on the Parthenon was raised. The Committee submitted an inconclusive interim report. The morality of the removal of important cultural objects from their place of origin is equally relevant to Raffles' activities. It did not worry him, or anyone else in London. The heads of the Buddha, like other pieces from Borobudur and most of Raffles' ethnological importations from the Eastern Isles, would eventually find homes in the new-built British Museum and its satellite depositories.

The History of Java had been issued in an edition of 900 quarto copies, with a folding map and 66 engravings and aquatints. The artist commissioned by Raffles, William Daniell, was a great draftsman who had himself been in Java. The publishers were the Company's booksellers, Black, Parbury and Allen, and John Murray of Albemarle Street, Byron's publisher. The price was six guineas – not cheap. Two hundred and fifty sets of the 900 were printed off first, on better paper (so the reproduction of the illustrations was sharper than in the rest), calf-bound and in larger format, at eight guineas. One of these Raffles inscribed to his new mother-in-law: 'Presented to Mrs Hull, by her Affectionate Son, Tho's S. Raffles' – evidence of Raffles' adoption of Sophia's family as his own.

By the time Raffles was leaving for Bencoolen, 200 of the 900 sets of *The History of Java* remained unsold. There was a strong vogue for traveller's tales and accounts of exotic peoples and regions among the educated population, but *The History of Java* did not gain a wide readership. It is salutary, in estimating public taste, to recall that Cousin Thomas' account (1813) of the life of the charismatic teenage preacher Thomas Spencer – a Liverpudlian prodigy who drowned at the age of twenty – is said to have sold 6,000 copies. Java was of consuming interest only to those concerned. Major William Thorn, Brigade Major in Gillespie's division, pipped Raffles to the post by publishing in 1815 his *Memoir of the Conquest of Java*, a blow-by-blow battle-book with topographical essays and coloured engravings, and minimal reference to 'Mr Raffles'.

Raffles left his cousin Elton Hamond with the task of preparing a second, improved and corrected octavo edition, relying on Cousin Thomas to collaborate in the editing: 'You must recollect that it is a great point in my interest, character and fame, that during my absence, all my friends act in unison – it will delight me to hear that my two literary Cousins are giving their mutual aid towards the correctness of the second edition.'

It was rash of him to entrust his second edition to Cousin Elton, and little wonder that he pressed Cousin Thomas to remain involved – that is, if he realised how disturbed Elton had become. Elton had planned to commit suicide back in 1813, and told the diarist and journalist Crabb Robinson so. In October of that year, Raffles wrote Elton a long letter. From internal evidence it is clear there was an ongoing correspondence, and that Raffles respected Elton Hamond's views. Raffles explained to him the currency crisis, the problem of the devalued paper money and his decision over the sale of lands. He promised to go further into the subject of land tenure in a later letter, and that 'when I may make up my mind to write a book on Java,' he would develop these important points.

It seems from the letter that it was Elton who sowed the seed of the book: 'I observe what you mention respecting the advantages attending a literary work, such as a statistical account of Java,' Raffles wrote, 'and, although I am fully sensible of my incapacity to appear before the public as an author, I feel some inclination to the undertaking... I believe there is no one possessed of more information respecting Java than myself: – but how far I may be able to put it together, and to bring it before the public, I know not.'

Elton's behaviour became more and more odd. Inheriting his father's tea business in Milk Street, he sacked the employees because the business interfered with his life. He told Raffles in London that, since Raffles owed everything to his father Charles Hamond – he was thinking of the £500 bond to the East India Company for which Hamond had stood guarantee back in 1795 – Raffles was morally obliged to give him, Elton, half of his earnings as Lieutenant-Governor of Java. Raffles gave him an order for £1,000, out of pure good humour. Elton, mercifully for Raffles, disdained to cash it.

Somehow Elton retained the increasingly bewildered friendship of Jeremy Bentham, the poets Coleridge and Southey, and Sir Frederick Pollock – top lawyer, MP and mathematician – who said that Elton had 'in the highest degree one mark of insanity, viz, an utter disregard of the opinion of the rest of the world on any point on which he had made up his own mind.' He was driven by an insistence on the truth as he saw it. When Elton was eleven, he had told his sister Harriet that he was going to be greater than Jesus Christ. 'His after-misery', wrote Crabb Robinson, 'lay in this, that while he had a conviction that he was to have been, and ought to have been, the greatest of men, he was conscious of the fact that he was not.'

Literary women clucked around Elton Hamond. Anna Letitia Barbauld, elderly poet and pedagogue, took on his sister Harriet as her companion. Mrs Barbauld's parson husband had become insane, attacked her with a knife, and then killed himself. Crabb Robinson found among Elton's papers after his death 'one which discussed at great length the best way of *"putting an end to Mrs Barbauld's life".*' Maybe there was something peculiarly maddening about Mrs Barbauld. Elton turned down various job offers over the years. Instead, he covered hundreds of quarto pages with unpublishable autobiographical and philosophical writings.

Raffles perhaps hoped that revising *The History of Java* might focus Elton's literary energies. Maybe he thought to help Elton's mother, his Aunt Elizabeth, by helping Elton. Whatever Raffles' reasons for entrusting his 'interest, character and fame' to his troubled cousin, they were nothing but benevolent. Any profits from the second edition were to be Elton's. The something excessive in Sir Stamford Raffles was sympathetic to the something excessive in hapless Elton Hamond.

Raffles was only returning to the East in order to make and save enough money on which to retire. He wrote to the Duchess of Somerset: 'Oh! That this leave-taking were at an end; my heart is sad, and yet what avails it to repine? I must go, and the sooner I am off the better; my house is filled with those who are all determined to say good-bye, and make me more miserable when it requires all my fortitude to keep my spirits calm and uniform.'

The Lady Raffles, commanded by Sophia's brother-in-law Harry Auber, picked up its passengers at Portsmouth, where Maryanne came to see the party off. The newly-weds, Travers and his wife Mary, joined Raffles, the pregnant Sophia and their servants, plus the Radin, and Dick the Papuan boy. Loaded on board was a quantity of livestock, and seedling plants for Bencoolen.

From the George Hotel in Portsmouth, on 22 October 1817, Raffles wrote to his mother, thanking her for an 'affectionate letter': 'You don't know how it has soothed me and how it has lightened my heart in going away. My only uneasiness was your feeling too much for your strength. It is only a little time and I will be with you again. Nothing can keep me beyond five years and I may be home much sooner. In the mean time we shall always be thinking of you and anxious to hear how you are going on... Keep up your spirits my dear Mother – there is much happiness and comfort in store for you.'

John Tayler, the agency friend who had looked after his affairs in London, 'will take care you want for nothing. Should any accident happen to me your £400 a year is still secure, therefore you can never I hope be again distressed for money. Sophia desires her kindest love and affection...'

This is the first extant letter from Raffles to the mother he loved. Sophia, after his death, destroyed all family correspondence (except that with Cousin Thomas and with a few peripheral relatives) from the time before Raffles knew her. For sure, neither she nor he would have wanted anything to remain which betrayed the misfortunes of his father, but she was seemingly motivated by resentment of Olivia, and of the life he had before his second marriage. There is only one reference to Olivia in her monumental *Memoir* of her husband. It is a footnote, and inaccurate. Sophia presented his private life, for posterity, as beginning and ending with herself.

The Lady Raffles encountered heavy gales and rough seas in the Channel. Off Land's End in Cornwall, she was struggling, and making no progress at all. After four days, everyone on board was exhausted and seasick, and the ship had to put in at Falmouth.

Raffles profited from the delay by rushing off inland to go down another tin mine, and on 30 October wrote again to Elton Hamond about his second edition, sending him copies of two papers by John Crawfurd, on Prambanan and Borobodur, which Crawfurd had 'allowed me to take for my information.' Acknowledging that his account of Borobodur was 'very scanty' and inaccurate, he desired Elton to make good the deficiencies from Crawfurd's papers. 'You may borrow freely – but if you adopt any opinion state the authority in a complimentary manner to Crawfurd.'

Sophia wrote to Maryanne, envisaging some future time when they would all live happily together with their children. 'You were always a little dear, and now more than ever.' She was quite well again: 'My strength has returned like magic and I am quite equal to a second edition of seasickness.' She indeed suffered a second edition, and a third, and lost a lot of weight. Their ship set sail again on 6 November, with a fair wind – which changed almost at once, and they were driven back once more into Falmouth.

Raffles took the opportunity to write to Elton yet again, with instructions about William Daniell's illustrations; the landscapes to be engraved were with the Duchess of Somerset, and she and the Duke would advise on what to include. He was still exercised about his use of Crawfurd's material, which reflects the touchiness of their relationship: 'There is no occasion to mention Crawfurd's name unless opinions are quoted or unless you make extracts from the papers,' in which case 'it perhaps would be right to notice in a note that they have been consulted... I would willingly do what was right.'

While in Falmouth they heard some terrible news. Princess Charlotte went into labour at Claremont on 3 November. The baby was large and in the breech position. She suffered for two days and nights and then gave birth to a stillborn son. She died the next day. The popular Princess was mourned by the public in a hysterical outpouring of grief.

Raffles too was 'shocked beyond measure,' as he told the Duchess of Somerset. 'I dare not dwell on it.' He had lost a friend. He had also lost an influential supporter, the presumptive heir to the throne. He never expressed this, but Cousin Thomas was less delicate. While acknowledging that Raffles' regard for the Princess was 'beyond any consideration of rank, or wealth, or honor, which he might have attained, had both their lives been prolonged,' the idea was 'no doubt entertained at the time, that had he lived, he would have been Governor-General of India – while she would have been too much delighted to have raised him to the Peerage in that capacity.'

Another attempt to make way was again foiled by strong west winds. The ship was driven back miles in the wrong direction; this time they put in at Plymouth. They passed the time by visiting the Somersets who happened to be at their Devon House, Berry Pomeroy; and then went to see Sophia's sister Alice and her husband Richard Mudge at Beechwood in Plympton St Mary, which belonged to the banker Richard Rosdew. The Rosdews and the Mudges were much inter-married, and Alice and Richard were to inherit Beechwood.

'Once more we are off,' wrote Raffles to the Duchess on 19 November, 'and as we must go, God grant it may be for good!' He despatched a last letter to Elton Hamond as they left the harbour: 'I write these hurried lines for the pilot who is now waiting on the gangway – your letter has only been with me for an instant and we are once more off.' Fretting about the illustrations, he told Elton: 'The Ronggeng I decidedly think must be left out.'

This onset of propriety is funny. Daniell's aquatint of 'A Ron-ggeng or Dancing Girl' was to prove the most popular of the illus-trations in *The History of Java*. Raffles recorded in his Chapter 7 how the *ronggengs* were the 'common dancing girls of the country,' whose conduct was 'generally so incorrect, as to render the title of *ronggeng* and prostitute synonymous.' He devoted a page to their costumes and coiffures, and to the style of their dancing and singing, sometimes 'rude and awkward, and on that account dis-gusting to Europeans.' ('Disgusting' then meant merely distasteful, or disagreeable.)

The *ronggengs'* costume was a less opulent version of that of the bejewelled court dancing girls: a long, decorative open sarong, its folds revealing the leg when dancing, and the upper body 'enclosed in a kind of corset (*pemakak*) passing above the bosom and under the arms, and confining the waist in the narrowest possible limits.' In Chapter 2, in a passage praising young women's slender wrists and ankles, he had complained that the cloth which narrowed the waist was 'injurious to female elegance' by 'drawing too tightly that part of the dress that covers the bosom.' The illustration is graceful and not remotely pornographic. Perhaps Sophia objected to the repre-sentation of a loose woman.

⌒

They were at last on their way. By 1 December 1817 *The Lady Raffles* had weathered the Bay of Biscay. Sophia had 'still not left her couch' but everyone and everything on board was recovering, as Raffles assured the Duchess: 'the cows, dogs, cats, birds, the latter singing round me, and my nursery of plants thriving beyond all expectation; the thermometer is at 76. What a waste of waters now lies between us, and yet the distance daily widens, and will widen still until half the world divides us.'

Chapter 10

The Golden Opportunity

Bencoolen and Calcutta 1818–1819

In February 1818, three and a half months after they left Falmouth, Raffles announced his great news to Maryanne from *The Lady Raffles*: 'As it was decreed so it has happened, Sophia was confined on board… Miss Charlotte has made her appearance – on the 15th of this month, without any previous illness and I may say with less suffering than most women undergo…a beautiful little girl, the very image of yourself – with blue eyes, beautiful features and crooked toes.'

Sophia, after a labour of only two hours, was receiving 'the visits of all the party aboard, seated on the couch to see them enjoy Cake and Caudle.' (Caudle, served at christenings, was a sort of egg-nog.) Everything went so smoothly that Raffles thought he might arrange for their next baby to be born at sea too. Mary Grimes, whom they employed to be the baby's nurse, was 'excellent'.

'We have now thrown the whole of the roundhouse into one cabin, which is occupied by Sophia and the child, and the cuddy is given up to us as an audience or antechamber, in which I sleep. The little darling has been baptised Sophia Charlotte.' At the suggestion of the Radin Rana Dipura, she also received the name 'Tunjong Segara', Lily of the Sea.

He wrote to his mother the same day: 'My dear Sophia has followed your example,' i.e. in giving birth at sea. 'You don't know how
proud we are of the little darling and what a beauty it is – tho' I say
it who should not say it, for they say it is the image of me.'

Bencoolen on the west coast of Sumatra was a shock after Java.
The only way out was along the surf-battered beach, or by sea.
Outside the town, the Company controlled most of a thinly popu-
lated three hundred-mile coastal strip, extending forty miles or so
into the interior. There were no built roads either across the island
or along the coast. Bencoolen's Fort Marlborough had an unnerv-
ing 180-degree prospect of the Indian Ocean, broken by Rat Island
six miles offshore.

The price of pepper had sunk in London. Yet pepper was about all
that Bencoolen had to offer. Free-trading Americans were buying
pepper from the ports of Acheen in the north of Sumatra, without
the cost of maintaining establishments, and were undercutting the
market. The settlement could not even feed itself; rice was imported
from Bengal.

Thomas Parr, Resident in the early years of the century, banned
Company servants' private trading and, to repair the economy, set
up forced deliveries of coffee. He was hated. Men of the Pasumah
people broke into his house and decapitated him. The Company
responded with reprisals of an extreme and brutal kind. All this
happened a decade before Raffles arrived, but Bencoolen reeked of
unease and economic failure. Malaria and smallpox were endemic.

The Lady Raffles anchored on 19 March 1818. There was a major
earthquake the day before, and Government House was too damaged
to receive them. 'This is,' Raffles wrote to William Marsden,
'without exception, the most wretched place I ever beheld. I cannot
convey to you an adequate idea of the state of ruin and dilapidation
which surrounds me… The roads are impassable; the highways in
the town overrun with rank grass; the Government-house a den of
ravenous dogs and polecats… In truth, I could never have conceived

any thing half so bad. We will try and make it better; and if I am well supported from home, the West coast may yet be turned to account.' He and Sophia would try to make themselves comfortable, and 'happy we always are.'

'Never was there such a pair of darlings,' he wrote to Maryanne on 12 April. Sophia was feeding Charlotte herself, and at two months she was 'as intelligent and large as most children at six [months], – and such a beauty!' There is no record of Sophia complaining, as many new mothers would, even though 'Government House is nearly a ruin, full of rents and cracks, and shaking with every blast.' There were constant aftershocks. 'We have seldom been a day or night without them. The lamps in the hall are thrown across each other...The couch pillows and mattress cast into the middle of the rooms as well as all the books from the shelves.'

There were in Bencoolen, apart from Malays and Sumatrans, several hundred Chinese and Bugis, and around five hundred convicts from Bengal. There were native slaves, and slaves from Africa imported by the Company. As well as forced cultivation, there was a system of 'free gardens': cultivators were paid lump sums of money in advance in exchange for pepper. Most never grew enough pepper to pay off the advance and became 'slave-debtors' to the Company. If they decamped their families, and, ultimately their villages, remained liable. Raffles' brief, inevitably, was to reduce costs. Even he did not feel that even more investment from the Company was the immediate answer, informing the Court of Directors: 'It is in the principle of Government, and in the management of the country that the evil lies.'

He emancipated the slaves and set up a school for their children, the African ones being 'in a state of nature, vice, and wretchedness' according to Sophia. She took on one 'little bright-eyed girl' for Nurse Grimes to train as a nursery maid. When Raffles reported the emancipation of the slaves to the Court of Directors, they let him know that he had been 'precipitate'. Any decision should properly have been referred to them beforehand. No surprises there.

Raffles made a regulation that the slave-debtors could not be bound for more than ten years. He 'graded' the convicts, and awarded privileges and opportunities accordingly. The Europeans, nervous since the Parr murder, had razed all vegetation near the Government buildings so as to afford no cover. Raffles ordered trees and a garden to be planted.

He banned cockfighting and gaming, a measure that lost the Government money, since the 'farmers' who licensed those activities bid competitively for the privilege. He let go his personal bodyguard and made administrative cuts. The trouble was that he could remove a civil servant from a post and abolish the post, but the man remained a Company employee – paid for doing nothing.

Raffles annulled former treaties with the Sumatran Chiefs, and declared the free cultivation of pepper. There would be no forced deliveries, but a 'free' delivery of so much pepper per cultivator, or 'tribute' in lieu. Not much change there, then. The Chiefs, as in Java, were paid salaries to compensate for the loss of their cut on deliveries. Their salaries came out of the Government Treasury, so the price Raffles could afford to pay for pepper was reduced, making the cultivators' situation worse. Raffles' ventures in Bencoolen have an *Alice's Adventures in Wonderland* quality, and not only because the Duchess' cook filled the kitchen with incapacitating clouds of pepper.

Nothing Raffles did in Sumatra saved the economy. *Mutatis mutandis*, 'It was the story of Java all over again,' as John Bastin has written. Add to this the horrid fact that when Captain Travers checked the Treasury accounts he discovered a deficit amounting to the equivalent of £40,000.

Nevertheless, Raffles could not resist projecting expansion. He sent Captain Travers to Batavia to negotiate with the Dutch for an extension of British lands in Sumatra, and to argue against ceding, as instructed, the port of Padang north of Bencoolen. Travers got nowhere. It was strange for him to see under the new regime the 'wonderful changes' at familiar Buitenzorg, where by chance he was given his old room to sleep in. The house was much improved, and would be 'superbly finished', while the gardens and grounds were 'altogether altered, and very much for the better.' Buitenzorg, though a happy house, had never been comfortable or well-maintained in Raffles' time.

Maryanne was in England without an income. 'I calculate you will be coming out,' Raffles wrote, 'because I don't know what you can do at home – and yet I fear I shall have but little to give you but eating and drinking and a broken-down home.' He was, as always, responsible for his family, and wrote to his mother: 'It is a heart-breaking thing to be so far apart and yet I am satisfied it is for the best – it is necessary – we could not live without it – to be in England without money would never do.' The time was not far distant 'when I shall return for good and all – never more to part... There is nothing to keep me in this country beyond the necessity of obtaining the means without which neither you nor I could live in England.'

He missed Maryanne. 'We often long for my dear Pussy, that we may have some fun.' She had no idea 'what a prosing domestic couple we have become. We really want you to entertain us.' The only familiar female friend the Raffleses had was 'Mrs Tot' – they called Mary and Thomas Otho Travers 'the Tots'. But as before, Raffles assembled a 'family'. His old friend Thomas McQuoid was in Bencoolen in the hope of private trading, and the Tots brought back from Java the naturalist Dr Horsfield – and '23 horses, birds without number, beasts of every kind and plants, seeds, etc in abundance.' Java, the Land of Promise, was now a Paradise Lost.

Mrs Tot had a baby within a week after their return – a girl, and 'a very ugly child,' as Raffles, the prejudiced new father, told Maryanne. Sophia lent Nurse Grimes to Mary for the event, and 'came over and watched my Mary as she would have done a sister,' wrote Travers in his journal. (This baby died at four months.) Sophia had told the Duchess that 'Sir Stamford will not long remain stationary, and when he is ready to move I am to wean my Baby that I may accompany him.' The result of weaning Charlotte was that Sophia fell pregnant again at once.

That did not stop her from travelling rough with Raffles into the interior. 'There is nothing to tell,' she wrote to Maryanne with maximum insouciance, 'except that we have walked all over Sumatra, and the people look upon us as a sort of wonder for returning alive.'

For three weeks in May 1818 they walked between twelve and fifteen hours a day. 'Here am I alive and well – tho' of course I suffered a great deal at the time, and sometimes thought I would have died of fatigue.' Where the way was very steep, 'I had a man to hold my hands, one before the other behind.' Everyone had told them it was impossible for Europeans to penetrate the jungle. 'Tom would not listen to difficulties...and I would not be separated from him merely for my own convenience, and there ends my story.'

Raffles' letter to Maryanne told how 'Sophia stood the fatigue and exposure like a heroine.' He reserved his best account for the Duchess of Somerset, knowing she would share it with the Duke and with botanical circles in London.

Raffles' primary purpose on the expedition was to assess conditions in the southern out-Residences and villages and, in Pasumah, to 'reconcile conflicting interests which had long distracted the country' (after the murder of Parr).

They rode eighty miles along the beach from Bencoolen to the out-station at Manna, where they turned inland, following the course of the Manna river, accompanied by Dr Joseph Arnold, Edward Presgrave (the young Resident at Manna), six native officers, and fifty Malays carrying equipment and supplies. Leeches 'got into our boots and shoes, which became filled with blood; at night, too, they fell off the leaves that sheltered us from the weather.' Sophia's letter to Maryanne did not say what she wore. Presumably she had long pantaloons under her muslin gowns.

On the third day Dr Joseph Arnold's attention was drawn to

something extraordinary. We know the details from an unfinished letter found after his death:

> I had ventured some way before the party, when one of the
> Malay servants came running to me, with wonder in his
> eyes, and said, "Come with me, sir, come! A flower very large,
> beautiful, wonderful!" I went with the man about a hundred
> yards into the jungle, and he pointed to a flower growing close
> to the ground, under the bushes, which was truly astonishing.
> My first impulse was to cut it up and bring it to the hut. To
> tell you the truth, had I been alone, and had there been no
> witnesses, I should, I think, have been fearful of mentioning
> the dimensions of this flower, so much does it exceed every
> flower I have ever seen or heard of, but I had Sir Stamford
> Raffles and Lady Raffles with me, and Mr Presgrave, who
> though equally astonished with myself, are able to testify to
> the truth.

What they saw was a giant flower which the Sumatrans called 'Petimun Sikinlili', the Devil's Betel Box. No larger flower has yet been discovered anywhere in the world. 'It measured across from the extremity of the petals more than a yard,' Raffles told the Duchess. 'The nectarium was nine inches wide and as deep; esti-mated to contain a gallon and a half of water, and the weight of the whole flower eighteen pounds.'

It was a parasite, growing on the exposed root of a vine. 'The inside of the cup is of an intense purple; and more or less densely yellow, with soft flexible spines of the same colour… The petals are of a brick-red, with numerous pustular spots of a lighter colour. The whole substance of the flower is not less than half an inch thick, and of a firm fleshy consistency.'

Dr Arnold described how it had no roots, no leaves, no stem, and was just 'seated' on its host, with a swarm of flies hovering over it. Porters carried it in a crate back to Manna, but most of it rotted away. 'The chemical composition being fungous, it would not keep; and not having sufficient spirits, we could not keep it entire. A part of it, and two buds almost as big as a child's head, will be sent home.'

The giant flower was named *Rafflesia arnoldii*. Neither Raffles nor Arnold named it thus, but Robert Brown, in a paper read to the Linnean Society of London in 1821. Brown was the Keeper of Sir Joseph Banks' Herbarium and Library, and specialised in the classi-fication of plant families; he considered that Dr Arnold would have chosen that name 'had he lived to publish an account of it.'

Since Raffles was better known than Arnold, and since Brown chose *Rafflesia* as the generic name, Raffles got the credit and renown. This injustice was not of his making. He always acknowledged the discovery to be Arnold's, as in his letter to Colonel Addenbrook, former Equerry to the late Princess Charlotte, mentioning the sad death of Dr Arnold – 'but not until he had immortalized his name by the discovery of one of the greatest prodigies in nature…I sent a short description of this plant, with a drawing, and part of the flower itself, to Sir Joseph Banks…' Yet even Edward Presgrave, making a similar expedition later in the year, referred in his journal to seeing 'several of the magnificent flowers found by the Governor' – and he had been present when Dr Arnold came back to the hut with the fleshy monster.

The giant flower was not exactly beautiful, and it smelt vile – 'precisely the smell of tainted beef' according to Dr Arnold. Sir Joseph Banks thought it 'by far the most extraordinary vegetable production I have seen.' The publication of Brown's paper in the *Transactions* of the Linnean Society included engravings and dissec-tions of the flower and a bud, and the impact was international. The Dowager Empress of Russia was so impressed that she sent Robert Brown a topaz and diamond ring; he gave it to Sophia, tardily, shortly before he died.

The expedition continued, sometimes with Sophia carried on a man's shoulders. They subsisted on rice and claret. The cavalcade struggled over the mountains into Pasumah, and a wide smiling valley where the Chiefs were gathered to meet them.

A decade of hostility seemed wiped away. Raffles made a treaty with the Chiefs 'by which they placed themselves under the protection of the British Government, and thus all cause of dispute and misunderstanding was at once set at rest.' Many 'cheerfully agreed' to be vaccinated by Dr Arnold. Raffles, always on the look-out for religious survivals behind nominal 'Mahometism', 'clearly traced an ancient mythology, and obtained the names of at least twenty gods, several of whom are Hindus.'

On the return to Manna by a different route it poured with rain, the baggage-bearers lagged behind, and they slept in their wet clothes. 'By perseverance, however, I made a tolerable place for Lady Raffles, and, after selecting the smoothest stone I could find in the bed of a river for a pillow, we managed to pass a tolerably comfortable night.'

Sophia took up the tale from where her husband's letter to the Duchess left off. Next day Raffles and Dr Arnold went on ahead and the party became dispersed, until 'Mr Presgrave and the Editor' found themselves alone. (Sophia referred to herself as 'the Editor' in the *Memoir.*) In the dark, Mr Presgrave fell into a large pit – 'and disappeared entirely, and with him sunk the hope of concluding the day's journey, and his companion's spirit.' The Editor had a sense of humour.

When the party came back together, they hurtled down the rapids towards Manna on rafts. They still had to ride back to Bencoolen along the shoreline – 'Very trying,' wrote the Editor, 'in the middle of the day, on account of tigers; the glare from the sea, the heat of the sand on the beach, the vertical rays of a tropical sun, without any shade…after the fatigue and exposure already experienced, were distressing to all, and proved fatal to one of the party.' By the time they were half way, Dr Arnold was running a high fever.

Sophia was as strong as an ox. It is amazing that she did not miscarry. Dr Arnold survived this bout but, to quote Travers, he 'gradually decayed.'

⌐

On a more modest inland excursion, Raffles climbed hills behind Bencoolen, and about twelve miles out of town on the 'Hill of Mists' (Bukit Kabut), 'where no European had before ever set foot,' he decided to build his country house. There was a fine view, and the temperature was six degrees lower than on the coast. The forests around bristled with elephants and tigers. 'One of the villagers told me that his father and grandfather were carried off by tigers, and there is scarcely a family that has not lost some of its members by them.' Raffles did rather like scaring the Duchess.

He cleared his Hill and put up a bungalow. 'To be sure we are not so grand as in Java,' he wrote to Maryanne, 'but then we are more retired, and as I advance in age' – he was writing on his thirty-seventh birthday – 'retirement becomes more and more congenial to me.'

But not yet. There was fresh trouble in Palembang. The Dutch claimed it, with the island of Banca, as a natural dependency of Java, and sent out Raffles' old colleague H.W. Muntinghe as Commissioner. Muntinghe turned Sultan Najmuddin out of the royal palace, claiming the pre-existence of a treaty transferring authority to the Dutch. Najmuddin appealed to Raffles, who despatched a mission led by Captain Francis Salmond to 'offer protection' to Najmuddin; Salmond made a treaty with him, 'having ascertained that the Sultan had in no way committed himself to the Netherlands Government by any legal act,' and hoisted the Union Jack on the Fort. Obviously Muntinghe would not stand by under such provocation.

But before the drama played out, Raffles was off again. Two days after telling Maryanne about the congeniality of 'retirement', on 8 July 1818, he, Sophia, Dr Horsfield and Dr Arnold sailed on *The Lady Raffles* for Padang on another pioneering expedition.

Raffles was bent on exploring on foot the ancient kingdom of Menangkabau (the Menang Highlands), over the barrier of mountains and almost in the centre of the island. Menangkabau had long ago ruled over all Sumatra, and still, in William Marsden's nice phrase, received 'a shadow of homage' throughout the island. Raffles knew that Menangkabau people had built a city on an island they called Singapura, provoking hostility from the Kingdom of Majapahit in Java. The last King of Singapura fled in 1252.

Raffles found the British Resident at Padang, Charles Holloway, profoundly unhelpful. No Europeans ever went to Menangkabau. Access was impossible. Raffles took no notice. The main group – two hundred coolies with their loads, a fifty-strong military escort, and personal servants – left on 14 July: 'A most ridiculous cavalcade,' Raffles told the Duchess, 'the interest of which was much heightened by the quixotic appearance of my friend Dr Horsfield who was borne along on the shoulders of four of the party in order that preceding us he might gain time for botanizing.'

Dr Arnold was too unwell to go when Raffles and Sophia with their escort left two days later. Dr Horsfield sent a note back to Raffles: 'I must inform you that there are many difficult passages; I should not, however, despair of your progress…but as for Lady Raffles, I almost doubt whether, in favourable weather, she could come on, as in many places *a lady cannot be carried*.'

Sophia was an obstinate woman. On she went. They were away for fifteen days, struggling across the mountains and then emerging into the rich agricultural Tiga-blas country and on into the heart of Menangkabau, where they found 'the wreck of a great empire'. Raffles described all he saw to the Duchess in a detailed diary-letter, now of considerable historical interest.

They came across ancient inscribed stones, and a Hindu image. For Raffles, this was 'classical ground'. His beliefs about the origins of the pre-Islamic Malay world seemed justified. He entered into a treaty of friendship with the Sultan of Menangkabau, naming him the Lord Paramount of all the Malays; for Raffles envisaged the ancient sovereignty of Menangkabau being re-established, and all Sumatra unified under British influence. Padang was the gateway to Menangkabau, as he informed the Secret Committee in London, 'and it is my intention to refuse admission to the Dutch at Padang until I receive further orders from England.'

Back in Padang they heard that Dr Joseph Arnold had died, and Charles Holloway, the unhelpful Resident, had drowned at sea.

In Bencoolen there was news from Palembang. Captain Salmond, having refused to lower the Union Jack, had been taken prisoner by Muntinghe, then shipped out and delivered back to Bencoolen.

Raffles wrote an angry and eloquent letter to the Dutch authorities. This became dignified as the 'Protest'; he got it published in the principle London newspapers and reprinted in the *Annual Register* for 1819. In the middle of composing it he found time to write to his mother, on hearing of the deaths of his sister Harriet and her new baby – 'poor girl... You see it is not those who are exposed to most dangers who suffer first.'

His Protest attracted attention, but not in a good way. Lord Lansdowne in the House of Lords raised Salmond's arrest as an outrage against the British Government, but was squashed by the Secretary for the Colonies: Sir Stamford was merely a commercial agent with no political authority, and the mission to Palembang should never have taken place. The Secretary to the East India Company, now Joseph Dart, wrote to Calcutta recommending that Raffles be better controlled, his 'proper functions' being only those of 'the Company's commercial Resident' at Bencoolen. The Board of Control remarked on the 'inconvenience' of the continuance at Bencoolen 'of a person, however individually respectable, who has in so many instances overstepped the limits of his duty.' The Netherlands Ambassador in London delivered his own protest. The political climate in London was entirely in favour of conciliating the Dutch for fear of jeopardising a major Anglo-Dutch Treaty. The Marquess of Hastings (as Lord Moira had become) wrote to the Dutch Governor of Java disassociating the Supreme Government from Raffles' actions.

Raffles had precipitated a diplomatic disaster, and then made things worse. In order to frighten the Dutch in Palembang he sent off an armed force to which he gave the jolly name of Sumatran Hill Rangers. Muntinghe responded to their approach by calling for reinforcements from Java. The former Sultan Badaruddin, in a bid to clear his name with the Dutch, then stuck his oar in, saying that the massacre of the Dutch garrison in 1811 had come about because Raffles had written to him from Malacca encouraging him to kill all the Dutch. So it was all Raffles' fault. (Raffles' message had been highly ambiguous, his precise meaning adrift in translation.)

Raffles was in hot water. He applied for permission to travel to Calcutta in order to explain about Palembang, to argue for the retention of Padang, and to impress upon the Governor-General the potential value of Sumatra. The omens, surprisingly, were good. 'It was painful to me,' replied the Marquess of Hastings, 'that I had, in the course of my public duty, to express an opinion unfavourable to your measures in Java.' His disapprobation 'affected their prudence alone,' and credit was due to Raffles' 'anxious and unwearied exertions' with results 'highly creditable to the British Government.'

Sophia and Raffles, with Sophia's brother William Hull, sailed for Calcutta, leaving Charlotte in Bencoolen with Nurse Grimes, 'quite a treasure'. 'Do you not pity Lady Raffles,' her husband wrote to the Duchess of Somerset, 'and think me hard-hearted to drag her about in her present state, but she will not remain from me, and what can I do?'

Every woman prioritises either the man or the child, and Sophia was definitely a woman for the man.

Raffles could not persuade the Supreme Government in Calcutta to hold on to Padang, and was instructed to have absolutely nothing more to do with Palembang. The Sumatran Hill Rangers were to be recalled. Lord Hastings would not honour the treaty Raffles made with the Sultan of Menangkabau, or agree that the whole island of Sumatra should be played for by the restoration of Menangkabau sovereignty.

Raffles bit on the bullet and in November apologised formally. 'His Lordship in Council may be assured that my proceedings will be entirely influenced by the orders which I have now received and that in all future communications with the agents of the Dutch Government the most conciliatory and amicable spirit shall be manifested.'

He added that 'I left England under the full impression that I was not only Resident at Bencoolen but in fact Political Agent for the Malay States' and attached a copy of the briefing letter issued to him in 1817. While this required him to collect and transmit intelligence on the operations of the Dutch and Americans in the Archipelago, it certainly did not authorise military or even diplomatic interventions. He heard however that his explanation was 'perfectly satisfactory to the Governor-General.'

Raffles was already on to something else, and would soon transform a humiliating episode into a personal triumph.

Penang and Bencoolen were the only British positions remaining in the Archipelago following the post-war concessions to the Dutch. British trade, and the most profitable branch of it – between India and the Far East – was threatened. This anxiety was expressed by the Government in Penang and taken on board by the Governor-General. The acquisition of some modest trading-point south of Malacca, roughly equidistant between India and China, was essential if the Company was not to be excluded entirely.

Raffles, with his charm and his zeal, was co-opted by Lord Hastings as the key figure in this project. Writing that November to the Secret Committee, Hastings regretted being 'compelled to adopt a tone of censure on the conduct of Sir Stamford Raffles' over Palembang. Although 'we conceive him to have misconstrued his powers...we are fully persuaded that he was influenced by motives of unquestionable zeal for the interests of the Honourable Company and the nation.' His confidence in Sir Stamford was such that 'we have actually entrusted to him the conduct of an important service to the Eastward.'

Major William Farquhar, with Malacca returned to the Dutch, had arranged to take home leave. But Lord Hastings and Raffles agreed that he was the man to investigate the islands at the southern end of the Malacca Strait and head up any new station; Farquhar had already tabled his own memo about the need for a settlement somewhere at the entrance to the Strait, and Colonel Bannerman, the Governor of Penang, had instructed him to make commercial treaties with islands near Singapore. Farquhar had success with the islands of Lingga and Rhio, where he concluded a treaty with the Chief acting on behalf of Sultan Abdul Rahman of Johore on the Malaysian mainland. All this he communicated to Raffles. The two were associated in the adventure from the beginning.

In mid-December 1818, when he and Sophia sailed from Calcutta for Penang, Raffles wrote to Marsden, 'We are now on our way to the Eastward, hoping to do something, but I much fear the Dutch have hardly left us an inch of ground to stand upon. My attention is principally turned to Johore, and you must not be surprised if my next letter to you is dated from the site of the ancient city of Singhapura.' Lord Hastings' last words to him in Calcutta were 'Sir Stamford, you may depend on me.'

Lord Hastings was giving Raffles a golden opportunity.

For his other mission from Hastings, to 'form a connection' with Acheen, Raffles had a co-Commissioner, Captain John Monckton Coombs. John Palmer in Calcutta was conspiring to thwart Raffles' 'impertinent Intrusion' over the contested throne of Acheen, and his equally impertinent intrusion into the plan for a new trading-post.

Palmer nobbled Captain Coombs in Penang: 'I would fain have you prepared for the reception of our Knight, if ever he contrives to get amongst you [in Penang]... But I am doing what I may to spike a too rapidly revolving Wheel.' As for the project of raising the British flag somewhere south of the Strait of Malacca, in a discussion with 'A' (the Secretary to Government in Calcutta, John Adam) he had 'ventured to assume that it were the very height of injustice to F [Farquhar]...to foist a fresh man on the fruits of his labour; and when in truth all is accomplished that even the eminent endowment of Sir Knight could by any possibility effect.' Farquhar was eminently qualified to carry it through 'on his own.'

'I had proceeded this far,' continued Palmer after more verbiage, 'when I was favoured with a call from Sir Knight, who stayed a couple of hours at my desk musing pretty largely into all the details of projected measures.' Palmer warned Coombs, and therefore all Penang, that Raffles 'carries instructions of his own drafting, to form stable connexions, political and commercial, where F has already put his seal, and the object of his visit appeared to be to ascertain my notion upon the nature of these relations... I had in view, however, to get the Knight out of your waters, for though I fear I may not *preclude* him, I trust I may shorten his stay among you.'

What Palmer picked up from his contacts in the Supreme Government confirmed 'my apprehension that the Knight is netting out for himself an Empire east of yours' (i.e. Penang's). 'This last, unless an entire and exclusive Dominion, evidently will not satisfy his ambition; nor even yield that occupation which a restless mind and frame seem to exact.'

Raffles was naturally open and communicative. It is painful to see him, leaning against Palmer's desk, confiding in that snake – who ended up disarmed by Raffles' directness: 'I have no wish to depreciate his talent or fitness...he has been either remarkably candid or remarkably artful in the readiest acknowledgment of more than one instance of erroneous policy in Java and Sumatra...he frankly threw off his disguise as well as his reserve... He is a kind hearted man, a little selfish in his views of ambition and policy – perhaps from a conviction that the whole range of Eastern subjects does not require more than the talent of more than one ordinary man – and that man he desires to be.'

That is not an unfair assessment, from an enemy. Palmer actually facilitated Raffles by procuring – so with profit for himself – a ship, the *Indiana*, to be brought round to Penang for Raffles' use.

There was even more than this to engage Raffles in Calcutta. He saw in the Asiatic Society Museum 'the head of a tapir', as he wrote to Marsden in December. When he first was in Penang, back in 1805, he had heard tell of a tapir, 'an animal in every respect the model of an elephant, but of diminutive size,' but it died, and the servants threw its body into the sea. He had now seen a live one, at the Governor-General's country place at Barrackpore. He was sending Marsden a 'correct drawing' of it. 'It is the most docile creature I ever met with.'

He made two new naturalist friends. Nathaniel Wallich, the recently appointed Superintendant of the six hundred-acre Botanic Garden in Calcutta, was a Dane, five years younger than Raffles. Staying with Wallich was a twenty-three-year-old doctor on sick leave – William Jack from Aberdeen, an ardent and gifted botanist. Raffles engaged Dr Jack as his personal physician and scientific collaborator, in place of the much-missed Dr Arnold.

Raffles, Sophia and Dr Jack arrived in Penang on the last day of 1818, and William Farquhar shortly afterwards. On 4 December John Palmer had written to Major Farquhar: 'I do hope, my Friend, that you will be employed to complete and perfect the only substantial measures which have been attempted since the peace with Holland in these seas; and that even Sir Stamford may not be used to diminish the value of your previous services.' Raffles was only a liability in dealing with the Dutch, since that 'worthy little statesman cannot budge a peg without exciting their suspicion and inspiring their Terror and Hatred and Hostility.' This opinion, Palmer added, was 'little less than High Treason' in Bengal, and Farquhar was to keep it to himself.

On their first day, Raffles and Sophia were among those dining with Governor Bannerman in the Marble Hall at Suffolk House. A Captain J.G.F. Crawford was among the dinner guests. Sir Stamford, he wrote in his journal, 'exposed himself greatly today, when speaking of his former chum Mr Phillips, by remarking that he was a worthy good fellow,' but that he did not 'possess capacities to set the Thames on fire.' Then, according to Crawford, Raffles said, after a short pause, 'Well, Colonel, you know I cannot be idle, I must always be doing something.'

This was not clever, since Phillips, whom Raffles never liked, and who never liked him, had just married Governor Bannerman's daughter Janet; and Suffolk House itself belonged to Phillips.

Captain Crawford saw Raffles as 'a courtier in action' and 'an excellent worthy man, possessing great abilities, and of a bustling active disposition' – and, significantly, with 'credentials from the Marquess of Hastings constituting his Representative and Agent among the Malay Chiefs.' Strategies were discussed at dinner, including the establishment of a 'factory' at Acheen.

The complication at Acheen was the long-running rivalry for the throne. Local chiefs had ousted Sultan Johor Alum in 1816 in favour of Syf-ul-Alum, son of Syed Hussein, the rich and now tottering merchant in Penang. The former Sultan and his supporters did not give up, and there was bloodshed.

Raffles strongly supported Sultan Johor Alum, the Anglophile, not very bright but legitimate ruler. (It was he who had awarded Raffles his Order of the Golden Sword.) John Palmer had been Syed Hussein's agent and supporter over many years. Governor Bannerman, like Palmer, backed Syed Hussein's son.

If a trade treaty were to be made with Acheen, one of the contenders had to be recognised as the proper authority. Captain Coombs, Raffles' co-Commissioner, shared Penang's prejudices. Hastings, appointing the two, was hoping for balance.

Raffles and Governor Bannerman argued over whether Raffles should go to Acheen to find out which contender was currently occupying the throne. Raffles wanted to go, Bannerman told him he should not. Bannerman deserves some sympathy. In a book written in Raffles' time (unpublished until 1840), John Anderson, who served for seventeen years in Penang, remarked that Governors of Penang were hampered by never being allowed to make their own decisions. They had to refer everything to Bengal.

'The superior merit of Sir S. Raffles,' wrote John Anderson, 'consists in acting for himself, as his enemies would express it, "in utter contempt of orders from his superiors"; as his friends would say, from "that decision of character, confidence in his own local knowledge and opinion that would lead him to decide and act, instead of asking for orders, or even against them, if he thought them wrong."'

Bannerman and Raffles were united only on the importance of the projected settlement to the south of the Malacca Strait – Bannerman thinking it would enhance the prestige and commercial success of Penang, under whose authority the settlement must surely be, as the area under consideration was only eight days' sail away. He provided two survey ships, commanded by Captains Daniel Ross and J.G.F.Crawford, to make a survey of the relevant islands. Ship's captains were of all kinds: Captain Ross was a distinguished hydrographer and a Fellow of the Royal Society.

'Sir Stamford, at the instigation of Major Farquhar, picks on the Carimons,' noted Captain Crawford. According to the instructions from the Supreme Government, he and Ross were 'to comply, as far as our services will permit, with the wishes of Sir Stamford.'

Governor Bannerman still recognised Major William Farquhar, not Raffles, as the man in charge. According to Sophia, the Penang Government 'protested in the strongest manner, and exercised its power and influence in every possible way, against the attainment of the important object entrusted to him.' Dr Jack was shocked but not surprised: 'For they cannot but feel how little and insignificant they are in comparison with the energy of Sir Stamford,' he wrote to Nathaniel Wallich. 'I cannot express to you how much I am delighted with him. He is of the *real* sterling stamp, and of that active and comprehensive mind that diffuses a portion of its energy all around.'

Instead of taking the heavily pregnant Sophia home to Bencoolen for the birth of the baby as they had arranged, Raffles decided she must remain in Penang because – against Governor Bannerman's wishes – he wanted to go and see what could be achieved in Acheen while Farquhar was reconnoitring in the south. He installed Dr William Jack with her as medical supervisor, botany instructor and companion. Sophia made the best of this as she did of everything. Dr Jack was happy too. 'Think how comfortable I am,' he wrote to Nathaniel Wallich, 'with so agreeable a woman as Lady R., abundant leisure to examine the productions of this Island: in short I am delighted, and the day is not half long enough for all that I have and wish to do.'

In view of controversy about the 'ownership' of the founding of Singapore, it is worth examining the Marquess of Hastings' instructions to Raffles, drafted by Raffles when he was in Calcutta. The arrangements had been made 'without further reference to the Authorities at home.' The Governor-General considered the port of Rhio to be the most advantageous position, 'just before the entrance to the Straits, exactly in the track of shipping passing in or out of them,' effectively in command of 'both the Strait of Malacca and Sincapore.' Major Farquhar's 'long experience and peculiar qualifications…eminently fit him for the command of the Post which it is desirable to establish and the local superintendence of our interest and affairs.' Sir Stamford was to 'leave that officer at Rhio… and consider yourself at liberty to return to Bencoolen, where your presence will be required.' Most importantly, the 'general management of our interests beyond the Strait of Malacca' were to be under Sir Stamford's 'immediate control as Lieutenant-Governor of Bencoolen.'

So Raffles – with Hastings – had established that the proposed new settlement would be under Raffles' personal authority, from distant Bencoolen, cutting out Penang.

Farquhar was instructed to accompany Raffles to Rhio 'with a view to your remaining in the local charge of the British interest in that quarter, under the general superintendence of the Lieutenant-Governor of Bencoolen.' (Rhio turned out to have been grabbed by the Dutch, but so far as islands were concerned the Governor-General's instructions were transferable.) There was thus no ambiguity about the division of responsibilities, or the ranking of the two principals.

The plan was for Farquhar to sail with troops, meet up with the surveyors' ships, and do some exploring. His instructions from Raffles were not to establish any settlement; he was to proceed eastward, and 'having ascertained the capabilities of Sincapore and its vicinity, and the result being satisfactory,' to 'make such arrangements for securing to us the important Command of that Station.'

Raffles did not, after all, go to Acheen before joining Farquhar. He could not miss out on the great adventure.

Major Farquhar sailed from Penang at dawn on 18 January 1819. Raffles, the previous night, had secretly loaded up the *Indiana* (not forgetting a red carpet) and its escort schooner the *Enterprise*. He left a note for Bannerman saying he was acceding to his wishes by not going to Acheen, sent a message to Farquhar to say he was on his way – and slipped off, just catching the same morning tide.

Chapter 11

Founding Father

Singapore and Bencoolen 1819–1821

Raffles' ships caught up those of Farquhar and the surveyors off the Carimon Islands, and there was a conference on the *Indiana*. In Farquhar's 'Memorial' to the Company (1824), he asserted that 'at the suggestion of your Memorialist [himself] they stopped… at Singapore.' It was actually Captain Ross, according to Captain Crawford, who pointed out Singapore's good harbour – where, on the evening of 28 January, the posse of vessels weighed anchor.

Mystified island people rowed out to meet them. Raffles ascertained that the local chief on the island was the Temenggong, and that no Dutch had ever been there. So next morning he and Farquhar, the small man and the tall, stepped out on to the beach where the river met the sea.

Singapore was a dependency of Johore on the mainland, and no exception to the customary issues of disputed succession. The Sultan of Johore named his eldest son, Tunku Long, as his heir. An uncle, the Rajah Muda of Rhio, challenged Tunku Long, declaring his nephew to be the rightful Sultan of Johore. Stalemate.

On Singapore the Temenggong, as a supporter of Tunku Long, was prepared to treat with Sir Stamford. But to cover all eventualities, Major Farquhar sailed from Singapore that afternoon to call upon the Rajah Muda at Rhio. In the presence of the watchful Dutch, the Rajah Muda refused permission for a British post on Singapore. Privately he said just the opposite to Farquhar, though he would have to lodge a protest, to placate the Dutch.

Raffles had no doubt that Singapore was the right place for the new settlement. The next day, 30 January 1819, he made a provisional treaty with the Temenggong, promising him in return 3,000 Spanish dollars a year and half of all port duties, in perpetuity. He wrote to William Marsden, triumphantly inscribing 'Singapore' at the top of the paper: 'Here I am true to my word, and in the enjoyment of all the pleasure which a footing on such classic ground must inspire. The lines of the old city, and its defences, are still to be traced, and within its ramparts the British Union [flag] waves unmolested.'

The straits separating Singapore from the Malaysian mainland are nowhere more than a mile across. The island is at most twenty-six miles long from east to west, and a maximum of fourteen miles north to south. Few vestiges of the ancient city were discernible in 1819, apart from a long mound – the 'ramparts' – where the flag was flying. 'Most certainly the Dutch never had a Factory in the Island of Singapore,' Raffles told Marsden, 'and it does not appear to me that their recent arrangements with a subordinate authority at Rhio can or ought to interfere with our permanent establishment here. I have, however, a violent opposition to surmount on the part of the Government of Penang…This, therefore, will probably be my last attempt. If I am deserted now, I must fain return to Bencoolen, and become philosopher.'

He had to hurry back to Penang 'where I have left Lady Raffles, and my anxiety to get there, on her account, is very great. If I keep Singapore I shall be quite satisfied; and in a few years our influence over the Archipelago, as far as concerns our commerce, will be fully established.' And later, to Colonel Addenbrooke, Prince Leopold's right-hand man: 'But for my Malay studies I should have hardly known that such a place existed; not only the European, but the Indian world was also ignorant of it.'

That statement, as it stands, is nonsense. Everyone knew where Singapore was. It had more than once been considered by Europeans as a strategic settlement. Raffles was eliding his facts. What most Europeans and many East Asians did not know was Singapore's significance as the site of the 'Lion City', the great citadel abandoned six hundred years earlier and full of ghosts – 'Bukit Larangan', the Forbidden Hill, to the local inhabitants. This captured Raffles' imagination. The rebirth of the ancient centre of Malay civilisation as a centre of British influence meant much to him.

Raffles still had to achieve a Treaty of Alliance with Tunku Long, who came secretly by night, fearing, like his rival, repercussions from the Dutch. But he had no trouble declaring himself the lawful sovereign of Singapore and Johore, wickedly cheated by his relations. By the time Farquhar returned from Rhio, Raffles – with his talent for theatre – had invited ashore the commanders and officers of the ships to witness the signing of the great treaty between Sir Stamford Raffles on behalf of the East India Company and Tunku Long, now confirmed as Sultan of Johore, with the title of Sultan Hussein Mahummud Shah.

The sixth of February 1819 was a beautiful day. Ships and boats were decorated with pennants. Field guns were mounted on the beach. Cold lunches were provided. At the river's mouth, chairs were set outside the state tent, from where the red carpet stretched for a hundred feet along the river bank. There was some unruly firing of guns from the ships in the bay as the new Sultan, perspiring heavily, made his appearance.

Raffles stood, and presented his commission from the Marquess of Hastings. The Treaty of Alliance was read out, signed and sealed. Gifts were presented – opium, guns, scarlet wool cloth. The whole company moved on to the ramparts to watch the Union Jack being hoisted. (It had been hauled down earlier, just so that it might be ceremonially raised.) The sepoys fired a volley and the Artillery a royal salute; the guns on the ships in the bay followed suit, and everyone had a drink, the Malays sitting down with the English.

Afterwards Captain Crawford proposed giving Sir Stamford three cheers and 'after a little demur' – from whom? – this was 'done with spirit'. That night Raffles gave a dinner party on the *Indiana*. Major Farquhar was not present. As Resident and Commandant of Singapore, he remained on the island as darkness fell, with his suite, his officers, the sepoys, the local inhabitants, and the rats with which the foreshore was infested.

In nine days Raffles and Farquhar had achieved something which would change the economic and political geography of South-East Asia. As well as imposing his will on the native rulers with maximum persuasiveness and skill, and stage-managing the climactic events, Raffles had much paperwork to do before he sailed.

He issued a brief Proclamation for public distribution, announcing the signing of the Treaty and the appointment of Major William Farquhar as Resident and Commandant 'and all persons are hereby directed to obey Major Farquhar accordingly.' And – just in case there was any doubt – 'the Residency of Singapore has been placed under the Government of Fort Marlborough [Bencoolen] and it is to be considered a dependency thereof; of which all persons concerned are desired to take notice.' He produced a Memorandum of Instructions for Major Farquhar, dated 6 February, the day of the treaty-signing. This document extends to twenty-three numbered paragraphs, and could not have been written in advance as the references are site-specific.

The instructions stressed the 'high importance of avoiding all measures which can be construed into an interference with any of the States where the authority of his Netherlands Majesty may be established.' Equally, 'caution and delicacy' must be observed in communications with native rulers under the immediate influence of the Dutch, as with those 'free and independent tribes' which might come to the port for reasons of trade.

Raffles was leaving Lieutenant Crossley with Major Farquhar, to be his Assistant and to direct the Pay Department, Stores and Commissariat. Captain Bernard (Farquhar's son-in-law) was 'provisionally' appointed Acting Master Attendant and Marine Storekeeper. (Raffles wanted this post for his brother-in-law William Flint.) He settled their allowances – i.e. salaries – subject to approval from the Supreme Government. Constructing a harbour and providing watering facilities for visiting ships was a priority. On the Hill overlooking the beach, 'a small fort or commodious blockhouse' should be built; and defensive batteries on each side of the port, and a palisade round the Cantonment. A Martello Tower should be erected at Deep Water Point.

'I should not think myself justified at the present moment in authorising the erection of a house for the accommodation of the chief authority,' but would take an early opportunity of recommending it to Supreme Government. This was a bone of contention with Farquhar already. The Resident could not be expected to live in an *atap* hut. Farquhar was to build himself an appropriately commodious bungalow.

No port duties were to be exacted from visiting vessels so as not to inhibit trade. Quarterly accounts must be submitted to Fort Marlborough, 'to me', and the 'usual return' to the Presidency of Fort William in Calcutta. 'I shall probably return to this Residency after a short absence;' meanwhile he had 'a perfect reliance' on the Resident.

He even found time to explore, coming across three species of Nepenthe (pitcher-plants, one of which received the epithet *rafflesiana*). And then on 7 February, the morning after the signing of the Treaty, Raffles sailed with the *Indiana* for Penang.

The newly appointed Sultan of Johore was sweating during the Treaty ceremony because he was scared. Neither he nor the

Temenggong knew how the Dutch would react to the British landing on Singapore. To keep their options open, it had to seem to the Dutch as if they had acted under compulsion. The Sultan sent a letter to the Dutch authorities in Rhio explaining how, when he heard that Raffles was landing stores and soldiers on Singapore, 'I completely lost my head and never thought of letting you know.' Raffles had 'laid hold of me and would not let me go again but insisted on making me Rajah of the title of Sultan.' He had no option but to comply. The Temenggong, equally apprehensive, wrote to the Dutch: 'All of us who were at Singapore were much startled' when they saw the British landings. 'We were powerless to say anything... We in no way separate ourselves from the Dutch. As it was with us in the beginning, so it shall be to the end as long as there are a sun and a moon.'

When Raffles got back to Penang on 13 February, Sophia's baby had still not arrived. She seemed content, deeply into natural history studies with young Dr Jack. The ground floor of the house, he told the Duchess, 'is more like the menagerie at Exeter Change, than the residence of a gentleman. Fish, flesh and fowl, alike contribute to the collection; and above stairs the rooms are variously ornamented with branches and flowers, rendering them so many arbours.'

He arranged for tools and materials to be shipped to Major Farquhar, and wrote his official report of the events at Singapore for Bengal. He asked Governor Bannerman for more sepoys to be sent to Singapore. Bannerman flatly refused. Singapore would obviously have to be abandoned, so the smaller the military force to be evacuated the better. He bluntly accused Raffles of 'personal ambition and a desire for aggrandizement', infuriated that Singapore had been placed under the control of Raffles at Bencoolen.

A strong protest against the occupation of Singapore arrived from the Dutch in Malacca, citing the letters written by the Sultan and the Temenggong. This crisis was defused by Major Farquhar, who got the Temenggong to put his seal and the Sultan's to a paper

22/23. Raffles' homes: Above, Buitenzorg, his country residence when Lieutenant-Governor of Java, and where Olivia died. Below: 'I have cleared my Hill' – Permatang Balam, the house he built for his growing family when Lieutenant-Governor of Bencoolen.

24/25. Above: Malacca on the Malaysian pensinsula, from where the invasion fleet set sail for Java, showing the Dutch church and, on the right, Government House. Below: Bencoolen, the unpromising settlement on the west coast of Sumatra where Raffles was Lieutenant-Governor and where four of his little children died.

26/27. Singapore: Two views of the new settlement from Government Hill, where
Raffles built his bungalow. He described how he looked from his hill all the way down
the High Street to the bay, crowded with vessels coming in to trade. Nowadays you
cannot see the sea at all from Government Hill on account of the massed high-rises.

28. An imagined depiction of the fire on the *Fame*, from which Raffles and Sophia escaped with their lives but with the loss of his natural history collection, his drawings, maps and papers, and all their personal belongings.

29/30. The Asian Tapir, first described by William Farquhar, to Raffles' annoyance. The water-colour drawing is from Raffles' collection. *Rafflesia arnoldii*, the vast bloom found by Dr Arnold on Raffles' expedition into south-west Sumatra – 'the wonder of the vegetable kingdom', as Raffles wrote, 'it measured across rather more than a yard.' The fleshy flower smells disgusting.

31/32/33/34. clockwise: The Marquess of Hastings, Governor-General of India, initially hostile to Raffles but soon his keen supporter. Raffles' good friend the Duchess of Somerset, to whom he wrote some of his best letters. Sir Joseph Banks, famous naturalist, President of the Royal Society, and the most influential of Raffles' 'Great Men of the Town'. Captain Thomas Otho Travers from Co Cork, Raffles' ADC and his most loyal friend and admirer.

35. East Street in the village of Walworth, Raffles' modest boyhood home.

36. Highwood, his last home, the happy house on a hundred acres in Mill Hill. He died here, thousands of pounds in debt to his lifelong employers, the East India Company.

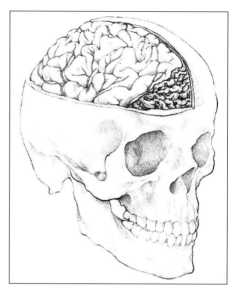

37. Sir Everard Home FRS, the comparative anatomist who performed the autopsy on Raffles at Highwood on the day of his death.

38. A modern artist's impression of the probable appearance of Raffles' open skull with the fatal arterio-venous malformation at the front.

39. Raffles' monument by Chantrey in Westminster Abbey. It is surrounded by massive memorials to grandees of the East India Company. The plaque on Raffle's monument lists his high achievements with no mention of the Company at all.

40. Raffles against the office towers on Boat Quay – a reproduction of the original statue by Thomas Woolner. The plaque reads: 'On this historic site, Sir Thomas Stamford Raffles first landed in Singapore on 28 January 1819, and with genius and perception changed the destiny of an obscure fishing village to a great seaport and modern Metropolis.'

stating that 'the English established themselves at Singapore with my free will and consent,' and that all had been done with 'the free accord of myself and the Sultan of Johore.' There was nothing that Raffles could teach William Farquhar about tact or conciliation. Raffles foresaw a 'paper war' with the Dutch over Singapore, but not an actual war. Governor van der Capellan in Batavia was trusting the Marquess of Hastings to bring Raffles to heel, and wrote to him in the expectation that 'a good and just Government such as the British would take immediate steps for the repression of the measures adopted by its subordinate agents.'

Hastings – unforgivably – wavered under pressure from the Dutch, from the violent disapproval of India House, and from Bannerman's drip-feed of antagonism. 'Sir Thomas Raffles was not justified in sending Major Farquhar eastward after the Dutch protested; and, if the Post has not yet been obtained,' Hastings wrote to Bannerman on 20 February 1819, 'he is to desist from any further attempt to establish one.' Too late. The Treaty of Alliance was signed and sealed already.

After three weeks in Penang and still no baby, Raffles left Penang on the *Indiana* with Captain John Monckton Coombs on 8 March 1819 for the postponed expedition to Acheen. Their instructions from Bengal were to make a settlement with whichever king seemed the best bet. Coombs had been on a mission to Acheen a year earlier and reported that, although the new Sultan, Syf-ul-Alum, son of the Penang merchant Syed Hussein, was on the throne, the real power was in the hands of the Chiefs; and Sultan Johor Alum was nowhere.

Syf-ul-Alum was becoming bolder in his piracy and plundering, but still the consensus in Penang was in his favour. Syed Hussein's determination to secure support for his son occasioned an attempted bribe of Raffles through Sophia, as she described in a footnote in the *Memoir*: she was presented with a casket of diamonds 'and it seemed to create much surprise that it was not even looked at.' Intelligence was received that a Dutch brig had been in Acheen offering assistance and armed forces to Johor Alum, and that he had declined in consequence of a supportive letter Raffles sent him as he was leaving for Singapore. According to John Anderson, who was present, Bannerman was apoplectic about Raffles' inappropriate intrusion in the matter.

Raffles desired to secure Acheen as part of his vision of a 'chain of ports' which would establish British hegemony throughout the Archipelago and beyond. In his letter to Marsden from Singapore he presented the mission as a duty: he would go to Acheen 'where I have to establish the British influence on a permanent footing.' He had grounds for the claim. He first met Captain Coombs in Calcutta, when Coombs was consulting the Governor-General about Acheen and giving the Penang line: 'and Lord Hastings asked my opinion. I had no hesitation in giving it as far as it was thus formed, and the Supreme Government was induced to pause.' To add to the insult to Penang, Raffles was appointed the senior of the two Commissioners, as a Lieutenant-Governor could not be subordinate to a Captain.

On arrival in the port of Acheen, Raffles and Coombs did not disembark. Raffles sent the three principal Chiefs an enquiry as to who they wished to be their ruler, Johor Alum or Syf-ul-Alum. They replied Syf-ul-Alum. Raffles was not given permission to land, so he invited the Chiefs to come down to the port to meet him. Accounts differ – either they did not turn up for a week, or Raffles kept them waiting around for a week. Raffles then sent a note saying he was ill, but that he had 'not broken off his friendship' with the Chiefs, though by now the Chiefs had broken off their friendship with him. Was Raffles ill, or unwilling to be told what he did not want to hear?

He never left the ship at all. To Robert Harry Inglis, the son of the old Company director, he wrote: 'We remained there nearly seven weeks, during the early portion of which we were directly opposed in our politics' – that is, he and Coombs were squabbling – 'but at length, after a paper war which actually occupies above a thousand pages of the Company's largest sized paper, he came round to my opinion.' The picture of Raffles and Coombs, cooped up on the *Indiana*, neurotically exchanging pages of polemic, is ludicrous.

Coombs caved in. They sailed down the coast to Pedir, where Johor Alum was living in exile, and signed a treaty with him, dated 22 April 1819. This gave the British exclusively the freedom to trade in all the ports of Acheen, and to instal a British Resident. In return, Johor Alum was given credit on the Bengal Government to the tune of a million rupees, and arms and equipment were left with him.

Raffles naively contacted John Palmer, and received a sarcastic reply thanking him for 'the promised detail of your proceedings at Acheen; and which I shall read with interest if not with pleasure; for *prima facie* I have not the satisfaction of an entire concurrence in them; and esteem the evidence of a thousand pages as extremely equivocal of a good cause. How a subject so comparatively [word missing] could have produced such a waste of time and paper is to me a riddle.' He suggested partitioning Acheen, which might just lead to Raffles' treaty being implemented, since 'I apprehend its abortion under the administration of Penang.'

Palmer was an instrument in that inevitable abortion. The day he wrote to Raffles, he wrote to Phillips in Penang: 'I think that between your communications and those of Coombs we have unmasked the artifices and charlataneries of the Golden Sword and left him his just title to repute for more talent than integrity.'

The treaty was never implemented, though Raffles initially represented this mission as a triumph. In his autobiographical letter to Cousin Thomas of 14 October 1819, he linked 'settling the affairs of the distracted kingdom of Acheen' with 'establishing the Port of Sincapore... Complete success attended both these important measures.' Later he wrote the episode off. In the comprehensive 'Statement of Services' which he wrote to the Court of Directors in 1824, he did not even mention Acheen.

Sophia's baby was born four days after Raffles left for Acheen – a boy, whom they named Leopold Stamford. The family and Dr Jack, returned from Penang to Bencoolen by way of Singapore, reaching the new settlement on 31 May 1819, and stayed a month.

Raffles was elated. His dream was coming true. To Colonel Addenbrooke, and therefore to Prince Leopold: 'Our object is not territory but trade, a great commercial Emporium, and a *fulcrum* whence we may extend our influence politically...and what Malta is to the West, that may Singapore be in the East.' Farquhar had achieved an amazing amount in four months. More than fifteen miles of roads had been laid, and more than five thousand people were already living in and around the new township. Singapore, Raffles told Addenbrooke, was 'a child of my own.'

Already the main topographical features of the place had acquired their permanent names. Raffles became a town-planner. The grid pattern of streets for Europeans that he envisaged was like that imposed on all the major settlements of East India and the Eastern Isles. The Europeans' warehouses would be in the Beach Road area. The Chinese *kampong* would be south of the river. The Malays and the followers of the Temenggong were to make their homes upriver. He designated the north bank, which was the firmest land, for Government buildings.

They were clearing jungle that June from Rocky Point (later Artillery Point, where the Fullerton Hotel now stands). Workmen uncovered a sandstone boulder ten feet high, ten feet wide, and very thick, split into two. It was inscribed with mostly indecipherable lettering, probably dating from between the tenth and thirteenth centuries. Raffles believed it to be Hindu. Fortunately he would never know that the 'Singapore Stone' was blown up in 1843 to clear the space for building. Three inscribed fragments were salvaged at that time and sent to the Royal Asiatic Society in Calcutta. (One of these is now in the National Museum of Singapore.)

The ship taking the Raffles family home to Bencoolen got stuck on a sandbank off Rhio on leaving Singapore, and was only re-floated by throwing overboard all the water loaded for the month's voyage. They sent a boat to Rhio asking to be re-supplied with water. The Dutch Resident refused. But 'a good Samaritan appeared in one of the beautiful American vessels,' as Sophia wrote in the *Memoir*. The Captain 'generously, and at considerable risk, for the wind was strong and in his favour, stopped his course, and with great difficulty, by means of ropes, conveyed some casks of water.' They never forgot this American kindness.

In the glow of Singapore's success, they were on their way back to Charlotte, their daughter whom they had not seen since the previous August. It was at this point in the *Memoir* that Sophia chose to put into words the 'pleasure of sailing through this beautiful and unparalleled Archipelago…the smoothness of the sea, the lightness of the atmosphere… Islands of every shape and size clustered together, mountains of the most fanciful forms crowned with verdure to their summit, rich and luxurious vegetation extending to the very edge of the water, little native boats, often with only one person in them, continually darting out from the deep shade which concealed them.' The beautiful Archipelago represented the emotional geography of their family happiness.

At noon on 31 July 1819, a vessel was spotted on the horizon from Fort Marlborough. Travers and the welcoming party waited on the wharf until ten at night, when the ship reached anchorage and Sir Stamford, Lady Raffles and four-month-old Leopold were ferried on shore.

Raffles found Bencoolen in bad shape. The young officials were bored and restless. Raffles told William Brown Ramsay in March 1820 that 'We have literally nothing for the civil servants to do at Bencoolen, and idleness is the root of all evils; they ought to be transferred to some other settlement, and not to be obliged to waste their time, life, and health here.' There was even a sour note in Travers' reverential attitude to Raffles: 'The constant reports of changes…and the attempt to introduce a new system without means of carrying any plan into effect, has operated much against the place. Sir Stamford, in my opinion, acted precipitately in almost all he has done, and this opinion, is, in fact, confirmed by his being compelled to relinquish some of his plans.'

Raffles had one more card to play. If it made sense for the supervising authority of Singapore to be in nearby Penang rather than in Bencoolen, then surely he himself should be appointed Governor of Prince of Wales Island (Penang) after Bannerman. He had this in mind during his second visit to Singapore, writing to his business agent in London: 'I have experienced a good deal of opposition and unfair treatment from Colonel Bannerman...I conclude he will be anxious to secure the succession to the Govt of Penang to his son in law Phillips, who I am told has applied for it, but I hope the point is already settled in my favour – at all events I rely on the strenuous exertions of my friends to secure the succession for me.'

On 8 August 1819 Governor Bannerman died at Penang, and W.E.Phillips was sworn in as Acting Governor. Raffles in Bencoolen did not hear of Bannerman's death until the arrival of a ship on 2 October. This was his opportunity, or so he thought. He told Travers that when he was in Calcutta, Lord Hastings had said 'that he thought the Government of our Eastern provinces should be placed under one head, and that no man was better qualified for the situation than Sir Stamford, and that on the removal or going away of Colonel J.A.Bannerman, he would certainly recommend the measure.'

Who knows what was said in Calcutta, or by whom. Lord Hastings was impressed and beguiled by Raffles, and he was a man open to free-wheeling discussion. In a fifteen-thousand-word memorandum to Hastings, Raffles set out his big idea. Both Penang and Bencoolen should become purely commercial stations, without the burden of maintaining full civil establishments. 'The residence of the superintending authority would not necessarily be fixed on either, he would occasionally visit them all and his principal residence would of course be in that which united the most advantages for his superintendence.' Singapore, 'once the great emporium of these seas, whose history is lost in the mists of antiquity,' was central to this plan (which was extraordinarily like the arrangement for the Straits Settlements made soon after Raffles left).

Raffles sailed for Calcutta in October 1819 to pitch for the gover-norship of Penang – without Sophia, who was pregnant yet again. He took along Dr William Jack and Captain Thomas Watson, who had been one of his ADCs in Java. Towards the end of December letters arrived in Bencoolen saying his return would be delayed. Things were not working out smoothly.

Hastings was in favour, in principle, of Raffles' radical idea: 'The consolidation of our Eastern possessions into one Government subordinate to the Supreme Authority would unquestionably be a desirable arrangement,' he wrote on 27 November. But until the future of Singapore was known, 'it would be premature to fashion, even provisionally, any plans.'

John Palmer, who as usual knew everything, wrote to Phillips: 'The Golden Sword came here posthaste... He comes on public grounds to show his pretensions to your Government, having dis-interestedly proposed long ago to the Court to reduce the Gov-ernment to a Residency and consolidate everything Eastward in one hand. I told him...that I had been turning Heaven and Earth to procure the confirmation of your pretensions both here and at home.'

One consolation for Raffles was the arrival in Calcutta of Mary-anne and William Flint from England. But his plan was not accepted and he was 'heavy and sick at heart'. In a uniquely expressive letter to the Duchess of Somerset in mid-December he said: 'I could lay me down and cry, and weep for hours together, and yet I know not why, except that I am unhappy. But for my dear sister's arrival, I should still have been a solitary wretch in this busy capital. I left Lady Raffles and my dear children at Bencoolen three months ago; and I have no one of congenial feelings with whom I can communi-cate.' Disappointed, suffering from terrible headaches, he longed for

England, where 'I must look out for some cottage or farm, and...
endeavour to sell butter and cheese to advantage – do you think this
would do?'

Raffles broke his return journey from Calcutta on an island in
Tapanuli Bay; the mainland there was Batak country, and the Bataks
ate human flesh.

English people were fascinated by cannibalism as the terrifying
'dark side' of dark people in faraway countries; though they were
not so far from it, since dried and powdered human tissue – known
as 'mummy medicine' – was still a traditional remedy in Europe.
Raffles determined to 'satisfy my mind most fully in everything concerning cannibalism,' and wrote the Duchess of Somerset a frisky
letter calculated to cause a sensation in Park Lane. He intended to
go back, with Sophia, 'and should we never be heard of more you
may conclude we have been eaten.' He told the Duchess how cannibalism was regulated by law and custom, in a public ceremony,
and unaccompanied by drunkenness. According to Raffles' Batak
contacts, they ate the raw flesh of criminals after a regular trial and
sentencing, cutting slices from the living body, and dipping them in
sambul (chilli, salt and lime). Women did not partake, or only sur-
reptitiously, and all agreed the flesh was delicious.

Raffles was 'enlightened' about cannibalism. 'However horrible
eating a man may sound in European ears,' he wrote to Marsden,
'I question whether the party suffers so much, or the punishment
itself is worse than the European tortures of two centuries ago [.ie.
during the Inquisition]. I have always doubted the policy, and even
the right of capital punishment among civilised nations; but this
once admitted, and torture allowed, I see nothing more cruel in
eating a man alive than in torturing him for days with mangled
limbs and the like. Here they certainly eat him up at once, and the
party seldom suffers for more than a few minutes.'

At home in England capital punishment was a cruel public spectacle. Cousin Thomas went out of his way to attend a beheading in

London on 1 May of that same year, 1820: 'This morning five of the conspirators of Cato Street were hanged, and their heads cut off, at the Old Bailey. The mob immense, but no riot; not many soldiers there, St Sepulchre's Church railing was stove in by the pressure of the mob, and several people hurt, but none killed.' Then Cousin Thomas trotted off to hear a sermon at St Bride's.

Raffles described the Batta way of disposing of one's elderly parents. They were suspended by their hands from the horizontal branch of a tree, and when they could hang on no longer, and fell, they were sliced and eaten. He told the Duchess about a neighbourly modification by which other people's old parents, not one's own, were disposed of in this manner.

He was not back at Bencoolen until mid-March 1820 after an absence, to no good purpose, of nearly six months. Phillips officially took over as Governor of Penang on 1 March. Raffles' vain bid was a salutary reality check. He brought with him on the *Indiana* Maryanne and William Flint and their little son Charley, with Dr William Jack and Captain Robert Hull, one of Sophia's younger brothers. Sophia's third child, a second boy, was born on 21 May. He was christened Stamford Marsden, but they called him Cooksey.

Major Farquhar, due for leave when he agreed to take on Singapore, said he would take up the leave in 1820. Raffles accepted this, and appointed Travers to take over as Resident and Commandant. Flint was going to Singapore too, to be Master Attendant and Storekeeper. Farquhar wished Raffles himself would come, 'from a conviction of the public benefit likely to accrue in the present state of the rising colony by your personal presence, even if for ever so limited a time,' in order to 'strengthen by every possible means the present ardour of feeling, increasing confidence and attachment towards the British Government and Nation.' It was Sir Stamford Raffles who had the real authority, and the glamour, however well-liked Farquhar was. Farquhar acknowledged with pride the success of Singapore, 'the extraordinary rise of which from a small fishing village into a considerable commercial port in the short period of fourteen months surpasses perhaps anything of the kind in Eastern records.'

For whatever reason, Farquhar announced he was postponing his departure until the end of August 1821, though he would welcome Captain Travers and family as his guests in the interim, and Travers could help out in the Pay Department. So when Travers arrived, he learned he was to have a long wait before he took office, and a dreary job. What's more, Farquhar did not go at the end of August. He did not go that year at all, nor the next year, nor the next. Travers did not wait that long. He packed it in and took his family home to Ireland.

Nevertheless the months Travers spent in Singapore were a revelation: 'A plain on the sea beach affords ample space for the troops. At the rear stands a hill commanding a most extensive and beautiful prospect.' Fresh water was available 'wherever you please to sink a well.' The population had now passed the 6,000 mark. Ships and boats arrived every day, loading and unloading goods, attracted by the exemption from port duties, 'a busy, bustling scene'. Maryanne and her son Charles – 'Charley Boy' – arrived to join William Flint, and 'we were constantly together.' Travers sailed for Europe with his family in December 1820, not before sending a memo to the Supreme Government seeking compensation for the disappointment and expenses incurred.

Raffles sent Maryanne potatoes to plant in Singapore, and 'several cases of Nutmeg plants which I hope will be the foundation of a valuable plantation at Singapore for Charley Boy.' And then, a PS: 'Elton Hamond has blown his brains out.'

He did it on New Year's Eve 1819. In a letter left for Crabb Robinson, Hamond pleaded 'not guilty' to self-murder. 'If anything is a man's own, it is surely his life... Go on, be as merry as you can. If you can be religious, good. But don't sink the man in the Christian.'

Raffles' mother, with her daughter Ann, went to lodge in Margate on the Kent coast with Elton's mother, her sister Elizabeth. 'Remember me kindly to my Aunt Hamond,' wrote Raffles. 'The melancholy fate of Elton must have affected her and god knows she has had her troubles – some she deserved but Heaven in mercy will forgive her.'

He had the grace not to mention that the melancholy fate of Elton put paid to the second edition of *The History of Java*. Elton held all the materials.

Raffles' worry about his book sharpened when he received in Bencoolen, in early 1821, a copy of John Crawfurd's *History of the Indian Archipelago*, published the previous year in three volumes, with maps and engravings. He wrote to Cousin Thomas in that state of nervous agitation peculiar to authors faced with a new work on their own subject. The second edition of *The History of Java* 'would certainly have superseded the necessity for Crawfurd's work – at least to a considerable extent.' Crawfurd's book 'will I dare say run through a second edition, and as it is written in a very popular style will I doubt not have a successful run.' It had 'all the characteristics of the author, that is to say, considerable talent, an imposing manner, much assurance and assumption, and very little principle. It does not contain one fact that is new to me and most of the reasoning and conclusions are founded on partial views. He has laid himself open to very serious attack by stating only as many facts and just such facts as suit his own theory and has either glossed over or omitted the others altogether.' He concluded it would be better to postpone his own second edition until he was back in England, and concentrate on collecting material for it.

Raffles did not review Crawfurd's *History of the Indian Archepelago* – or not exactly. The *Quarterly Review*, a Tory journal founded by the young publisher John Murray, carried in February 1823 a late notice of Crawfurd's book combined with remarks on the first volumes of *Proceedings of the Agricultural Society established in Sumatra*, and on *Malayan Miscellanies*, both published in Bencoolen.

The piece was written by John Barrow, who had been with Lord Macartney to China and was a Fellow of the Royal Society, which may be how Raffles knew him. It was not uncommon for the (always unsigned) articles in the *Quarterly* to be compiled by a regular contributor from 'fragments' supplied by an outside expert or interested party. The treatment of Crawfurd's book is dismissive. The reviewer was 'disappointed' that 'the author has not gone beyond those more civilised portions which had already been so fully treated, and has left the remainder nearly as much a blank as he found it.' The book suffered from 'insufficient data' and a 'pseudo-philosophical spirit.'

Special criticism was made of Crawfurd's argument for the inferiority of the 'East Insular Negro...supported by the description of a solitary individual brought to England by Sir Stamford Raffles.' (This was Dick, the Papuan boy.) In addition, Crawfurd had reproduced, without any acknowledgment, the drawing of this individual 'so recently published in Sir Stamford Raffles' *History of Java.*'

Commenting next on the *Proceedings* of the Bencoolen Agricultural Society, Barrow informed the *Quarterly*'s readers: 'It opens with a sensible and well-written address, by Sir T.S.Raffles, who probably will in no great length of time bring the districts of Sumatra contiguous to our settlement into the same state of prosperity as the island of Java enjoyed under his most judicious and active sway.' The information on Sumatra 'enables us to conclude that a great extension of European capital and enterprise is alone wanting to render Bencoolen a valuable and important possession.' Raffles must have sent Barrow a pretty comprehensive packet of 'fragments'; and a notice of Crawfurd's *History of the Indian Archipelago* was transformed into a promotion of Sir Stamford Raffles.

Anxiety remained that the expanding settlement in Singapore might have to be evacuated and handed over to the Dutch. The 'paper war' crackled on. The Dutch Ambassador in London, the British Ambassador in Brussels, Foreign Secretaries and statesmen in both countries, the Court of Directors, John Palmer, Lord

Hastings, the Java Government – all wrote hundreds of pages of protests and counter-protests, some on a lofty geopolitical level and some vituperative of Sir Stamford Raffles.

Raffles had a few supporters in India House, among them Sophia's brother-in-law Peter Auber, Charles Grant, and the hydrographer James Horsburgh FRS, who wrote to the Court of Directors that 'the settlement of Singapore, lately established by Sir Stamford Raffles' was in his opinion 'of the utmost importance both in a political and commercial point of view to the British Empire.' He wished this opinion to be communicated to Mr Canning. In fact the European powers had no intention of going to war over it, and the longer Singapore flourished, the less likely it was to be handed over.

In Bencoolen, Raffles retreated into a private Garden of Eden, planting coffee and spice-gardens on his property, and an avenue of cloves up to his country house. Sophia and 'the three pets' were well, Leopold 'the handsomest and the most princely little fellow that ever lived.' The house, Permatang Balan, was airy and spacious: 'We have a Noble Bed Room, 32 feet by 22 with a Verandah and Venetian doors all round.' Sophia was 'as big as the house.' As he wrote to his mother, 'My three little darlings are rapidly advancing to make way for a fourth – if we go on at this rate we shall require at least two ships to convey us home.'

Sophia wrote in the *Memoir* that 'the beauty, the retirement, the quiet domestic life, which he led in this happy retreat, soon restored his health.' He rose at four, worked in the garden until breakfast, and wrote and studied until dinner. Then he walked in his plantations, 'always accompanied by his children.' 'I have thrown politics far away,' he told William Brown Ramsay. And to the Duchess, in June 1820: 'My dear little Charlotte is, of all creatures, the most angelic I ever beheld...she has a soft heart, and is so full of mildness and gentleness that I fear she will have many trials to go through in this unfeeling world. Her brother Leopold, however, will take her part; for he has the spirit of a lion and is absolutely beautiful.' At two and a half, Charlotte chattered in English, Hindustani or Malay, depending on her company.

As for himself, 'I am no longer striding from one side of India to another, overleaping mountains, or forming new countries – I am trying to do the best I can with a very old and nearly worn-out one.' He did admit physical frailty to the Duchess; he did not think that he would last more than another two or three years in the Indies.

Besides, there were 'my dear little rogues' to consider. Charlotte was advanced for her age. 'In two or three years both her mind and body will require a colder climate.' But to send the children home 'as people usually send their children from this country, is out of the question.' Raffles could not think of breaking up the family. He planned for them all to leave together when the time was right. 'Leopold will also, in two or three years, have grown beyond my management, and it will be time to commence upon the rudiments of a better education than I can give him.'

Sophia, in retrospect, thought 'this was one of the most happy periods' in Raffles' whole life. She recalled how, after their dinner guests left, her husband was 'fond of walking out with the Editor, and enjoying the delicious coolness of the night land-wind, and a moon whose beauty only those who have been in tropical climates can judge of.'

He had attained his great object in the establishment of Singapore. He was on good terms with the natives and Chiefs in Bencoolen. He was taking a census of the settlement and its hinterland, and building new roads, and compiling a comparative vocabulary of the Nias and Batta languages. He had ordered an armed incursion into the offshore island of Nias, where slave auctions were attended by traders from all over the region, in the hope of suppressing the revolting trade. This was another of Raffles' unauthorised initiatives which infuriated his employers in London, and for which he was censured. And Bencoolen showed no profit. 'The charges of the establishment have, I fear, rather increased than otherwise,' he confessed to Peter Auber in July 1820. But then 'all changes and reforms' are expensive, and although 'all my plans lead to real and practical economy, some liberality in effecting them is indispensible in the nature of things.'

The fourth baby, Ella Sophia, was born on Stamford Marsden Raffles' first birthday. Sophia made a good recovery: 'She seems so contented that I am almost afraid there is another on the stocks and yet god forbid!' This letter to Maryanne, written 23 June 1821, has an undertow of foreboding. The Flints had complaints about Singapore. Raffles advised Maryanne and her husband to keep to themselves, and avoid quarrels. 'I wish to God Farquhar himself would be more particular in his own conduct.' Farquhar, now Lieutenant-Colonel Farquhar, was sending his reports to Bengal, with copies to Raffles, and not the other way round as instructed.

'Leopold has been unwell for the past fortnight and is a good deal pulled down, but we think he is getting better...'

Chapter 12

'My Almost Only Child'

Bencoolen and Singapore 1821–1823

On 27 June 1821, the day fixed for baby Ella's christening, their world changed. 'Our house of joy has been turned into a house of mourning.' The letters say it all.

'How shall I tell you,' Raffles wrote to Maryanne, 'that we have lost our dear darling Leopold… This awful event has overwhelmed us with so much sorrow and misery, that it is impossible to write – tis a cruel stroke and of all my Children, to take the flower – is cruel indeed, and our hearts are ready to break. My whole Soul was wrapped up in him…Poor Sophia is heartbroken and wretched…the other children are well – but really they are nothing in the scale to our dear Leopold…My heart is too full to add more.'

Two days later he added another letter to the packet to tell her that Captain Harry Auber, Sophia's brother-in-law who was staying with them, had also died; and that 'the loss of Sophia's milk has proved really serious to our last babe – Ella – poor little thing, we hardly know whether it will live or die, we think it better today.' Sophia was 'getting about' again but 'far from being herself.' Raffles himself had been 'desperately ill', his legs and feet swollen from the knees down. 'I am however getting better and do not mean to die this bout.'

By September, little Ella was now 'one of the finest and most lovely children that ever was seen,' but 'poor Cooksey' was teething and running a fever. 'Charlotte is becoming a great girl and is wonderfully improving... On the whole, we are beginning to revive.'

Not until November did Sophia manage to pick up her pen to tell her mother about the loss of Leopold. As for Raffles, 'I am at this moment under the operation of mercury, and maintain but a crazy existence.' Then on 20 December: 'Our dear Charlotte was suddenly taken ill in the same manner as poor Leopold and for about a week we had no hope for her life.' Against their principles, they were now set on despatching the three children home under the charge of Nurse Grimes. 'Poor dears, we should not be justified in keeping [them] here longer at such risk merely for our own gratification.' His handwriting was shaky.

Charlotte remained 'terribly pulled down and altered, no one would know her to be the same child.' The plan was for the children and Nurse Grimes to leave in March, 'so that you may rest assured we do not calculate upon any further increase in this country. What we may do at home [in England] is another thing – time enough for that.' Sophia liked being pregnant, and Raffles was uxorious. Sophia was in reasonable health, but 'for my part I am complaining [i.e. suffering] and fear I cannot stand the climate much longer... I hope Flint is making a collection of handsome Tortoiseshell for me. I don't mind what may be the quantity, but the quality must be the best... If he falls in with a lot of cheap diamonds, I would like to have them.' Raffles' great fear was of the whole family landing up back in England with nothing to live on. None of them had ever been any good at saving.

Then a 'new and most unexpected affliction' knocked them back. Fourth of January 1822, to Maryanne: 'Last night robbed us of our last and only remaining Boy.'

Cooksey's teething troubles seemed better, but then 'he was seized with a violent bowel complaint.' They had left him in 'apparently a tranquil and reviving sleep,' but were soon called up, 'and in less than half an hour he was a corpse – poor fellow he now lies in his coffin.' Charlotte was 'a perfect skeleton without life and spirits and scarcely knows anyone. All our hopes depend on our being able to get her off early for England' with baby Ella, but they still had to wait two or three months for the arrival of the *Borneo*. 'Poor Sophia – will you not pity her from your soul...but god's will be done and we must be reconciled.'

Sophia was 'in agony' at the idea of sending Charlotte home 'in a ship without a medical man and poor accommodation' but she did not think of accompanying the children herself. As Raffles wrote, it would be hard parting with them 'but as she prefers her husband to her children her determination to remain with me was no difficult matter.'

Ten days later he opened the letter to add a postscript: 'Charlotte has just been snatched from us. I have nothing more to add.'

Within six months, he and Sophia had lost three of their children. They were shattered in spirit and body, suffering themselves from the dysentery that had drained the life from the children, and poisoned by mercury treatments. Raffles had attacks of what he called 'brain fever' – the crippling headaches which confined him to the bedroom and 'almost made me mad.'

Raffles' response to the collapse of their hopes was to send in his resignation to the Company, giving extreme ill health as the reason and requesting to be relieved of his present charge 'at the close of the next year.' A few more years' salary seemed no longer a priority. As he said to Cousin Thomas, on 29 January 1822: 'We were never very covetous of affluence – and riches are now of less value to us than ever.' He was cultivating oats and barley on his estate on which he hoped to see a good return before he left, and experimenting with milling sugar, with no experience – 'We took our model from the Encyclopaedia.' The reply to his resignation letter from India House expressed conventional regret, and 'Although we have had occasion strongly to express our disapprobation of some of your proceedings at Fort Marlborough, we are disposed fully to acknowledge your integrity, zeal and ability.'

The *Borneo* carrying Ella – their 'last little prattler' – and Nurse Grimes sailed on 4 March 1822, carrying also a cargo of pepper and spices, part of which Raffles was trading on his own account. He had somehow to raise cash, for the reasons he explained to Joseph Dart, the Company's Secretary in London: 'In consequence of…the necessity I have felt myself under of providing funds for a portion of my family proceeding to and residing in England, I have availed myself of the opportunity afforded by the present consignment of spices to the Court to include a quantity to the value of 8000 d[ollars] on my own account, a measure to which I trust the Honble Court will not object under the circumstances above stated, and the more particularly as the said amount is in excess of what I was authorised by the Board of Trade to purchase.'

The *Borneo* slipped over the horizon. 'What a sad and lonely house, without nurse and the children,' he wrote to Peter Auber two days later, 'we wander from room to room, solitary and dejected. But God's will be done, and we must be content.'

Permatang Balang had only ever been an oasis in the festering society of Bencoolen. Two of Raffles' ADCs, Captains Watson and Methven, turned rogue, and Raffles dealt severely with them. Weakness was causing him to lash out – the one thing he was always warning William Flint not to do. 'I hope to god you and Flint keep quiet – avoid hot water – and tell him that if he keeps his temper he may be right, but if he loses it he must be wrong.' Raffles was not going to be capable of following his own advice.

Unlike Sophia, Raffles was not sustained by a strong Christian belief. His attitude to religion was pragmatic. Elton Hamond, in whose nonsense lurked some sense, had written in his farewell letter: 'If you can be religious, good! But don't sink the man in the Christian.' Raffles never sank the man in the Christian. He believed in the benign efficacy of Christian principles, but never referred to Christ, or salvation, or redemption, and – this was a statement of a sort – nearly always wrote 'god' with a lower-case 'g'. He used the

term 'Providence', as did many nominal Christians, more comfortably than the word God, or god.

He was a fatalist and keenly aware of hubris. Sophia in her *Memoir*
recalled that during the idyllic times with the children and animals at
Bencoolen, 'Sir Stamford never forgot that the scene was too bright
to continue unclouded, and often gently warned the Editor not to
expect to retain all the blessings God in his bounty had heaped upon
them at this time.' Telling Thomas Murdoch about the loss of the
children, he observed that 'We were, perhaps, too happy, too proud
of our blessings.'

The Company had never allowed Christian proselytising, though
it was permitted to appoint chaplains in their settlements for the
benefit of Company personnel. The renewal of the Company's
Charter in 1813 (which brought to an end the Company's monopoly of trade with India) brought about a volte-face, after pressure
on the Company from religious enthusiasts and evangelicals. By
the terms of the Charter, missionaries were encouraged to settle in
India (including the Eastern Isles), and the Company was required
to appoint a Bishop and three Archdeacons in Calcutta.

Pressure to admit missionaries came from within India House as
well as from outside. Charles Grant, Director and off-and-on Chairman of the Court over many years, was a member of the evangelical
Clapham Sect. A letter from Grant to Raffles dated 19 July 1820 is
nuanced, starting with a by-now familiar barrage of censure: 'You
are probably aware of the obstacles which have been opposed to
the adoption of your measures [re Singapore], and even threatened
your position in the service. Your zeal considerably outstepped your
prudence...'

But then came a paragraph to lighten Raffles' heart: 'The acquisition of Singapore has grown in importance... It is now accredited
in the India House. Of late, in an examination before a committee
of the House of Lords, I gave my opinion of the value, in a moral,
political, and commercial view, of a British establishment in the
locality of Singapore, under the auspices of the Company. From all

these circumstances and others, I augur well as to the retention and encouragement of the station your rapidity has pre-occupied. Accept of these few hints instead of an elaborate letter.'

Grant's final sentence may also be read as a 'hint' – or a word to the wise: 'I have heard of your efforts for introducing religious improvement into Bencoolen. I hope that disposition will follow you wherever you go.'

This was one way that Raffles could mitigate the Company's dis-approval, though he was not himself in favour of trying to impose Christianity. As he had written from Buitenzorg to Cousin Thomas: 'I am a good deal more inclined than you are to let people go to heaven in their own way. I foresee much mischief – much bitterness of heart and contention – by an inordinate desire after conversion.' He was '*Utopian* enough' to think that a system 'founded on the principles of Christianity, and modified according to the temper of the people, would be far better than the naked revelation at once, which they would neither admire or relish.' This was the only subject on which Raffles advocated caution and gradualism; he was not ego-involved.

Missionaries – non-conformist Protestants – became a presence in the Archipelago, distributing their Bibles, catechisms and tracts. Raffles reported to Cousin Thomas in February 1815 on a handful who arrived under the London Missionary Society's auspices: 'Your friend Mr Supper has been fixed at Batavia – he is a good simple creature, rather silly, but amiable.' The missionaries Raffles liked were the kind of men he would have liked in any walk of life. The Rev. William Milne was 'a liberal, well-informed, excellent man'; Milne had co-founded the Anglo-Chinese College at Malacca.

Raffles did not conceal from Cousin Thomas that he thought most missionaries were useless: 'Had I been a Missionary myself I think I could have evangelised the whole island by this time.' He approved of the Rev. William Robinson, who opened a school, seemed 'a good practical sort of fellow,' and preached in Malay. But most knew no Malay and 'so far as I can see, do nothing.' But with missionar-ies came printing-presses. Raffles caused some resentment among the Baptist missionaries in Bencoolen by hijacking their press for Government notices and proclamations, not to mention his own natural history material, using the mission presses as one would use a photocopier.

Raffles told Maryanne he had 'no particular inclination' to return to Singapore, suspecting he would be sailing into trouble. William Flint had set himself on a collision course with Lieutenant-Colonel William Farquhar. On arrival in Singapore, he took over the well-paid positions of Master Attendant and Marine Storekeeper, as promised by Raffles, which meant displacing the temporary holder of the offices: Farquhar's son-in-law Francis Bernard. That in itself required more tact than Flint possessed. Flint then proceeded to channel constant protests to Raffles in Bencoolen about his demeaning treatment by Farquhar – bureaucratic trivia.

Raffles, for Maryanne's sake, defended Flint. But in July 1822 he wrote her a exasperated letter: 'As you love and respect your brother – for God's sake restrain Flint from [illegible] himself with Farquhar – he has done so already and so seriously that I hardly know how to act – don't think of *yourselves* but of *me* – everything of the kind bars and neutralises all my intentions. You know not how seriously you are injuring me by these proceedings.'

There were other bones of contention. Farquhar allowed his son, Andrew, to export rice to Rhio against the regulations, and he himself had had imported nine chests of opium from Calcutta, passed them to Francis Bernard to sell, and placed the proceeds with an agency house in Singapore. Farquhar reported this transaction to Raffles as a private transfer of funds, but Raffles was angry.

He and Sophia were to have left Bencoolen for Singapore on 15 September 1822, but an adverse wind held them back. So they were there to witness another sad death – of Dr William Jack, their dear friend, who had kept Sophia happy during her pregnancy in Penang, and delivered baby Ella. He was all set to be Raffles' collaborator on his second edition.

They sailed a couple of days later on the *Minto* with Sophia's youngest brother Nilson Hull, Captain Salmond, and a doctor. Raffles planned to stay six months in Singapore (he stayed eight) with the intention – as he wrote to Cousin Thomas – 'of arranging and modelling something like a constitution for the place, and transferring its future management to a successor [to Farquhar].' They would return to Bencoolen 'for the purpose of winding up.' after which 'we contemplate the prospect of revisiting old England.'

They reached Singapore on 10 October. Raffles had not been back for two and a half years. The next day he wrote to a friend in England: 'The coldest and most disinterested could not quit Bencoolen and land at Singapore, without surprise and emotion... After all the risks and dangers to which this my almost only child had been exposed, to find it grown and advanced beyond measure, and even my warmest anticipations and expectations.' He had thought that the time had passed when he could take much interest in it 'but I already feel differently; I feel a new life and vigour about me.'

He went into action. Since Singapore was a dependency of Bencoolen, and Raffles was Lieutenant-Governor of Bencoolen, he was Lieutenant-Governor of Singapore as well. Nilson Hull was his Acting Secretary, through whom Raffles communicated with the Resident, Lieutenant-Colonel Farquhar, on all official business. Farquhar had no Secretary, although his sons-in-law Captain Davis and Francis Bernard acted as his Assistants. Only days after his arrival, Raffles 'discontinued' Bernard's post as Farquhar's Assistant.

The success of the settlement was not in question. In 1822, 139 square-rigged ships and 1,434 native vessels called in to trade. As Raffles told the Duchess on 30 November: 'Here all is life and activity; and it would be difficult to name a place on the face of the globe, with brighter prospects or more present satisfaction. In little more than three years it has risen from an insignificant fishing village to a large and prosperous town, containing at least 10,000 inhabitants of all nations, actively involved in commercial pursuits, which afford to each and all a handsome livelihood and abundant profit.' Any letter to the Duchess had a public-relations aspect; and there was a darker side.

Many of Raffles' instructions had been disregarded by Farquhar, and measures had been taken which he deplored and proceeded to overturn. Outraged to learn that slaves were being sold on the river near Farquhar's house, he called Farquhar's attention to the fact that slave-trading was a felony by Act of Parliament for any British subject. The Resident's response was that 'circumstances' accounted for the irregularity. Farquhar, in the thick of it, far away from both Bencoolen and Bengal, had made his accommodations pragmatically.

Raffles certainly did not want to antagonise Farquhar. He wrote to John Brown – one of his remaining friends in Penang – on 12 November 1822:

> I am afraid our friend Farquhar is a little annoyed because I
> do not approve of his European Town, as he calls it…but I
> trust it will not be long before he comes around to my opinions
> generally. It can never be my wish or interest to annoy him nor
> his to annoy me. We have both a great interest in the prosperity
> of the place and it must not be allowed to go into confusion
> for want of due precautions. You know that he is sometimes
> as good-natured as he is stubborn at others, and I don't think
> either of these failings decrease with his years [Farquhar was in
> his late forties] but he has a warm and kind heart and while that
> is the case we must make allowances for minor defects.

John Crawfurd called in at Singapore for a week that November, back from a commercial mission to Siam and Cambodia and on his way to Bengal. Crawfurd inspected the 'Singapore Stone' at the entrance to the salt creek; he took his morning walk round the Singapore Hill, now cleared and 'clothed with a fine grassy sward', and identified the boundaries of the ancient city. It can be inferred from Raffles' letters to Wallich that Raffles spoke to Crawfurd during this week about his taking over from Farquhar as Resident.

The most extreme – and the most costly – of Raffles' reversals of Farquhar's policy was over land allocation. Raffles had designated the north-eastern bank of the river for Government offices and public buildings. Farquhar had allowed European merchants to build their wharves and warehouses there; the stretch of shore which Raffles had allocated to the merchants in 1819 turned out to be impractical for loading and unloading because of the heavy surf. The south-west side of the river, where the Chinese were settled, was equally unsuitable because of its salt-marsh swampiness.

Raffles had also ruled that the original Cantonment – now the Esplanade – was to be kept clear as a public space; Farquhar had allowed haphazard domestic housing on it, and built his own spacious Residency bungalow there, as did Claude Queiros, a Eurasian protégé of John Palmer and his personal representative in Singapore. Though Palmer was still a gadfly to Raffles, his influence was waning. Associated with his half-Indian half-brother William in an agency house in Hyderabad, he was disgraced when a new-broom British Resident, Charles Metcalfe, discovered they were exacting from the Nizam excessive and illegal interest on loans.

Raffles ruled that all structures erected in the 'wrong' places in Singapore must be moved or demolished. He appointed a Town Planning Committee, and a young Second Lieutenant, Philip Jackson, as Executive Engineer and Surveyor. Raffles ordered the Chinese to be moved inland from the south-west bank to make space for the European merchants' warehouses and offices; the swampy land was made viable by raising levels, draining and infilling. Hundreds of labourers were employed to carry earth and rocks for the landfill, supervised by Raffles himself.

He rearranged the 'native divisions' or *kampong*s, which necessitated the removal of hundreds of people, quite apart from the Chinese, whom Raffles surmised, quite correctly, would 'always form by far the largest portion of the community.' The new villages for the Bugis, Arabs, Chuliahs and Malays were to be sited with care for their respective religious sensibilities; two hundred acres were cleared for a new village for the Temenggong. There were plans made for markets, police stations, a marine yard. The disruption was on a massive scale.

An architect, George Coleman – Irish, from Co. Louth, still in his early twenties – arrived in Singapore a few months before Raffles. Waiting for him, Coleman designed a Residency House. He was to have a major impact on the development of the town, and died in 1844 in a house designed by himself in Coleman Street, named in his honour. His main work was done after Raffles left, and included the Armenian Church. Young Coleman became Raffles' advisor on the grid of central streets, divided into first, second and third class depending on the width of the houses' frontages.

The shop-houses (shops or small businesses with living space above) were only twenty feet wide, apparently so as to match the standard length of the timbers cut from the jungle trees. The tight terraces were to have open verandahs forming a continuous arcaded walkway on both sides of the street – the 'five-foot way' – not unique to Singapore, but characteristic of the Singapore streetscape until the cataclysmic urban renewal of recent years. Raffles also commissioned a drawbridge over the Singapore River, which was completed in August 1823.

By that time, Raffles had gone. Philip Jackson drew up the first known map of Singapore, a speculative plan not quite transferred into reality on the ground. Coleman made better sense of his layout, mostly following Raffles' instructions, after Raffles left.

Nathaniel Wallich, like Coleman, arrived before Raffles, en route for China to collect plants. He stayed, spending his leave in Singapore instead and coinciding with Raffles for about six weeks – long enough to cement their informal and familiar friendship: 'Lady R. is dressing or would answer your note herself,' wrote Raffles; and 'Sophia tells me I may expect to see you at breakfast.'

A section of Singapore Hill – the Forbidden Hill (now Fort Canning) – became the European cemetery. Raffles recruited Nathaniel Wallich, who had with him two apprentices and the head overseer from the Calcutta Botanic Garden, to help him establish a Botanic and Experimental Garden on the other side, planned to cover the whole north-eastern slope and beyond. Houses within the perimeter had to be cleared, and their owners compensated and rehoused. The budget for the Garden's development was sixty dollars a month, to include ten labourers and an overseer. There were some six-hundred-year-old fruit trees on the site, in a decayed condition. Wallich assured Raffles he would find 'pride and satisfaction' in superintending the project.

But Raffles' Botanic and Experimental Garden did not thrive. He himself had the paths laid out, and Wallich left Dr William Montgomerie, Medical Officer of the settlement, in charge when he left for Calcutta – but then, Montgomerie never heard another word from Wallich about it. Montgomerie continued planting spices after Raffles left Singapore, but when he too left to take up a post in India the project languished, and in 1829 the Garden on the Hill was officially abandoned. (The great Botanic Gardens at Tanglin were not founded until 1859.)

When Raffles and Sophia arrived in 1822 they stayed with the Flints in their house at the end of the Point, a simple structure with matting walls and an *atap* roof. Raffles decided to build the Governor's Residence on Singapore Hill. After a farewell dinner the evening before he left for Calcutta, Wallich determined the precise site of the projected Residence. Raffles sent a note to him on shipboard next day: 'I marked out the site of a small bungalow on the Hill where you threw the stone last night...' Raffles already had Coleman's design, and the house, begun in November 1822, was finished by January 1823.

The materials were probably not as Coleman had specified. Raffles cannot be accused of extravagance. The bungalow had rough plank walls, verandahs at front and back, and an *atap* roof. Its frontage was a hundred feet, and its depth fifty feet. The interior consisted of two large rooms, with small square 'wings' on each side for bedrooms.

It was not substantial, and seemed sometimes in danger of being swept away by the wind. After Raffles left, Coleman supervised a makeover using brick and tile, and added a neo-classical pediment. With subsequent improvements, Raffles' Residency House lasted until 1859.

The project dearest to Raffles' heart was the Singapore Institution. Although it had been in his mind ever since 1819, he founded his 'native college' only towards the end of this last stay, holding the inaugural meeting on 1 April 1823. He invited all the principal inhabitants of the place, including the Sultan and Temenggong. The Institution could not have got off the ground without the input and co-operation of the missionary community; his main collaborator was the Rev. Robert Morrison, co-founder with Milne of the Anglo-Chinese College in Malacca.

The Institution was to comprise a 'literary and moral' department for the Chinese, a 'literary and moral' department for Siamese, Malays and others, and a 'scientific department' to serve both. The scientific department was to offer natural philosophy, natural history, chemistry and the elements of anatomy and medical science.

Natural philosophy, to include 'the Newtonian system of astronomy' and 'the mechanical and chemical properties of matter', was to be taught through the medium of English. But it was expected that professors in the scientific department should 'pay attention to the native languages' with a view to translating scientific books. 'When funds can afford it' there would be an observatory, and an astronomical clock.

The purpose was to 'educate the sons of the higher order of natives and others,' including Europeans who wanted to learn native languages. Raffles named and appointed 'native masters' for Malay, Javanese, Siamese, Bugguese, Arabic and Pali. Another object was 'to collect the scattered literature and traditions of the country' and publish and circulate the most important. There was to be a library.

Raffles was the Patron, and appointed Trustees, co-opting in absentia William Wilberforce, Charles Grant and William Marsden; he planned to establish a 'Committee of Co-Operation' in London. Among the resident Trustees were Lieutenant-Colonel Farquhar and Captain Flint, Captain Davis (another of Farquhar's sons-in-law) and British merchants who were Raffles' friends. He appointed a Secretary and a Management Committee, and made provision for a President, a Principal and a Treasurer – the latter two both the same person, the Rev. G.H.Thompson, who was also the Professor of Malayan Languages. Mrs Thompson was to organise a class for girls.

The Institution's motto was Raffles' own: 'Auspicium Melioris Aevi.' He compiled statutes and byelaws. 'It shall be the duty of the officers of the College to cherish, at all times, a paternal feeling of kindness to the students' and to 'set an example of patience, moderation, good temper, and assiduity.' 'Pagans, Christians and Mahomedans are all admissible as students.' The religious requirements were Rafflesian: 'The forms of Protestant worship will be observed…but neither native students nor Native Masters are compelled to attend Christian worship.' The European officers of the Institution were to be Protestant Christians; but the Native Masters 'may or may not be Christians,' but they 'shall be, when practicable, correct moral men, according to the opinion of their own nation.' The Rev. Mr Milton, in charge of the Chinese school and Professor of Siamese, was commissioned to purchase presses, and to supply fonts in English, Malayan and Siamese.

Funds were raised by subscription. John Palmer declined to contribute; he would have done so 'when all was Sunshine with me,' even though he feared 'the *precocity* of the scheme.' There was 'a donation from Lieutenant-Governor Raffles on behalf of the East India Company' equal to his personal subscription (2,000 Spanish dollars). Raffles had no authority to commit the Company but the Company honoured the commitment.

Farquhar subscribed 1,000, and Lady Raffles 200. The projected sale of the Anglo-Chinese College in Malacca, which Raffles planned to merge with the Institution (this never happened), ought to bring in 4,000. A fortnight after the first meeting subscriptions, actual or notional, amounted to 17,495 Spanish dollars. As a result, 15,000 dollars were voted for the construction of buildings to a plan drawn up by Lieutenant Jackson, to be completed within twelve months. The site, which Raffles and Farquhar chose together, was a hundred acres on Bras Basah Road (where Raffles Shopping City is now).

Raffles envisaged the Institution, through its generations of future alumni, as 'the means of civilising and bettering the conditions of millions' way beyond Singapore. It was his 'last public Act,' he told Wallich. 'It is here that I think I may have done some little good and instead of frittering the stock of zeal and means that may yet be left me in objects for which I may not be fitted, I am anxious to do all the good I can *here*.' He wished he could infuse into it 'a portion of that spirit and soul by which I would have animated it as easily as I endow it with lands etc.'

It was all projected at speed, within weeks of his departure. Dr William Montgomerie, who was to teach anatomy and medical science, also left Singapore soon afterwards, as did the Rev. Robert Morrison. Even though he was not even in Singapore in 1823, the designated Professor of Natural History was George Finlayson – a naturalist whom Raffles met with John Crawfurd when their ship called in at Singapore en route for Bengal, and to whom he instantly established a strong attachment. Finlayson was, Raffles later wrote, 'indefatigable' as a botanist and a gifted writer 'even though he may not rank with a Burns, or a Leyden, in point of talent.' In November 1823, when he was back in Bencoolen, he heard that Finlayson had died; he wrote a 'Memoir' of Finlayson to accompany his published Journal of the Mission to Siam; the *Literary Gazette*'s reviewer (December 1825) commented that 'the memoir speaks very feelingly, and the account is an affecting one.' Like so many of Raffles' arrangements for the Institution, Finlayson's appointment as professor had been purely aspirational.

Unsurprisingly, work on the Singapore Institution stalled after Raffles, Montgomerie and Morrison left. Construction did not get going until four years later, and was shoddily done. Grants continued to be made by the Supreme Government, but the project was mismanaged and virtually abandoned after some years. The buildings deteriorated and fell into decay.

But Raffles' vision of the Institution survived. It was rebuilt, with added wings, in the 1830s: this is the so-called 'old' Singapore Institution depicted in a watercolour of 1841. It continued to transform itself through Singapore's successive cataclysmic upheavals. Today, re-named the Raffles Institution, and affiliated to the Raffles Girls' School, it is an independent secondary school on a campus in central Singapore. It still claims to be animated by Raffles' 'spirit and soul', Raffles' motto is still the school motto, and Raffles' coat of arms is its crest. 'Old Rafflesians' distinguish themselves all over the world.

Raffles and Sophia found new friends in Singapore. The merchant David Skene Napier, a trustee of the Singapore Institution, was the son of Professor Macvey Napier, editor of the *Edinburgh Review*; and it was through Professor Napier that the honorary degree of LL.D from the University of Edinburgh was conferred on Raffles in 1825. David Skene Napier, with his first wife Anna – 'the Naps' – came to occupy the place in the Raffleses' and Flints' lives previously filled by 'the Tots'.

Maryanne's daughter, also Sophia but known as Sophie, was born while Raffles and Sophia were in Singapore. They had no word of their own Ella's safe arrival in England before they left Bencoolen. Raffles wrote to his mother that they were 'not a little anxious – at one time I thought she would be our only one, but I think there are at last certain signs of another forthcoming in about six or seven months… We are in hopes it may be a Boy – but I fear we shall never have another like our dear Leopold.'

The Raffleses were irredeemably philoprogenitive, but Sophia sadly miscarried that baby. On the way to Singapore, Raffles wrote to Cousin Thomas that 'the delicate health of Mrs Raffles [Thomas's wife] should be removed by breeding – at least so I find it with my Wife who is always best when coming into bearing and shewing fruit.' When in April they at last heard that Ella and Nurse Grimes were safe with Sophia's parents in Cheltenham, Sophia became pregnant again. 'Lady Raffles being in the family way,' Raffles wrote to Wallich, 'all other complaints seem to be absorbed as her pregnancy advances.'

The Rafflesian fertility was, to the Naps, enviable, and Raffles took on the role of counsellor in the matter of making babies. His advice was to keep trying, but not too stressfully. He wrote to Maryanne after his return to Bencoolen about 'my dear little friend, Nap's wife' who 'by listening to *my* counsel is again with child – these things come of course if people would only have patience and perseverance. Nothing is gained by being in too great a hurry...'

The Naps were good friends, but as always Raffles felt that he lacked informed, sensible colleagues on his own level. Maryanne and William Flint were anything but sensible. Nothing in Java or Sumatra had prepared him for the utter newness of Singapore. 'I assure you,' he told the Duchess, 'I stand much in need of advice, and were it not for Lady Raffles, I should have no counsellor at all. She is nevertheless a host to me, and if I do live to see you again, it will be entirely owing to her love and affection; without this I should have been cast away long ago.'

'A host to me'? He must have meant that Sophia sustained his life as the *Rafflesia arnoldii* was sustained by the tree on which it was poised, connected by tissue as fine as silk. Once, she had been dependent on him – parasitical. Now it was perhaps the other way round.

Whatever the quality of her advice, Sophia could not prevent the deterioration of the relations between Raffles and Farquhar. In the letter of 8 December Raffles said to Nathaniel Wallich: 'Since you left us, I have been compelled to some rather sharp correspondence with the King *Malachi* [i.e. Farquhar, 'King of Malacca'] of which and other things he will no doubt complain abroad – but I am happy to say that personally we remain as you left us and that I perceive symptoms which induce me to believe that he now takes a different view of my measures to what he did at first.' Farquhar, like Raffles, did not want a showdown.

Raffles and Sophia moved into their new bungalow on the Hill. 'Nothing,' he told William Marsden, 'can be more interesting and beautiful than the view from this spot.' They looked down on to the High Street and out to the harbour, alive with the movements of vessels from many nations – except from England. No English ships entered the port of Singapore in its first four years, officially discouraged so as not inflame the Dutch while the 'paper war' was ongoing.

'Our abode on the Hill,' was 'very roomy and comfortable,' he told Wallich. Ominously, he told his friend that he had had 'several alarming attacks since you left us – one not many days ago when the doctor wanted to hurry me off to England by a ship on the eve of sailing – but let what will happen I cannot move from hence until my place can be supplied here, even if it should be my fate to leave my bones below ground... The house is full of carpenters and bustle and my hand is unsteady.' The 'attacks' were his terrible headaches. It might have been better for Raffles' happiness if he had taken that ship for England, but it would not have made any difference to the headaches.

Between 1 January 1823 and his departure in June, while planning the Institution he rolled out a raft of regulations. The first concerned the registration of land, to control unauthorised building development. The second re-established Singapore as a free port, 'the trade thereof open to ships and vessels of every nation free of duty, equally and alike to all,' with special responsibilities for port management allocated to the Master Attendant (William Flint).

The third concerned the police, and the appointment of Magistrates. The fourth prohibited all gaming-houses and cockpits as

'being highly destructive to the morals and happiness of the people.'
The fifth concerned slavery 'which my Representative seems to have
permitted to an unlimited extent.' All slaves and slave-debtors in
Singapore were entitled to claim their freedom, apart from those in
the households of the Sultan and the Temenggong 'out of deference
to their authority, as not coming under the operation of slave laws.'
The sixth established the Resident's Court, with the assistance of
two Magistrates, and Raffles himself, to sit every Monday at nine
a.m., their business being to try causes beyond the jurisdiction of
the Magistrates' Court.

In his 'Scale of Crimes and Punishments' simple or culpable
homicide incurred solitary confinement. The punishment of murder
'by Amok' was 'To suffer death, with confiscation of property; and
the body to be ignominiously exposed on a gibbet for twenty-four
hours.' This constituted a post-hoc ratification of Raffles' extreme
reaction when in March that year William Farquhar was stabbed
by a Malay, causing much loss of blood but no danger to life. The
Malay was killed. Raffles, that very night, commissioned an iron
cage from the blacksmiths. The point, for him, was that an assault
on British authority in the person of the Resident was not to be
tolerated. The next morning he had the Malay's corpse drummed
round the town in a buffalo cart and then suspended from a gibbet
inside the iron cage. This was contentious. Raffles' actions could
have inflamed the Malays against all Europeans. Raffles was shrewd
enough to take counsel with the Sultan and the Temenggong; the
body was taken down, released to the Sultan, and buried 'with lus-
tration and prayers'.

Prince Leopold's niece Victoria was born in the year that Raffles
founded Singapore. Singapore represented for Raffles the glorious
realisation, in miniature, of his fantasy of good governance under
British rule with himself as the 'great Mogul' – as Queen Victoria would be as Empress of India. Raffles achieved his dream only
because, while Singapore had great geopolitical significance, it was

such a small-scale polity – not, like Java, a whole intractable country, nor, like Bencoolen, a run-down settlement on the edge of another large intractable country.

During the happy time at Bencoolen in 1820, he marshalled his thoughts in two letters to Thomas Murdoch, who was not in the political loop – an older man, a Fellow of the Royal Society, and a former wine merchant in Madeira. Raffles got to know him when he was in London on leave, and used materials on the Portuguese colonial period in Murdoch's library while compiling *The History of Java*. He wrote to Murdoch about the relationship between the rulers and the ruled.

His thrust was that there is no one template for Europeans who set themselves in authority over other peoples. The same system would not work in Sumatra as in Java. In Bencoolen, he had to assume 'a new character' among the people, 'that of lord paramount', because the Sumatrans were 'perhaps a thousand years' behind the Javanese. 'In Java, I advocated the doctrine of the liberty of the subject, and the individual rights of man – here [in Bencoolen] I am the advocate for despotism. The strong arm of power is necessary to bring men together, and to concentrate them in societies, and there is a certain stage in which despotic authority seems the only means of promoting civilisation.'

'There appear to be certain stages and gradations through which society must run its course to civilisation, and which can be no more overleaped or omitted, than men can arrive at maturity without passing through the gradations of infancy and youth. Independence is the characteristic of the savage state,' and only a despotic power can bind people into an economic and social entity. At a later stage of a society's development the 'seeds of internal freedom' are sown, in order to 'set limits to that power whenever it may engender abuse.'

Raffles did not reflect that the abuses of despots are not generally checked for the asking.

'I cannot be one of your tacit spectators of barbarism.'

Enlightenment – he used that word – must take precedence over ignorance. He saw hypocrisy and irresponsibility in a policy of 'affected respect for the customs of savages, of abstaining from all interference, and endeavouring to perpetuate the institutions of barbarism.' The British had used their power quite wrongly: 'We have employed it in the most arbitrary of all modes, in the exaction of forced services and in the monopoly of the produce of the country. While, as if in mockery, we have professed to exercise no interference with the native administration of the country, we have made ourselves the task-masters of the people, and with a false humility have refused to be their governors. Ought we not to discard this empty pretence?'

He used the phrase 'the rights of man', but not in the sense of the American Declaration of Independence, nor of the French Declaration of the Rights of Man, and he did not question the right of one people or nation to rule over another. He believed that large-scale colonisation was the way forward. In Sumatra he would, he told Murdoch, 're-establish the ancient authority of Menangkabu, and be the great Mogul of the Island. I would, without much expense, afford employment for twenty or thirty thousand English colonists…'

And then, like a great cry: 'In short, what would I not, and indeed what could I not do, were I free to act, and encouraged rather than abused?'

But it was now 'all very speculative, and I am sorry to be obliged to add, also very visionary, for there is no chance of my ever attempting anything of the kind – the time has gone by when I had the spirit for it.' That was before the children died. Afterwards, he had little spirit for anything at all, except for Singapore.

Chapter 13

Fame in Flames

Singapore and Bencoolen 1823–1824

R affles was anxious to appoint a successor to Lieutenant-Colonel Farquhar 'in whom he had little confidence.' He wrote to Calcutta recommending his supercession on 27 January 1823, stating that Farquhar was 'totally unequal to the charge of so important and peculiar a charge as Singapore has now become.' It had 'grown beyond his management,' and he brought up Farquhar's application for leave in 1820, already put off for three years. He wrote to Wallich asking him, if he should see John Crawfurd in Calcutta, to tell him he had sent in his 'recommendation for the relief of the present Resident – and that I am anxious to get away before May.'

The deterioration in the relationship between Raffles and Farquhar is documented in a non-stop tragi-comic exchange of letters. Every couple of days, sometimes two or three times in one day, messengers ran with agitated communications between the bungalow on Singapore Hill and the Residency House down on the Cantonment. All the while, Raffles' Regulations, annulling or reversing Farquhar's rulings and decisions, were being announced. Perhaps Raffles was trying to provoke Farquhar into resigning.

Raffles made a further point to Calcutta: 'The Malay connection in which Lieutenant Colonel Farquhar is involved, and the general weakness of his administration' made him open to pressures from 'peculiar interests' – favouritism, 'irregularities'. This was a reference to Farquhar's family life. He had with him in Singapore his *nonya*, with whom he had lived since his earliest days in Malacca. They had six children together. Farquhar was connected with the people in a way Raffles could never be, and was therefore tolerant of traditional practices such as gaming and opium-farming, and of course slavery. It was this, rather than any social-sexual objection, which made Raffles angry. Farquhar also considered the land to be ultimately vested in the Temenggong and the Sultan, and the port to be a 'native port' – an 'extraordinary principle' in Raffles' view.

With this orientation, Farquhar could claim a deep knowledge of the cultures of the Eastern Isles; and his natural history collections and drawings were almost on a level with Raffles' own. Raffles had the vision, and a mission, and authority. Farquhar, after more than thirty years in the East, had authority too, and a different, laid-back way of being, and a closer focus on the local and day-to-day.

The letters – an enormous mass of verbiage – reflect their differences, and their similarities. One of Raffles' stated aims was to wipe out favouritism and 'irregularities'. But he himself doggedly forwarded the interests of William Flint, for Maryanne's sake, just as Farquhar was transparently vulnerable through Francis Bernard, for his daughter Esther's sake. Each bristled at the other's partiality. Each fought for his near and dear and denigrated the near and dear of the other. Large strategic matters were not addressed nearly so passionately. The battleground was displaced to the personal.

Raffles, because he and Sophia had stayed with the Flints before the new Residency bungalow was built, insisted that Flint's rent for that period should be paid by Government, since he used Flint's house as his office. Meanwhile Flint, as Master Attendant and Storekeeper, was being allocated by Raffles more and more duties and allowances loosely connected with the port, assuming also the authority 'where necessary' of a Magistrate. Even the new office of Post Master was to come 'under the general superintendant of the Master Attendant.' At Farquhar's request, Raffles was forced to provide him with details of all Flint's considerable emoluments.

There was a ludicrous long-running letter-row about a consignment of flooring tiles, originating before Raffles' arrival. Some of the tiles were missing, and Farquhar blamed the shortfall on Flint in his capacity as Storekeeper. 'It could hardly be thought necessary, from an Officer of your Rank and Station,' riposted Raffles, 'that every particular tile or brick should be counted.' As they were to be auctioned immediately, 'the counting of them on delivery after sale would be sufficient... There seems to be little doubt that the deficiency arose during the period of your charge' – so, in writing off the loss, the Lieutenant-Governor 'can by no means consider this an indulgence to the Storekeeper but an act of liberal consideration to yourself.' This petty wrangle ran and ran.

Farquhar was gunning for Flint, and Raffles was gunning for Farquhar's son-in-law Francis Bernard, compelled to renounce his temporary positions as Master Attendant and Storekeeper in favour of Flint. Raffles moved Bernard to the Police Department. On 24 January Farquhar sent Raffles a thick sheaf of pages conveying furious resentment about Bernard's reduced salary and status: 'I cannot but consider this expression of *Head Constable* which he applies to Mr Bernard as intended as a premeditated insult and affront not only to that Gentleman but to myself and family to whom he is so nearly connected.' The Lieutenant-Governor well knew that 'no one with the slightest pretension to rank as a Gentleman in Society' could ever be so degraded as to be called a police constable. On this issue too, many letters flew back and forth. Since one of Lieutenant-Colonel Farquhar's particularly outspoken missives 'may have been written in haste and under misconception,' the Lieutenant-Governor 'trusts you will see the propriety as well as the advantage to the Public Service of reviewing it.' And then, the Lieutenant-Governor treading on very thin ice: 'It should be recollected that offices are not to be created to suit individuals or to serve the purposes of private patronage.'

Raffles rightly suspected that John Palmer was spreading gossip about Singaporean discontents in Calcutta, and wrote to Wallich on 8 February 1824: 'Of Singapore politics I suppose you will have various accounts. I continue to go on as steadily and quietly as possible – not so however our local Chief [Farquhar] who seems every day more and more to forget himself.' One of Farquhar's 'principle satellites' in Singapore was a protégé of Palmer's, Claude Queiros – Raffles called him 'Quier-ass' – through whom he hoped to 'impress Mr Palmer with an idea that he is sadly used by me…it is intended that Mr Palmer should be able to shew the Supreme Govt the ruinous consequences of my measures.'

Another sore was the removal of houses from the Cantonment. 'Mr Bernard is claiming compensation for the actual cost of his house [on the Cantonment] since he says that building costs were *more* when he built it than now!' Raffles' tone to Wallich was exasperated. 'The case will of course be appealed to Mr Palmer who will no doubt submit it to the Supreme Govt.' The whole thing was 'absurd in the extreme,' and he wanted Wallich to 'guard Mr Adam against Palmer's influence.' Bernard went on nagging Raffles about compensation in letter after letter.

Flint, as well as his house on the East Beach, had acquired Saligar Hill, and Farquhar questioned his right to it. The routine was to apply to the Resident for a land grant. No money changed hands, apart from financial arrangements made by the new owner with local inhabitants who were required to remove themselves. Raffles had given Flint informal permission to have a Hill and reminded Farquhar that 'by your own estimate the extent of his Hill is only estimated at 33 acres.' Flint held on to his Hill, built a house on it, and named it Mount Sophia.

Raffles wished Wallich to intimate to the Supreme Government the extent of Farquhar's own 'Hills of Babylon', as he called them, 'far more considerable' than was envisaged. He was happy to authorise 200 acres. Farquhar called his Hill – next to Flint's – Mount Emily; and in fact it comprised rather less than 200 acres. Farquhar expressed himself 'surprised and hurt' by Raffles' insinuations about land he claimed was 'appropriated' by himself and Mr Bernard. He had cleared ground at his own expense, and with the approval of the Temenggong. And it was unfair to penalise Mr Bernard financially since Captain Flint, the Master Attendant, held a post of 'far greater influence and importance than the Assistant in the Police Department.'

Farquhar was accustomed, when off duty, to wear informal clothes, probably a sarong – and probably Raffles was again obliquely referring to the Malay connection when he censured Farquhar's 'departure from the usual etiquette' in dispensing with his military uniform. Barbed exchanges about the dress code continued for a month. Then Raffles informed Farquhar that he had referred the matter to the Governor-General in Calcutta. Farquhar protested that such a measure should have been discussed with him beforehand, repeating that he dispensed with wearing military uniform only when not engaged in any duty 'connected with my office of Commandant of the garrison.'

A week after that, on 29 April, through Nilson Hull, Raffles sacked Farquhar:

'Inconvenience having arisen from your exercising the Office of Resident, during the personal residence of a Higher Authority at Singapore, I am directed to acquaint you that the Lieutenant-Governor has deemed it necessary to relieve you from the performance of all duties attached to that Office, from the 1st proximo [i.e. the day after tomorrow] and during his continuance at this settlement or until further notice.' The Lieutenant-Governor would take upon himself 'the direct exercise of all the civil duties of the station, agreeable to the enclosed General Orders of this date which you will be pleased to publish without delay.' Farquhar's informal resignation of 1820 was to be accepted from receipt of this letter.

In response to Farquhar's instant epistolary howl of protest, he sent a curt note: 'You are desired to pay due obedience to the Orders which have been this day issued to you.' Farquhar demanded repeatedly to know on what authority Raffles was removing him from office. Raffles did not tell Farquhar that John Crawfurd was already appointed to succeed him. Farquhar only heard this through private channels – presumably Palmer – on 19 May. Three days later he learned that he was expected to vacate his bungalow so that the successor could move into it. It was naturally not at all convenient for Farquhar to move out of the bungalow he had built at his own expense and where, in the compound, he kept his wild animals. Raffles persisted. The site, on the Cantonment, belonged to Government. Farquhar would be recompensed 'the present value of the buildings'.

With the arrival of Crawfurd imminent, Raffles informed Farquhar that 'as a public duty and mark of respect to his authority' he was to be present at the vacated Residency house on the landing of his successor, 'where the Lieutenant-Governor will himself take such measures as the occasion may require.' This elicited the nettled reply: 'It was not I presume at all necessary to point out to me the necessity of a public duty of respect and courtesy towards Mr Crawfurd on his landing here.'

Raffles still had not finished. On 22 May, he issued General Orders removing Farquhar from his additional post as Commandant of the Garrison: 'The Hon. the Governor-General in Council having accepted the resignation of Lieutenant-Colonel Farquhar, and Mr John Crawfurd having been appointed Resident of Singapore,' Lieutenant-Colonel Farquhar will 'deliver over charge to Mr Crawfurd on his arrival, and the Commander of the Troops will that day devolve on Captain [Thomas] Murray of the 20th Native Infantry.' This notice was sent to Farquhar with an instruction 'to publish without delay.'

Farquhar now was suffering a double humiliation. Over that week in May, letters between the two frenzied men were read, replied to, and despatched several times a day. Unless, wrote Farquhar, the Lieutenant-Governor could produce 'sufficient authority from the

Supreme Government or H.E. the Commander in Chief' in Calcutta for removing him from the command of the troops, he declined to relinquish it. The reply came through Hull: 'I am directed to convey to you his *positive command* that you forthwith publish the General Order of this date and obey them to the Letter – the contrary at your peril. On the arrival of Mr Crawfurd you will be released from all further duties and struck off the strength of the garrison from that date.'

Farquhar asked to see copies of any letter from the Supreme Government appointing Crawfurd to relieve him as Resident of Singapore. Back came the reply from Raffles that 'the General Orders of that same date [22 May] contain all the information required.' Farquhar, in face of the inevitable, agreed to comply with Raffles' 'peremptory commands' since 'an act of resistance on my part would be the means of occasioning interruption and inconvenience to the Public Service.' And then: 'To the highest tribunal in India, therefore, I will make a solemn appeal under a confident hope that ample redress will be sooner or later afforded me for all the severity and injustice I have received at your hands.' He was not going to let this go.

Raffles did not have the right to sack Farquhar, only to recommend to the Supreme Council that Farquhar be removed. The Supreme Government, regretfully, supported the Lieutenant-Governor's decision; the Governor-General in Council however deemed it 'an act of justice' to Lieutenant-Colonel Farquhar if the Lieutenant-Governor were to 'record his sense of the activity, zeal, judgment, and the attention to the principles prescribed for the management of the settlement, which has marked his conduct in the execution of that duty.' Raffles complied, almost word for word. It rang hollow to Farquhar, who still felt his dismissal was 'illegal and unauthorised'.

It is a sad, bad story. Raffles was peremptory, disrespectful, cruel. Why? Because he wanted Farquhar gone. Singapore was Raffles' last and best opportunity. He would never be the great Mogul of the Archipelago, but in this small, strategically placed island, this 'child of my own', his ideas and ideals had found their time and place.

He just could not bear it that his vision was being vitiated by Farquhar's laxness and pragmatism. He had very little time to set things right. He had nothing to lose in the stand-off. He was fighting for principles in which he believed while bedevilled by the constant shattering headaches which left him in shreds. At these times he was deranged, his common sense and human sympathies obliterated by the pain.

Back in Bencoolen in November, with time to think and his animus (but not his headaches) abated, he wrote to Wallich: 'God knows I have had but one object in view – the interests of Singapore – and if a brother had been opposed to them, I must have acted as I did towards Colonel Farquhar, for whom I ever had, and still retain, a warm personal affection and regard.' He said he did his best to 'prevent a rupture,' but when it did take place, 'I found it necessary to prosecute my cause with vigour and effect.'

Raffles, before the arrival of conscientious Crawfurd, had to rectify the 'irregularities' of his brother-in-law William Flint. On the very day he sacked Farquhar, he wrote to Flint officially, through Nilson Hull, about boat-repairing materials causing obstructions on Ferry Point: 'I am directed to desire you to explain how this has arisen, and that you lose no time in causing the same to be removed.' As to the silly skirmish about flooring tiles, still unresolved, Raffles told Flint that 'the amount short of the stated consignment will necessarily stand at your debt until explained.'

There was more, and worse. Raffles wrote to John Crawfurd – not through Hull but directly – about 'the accounts of the Storekeeper'. On receipt of the report of the officers appointed to examine them, 'the details' would be 'adjusted from Bencoolen.' Flint should open his books and provide all the information required to determine 'the amount of the balance' – consisting of a very large deficit due to the Treasury, which 'must be received from the Storekeeper.' He recommended to Crawfurd a regular examination of the Storekeeper's accounts. Maryanne's husband was unreliable and an embarrassment, and Raffles had indulged him.

～

John Crawfurd arrived on the *Hero of Malown* on 27 May 1823, bringing 'a bottle of ether for Sophia.' (If this was to ease the pain of childbirth, it is a strikingly early incidence, as the use of ether in childbirth is documented in the West only from the 1840s.) The same ship was to carry Raffles and Sophia, Nilson Hull, Captain Salmond, and the Flints' four-year-old son Charles to Bencoolen; for obvious reasons, it was agreed that the little boy should be taken on back to England, though baby Sophie remained with her parents.

The *munshi* Abdullah left an account of how he packed Raffles' treasures. The Malay books and manuscripts were wrapped in waxed cloth and packed into leather cases – three hundred bound volumes, plus many unbound, or in rolls and loose sheets, or on palmyra leaves. Abdullah packed shadow-puppets, craft objects, games and, in one huge chest, a gamelan orchestra. He packed hundreds of stuffed animals and birds, and bottles containing reptiles and insects preserved in spirit. It took twenty barges to ferry all the cases and boxes out to the ship. Raffles had brought his collection from Bencoolen to Singapore, thinking they might sail from there straight for Europe.

Four days before he left, he laid the foundation stone of the Singapore Institution at seven in the morning, witnessed by the Trustees, officers and friends. On the day of departure, Raffles formally transferred the charge of Singapore to John Crawfurd by Proclamation. His own connection was severed; the settlement was 'no longer to be considered as a dependency of Fort Marlborough,' but placed 'in direct communication with the Supreme Government' and considered 'an immediate dependency of Fort William.'

Abdullah's sadness on saying goodbye to Mr Raffles – he never took on board the change to 'Sir Stamford' – 'was not due to the fact that I had gained such benefit from him nor because of his greatness and pre-eminence but because of his courtesy and understanding... a nature so good at winning the affection of others and so noble as that of Mr Raffles I never found.'

From the wharf, he saw Mr Raffles standing all alone at a window on the *Hero*, raising his hand in farewell to Singapore.

Abdullah, who never seemed to make a distinction between the first and the second 'Mrs Raffles', remembered them in a poem:

> The plover seeks the wayside tree,
> The *rambai* in green pastures grows,
> Mr Raffles – wise is he,
> How well the hearts of men he knows.
>
> The *rambai* in green pastures grows,
> Delicious fruits the taste beguile,
> How well the hearts of men he knows
> How natural his charm and smile.
>
> Delicious fruits the taste beguile
> Like bramble with its prickly hairs.
> How natural his charm and smile,
> The grace his wife so nobly shares.
>
> Like bramble with its prickly hairs,
> The lane with trailing branches strewn,
> The grace his wife so nobly shares.
> Unites them as the sun and moon.

At sea off the coast of Borneo, Raffles assured Wallich that all his arrangements were 'approved by Bengal.' As for Farquhar, 'It would make your hair stand on end were I to mention half of what took place…they have shocked every reasonable man in Singapore… with the exception of his immediate family, no one seems to have the least feeling for him.' That was wrong, even though the European merchants who were Raffles' friends shared his views. Raffles underestimated Farquhar's popularity, and the reasons for it.

'I give you this parish news,' Raffles continued to Wallich, so he might know 'that however annoyed I have been for a time, the close of my administration at Singapore has been just what I wished.' On

the way to Bencoolen, the ship was stopping off at Java for a week
as the Captain had goods to land there. The Dutch 'will be a little
astonished but I cannot help it.'

When the *Hero of Malown* anchored off Batavia, Raffles sent
Nilson Hull ashore with two letters to deliver. One was a courtesy note to Governor van der Capellen, who replied brusquely that
he was unable to welcome Sir Stamford in Batavia. Raffles himself
had never intended to disembark, but was anxious for the pregnant
Sophia to have a few days on dry land. The second letter Hull delivered was to Thomas McQuoid, who was making his living – just –
as a private trader in Batavia. Because of 'the delicate state of Lady
R.'s health,' might the McQuoids put her up for a few days? And 'as
a first requisition, I beg of you to send us off a loaf of Bread without
delay.' He wrote again, once the *Hero* was continuing on its way, to
thank the McQuoids for their kindness. They had given him such a
'feeling of happiness and comfort' on Sophia's behalf.

Because, owing to shock and grief, her milk had dried up when
Ella was a new baby, they were anxious about feeding the next
one. As the *Hero* traversed the Java Sea, he wrote again to Wallich:
'Lady Raffles will be infinitely obliged by your sending her by the
first opportunity two glass sucking bottles for infants – they are
obtained at the chemists and you will easily know what she means.
She knows no one to whom she could make such a request but yourself.' The baby was expected in October, and they hoped to sail for
England the following January, 'so we must look forward to the
necessity of bringing up the child by hand' i.e. by bottle.

The *Hero of Malown* reached Bencoolen on 17 July, and they
moved back into their own house, Pematang Balam. They were now
desperate to hear of a ship to take them back to England, There was
nothing scheduled before the end of the year, when the *Fame* was
expected.

Sophia's baby was born prematurely, on 19 September. It was
a girl, and they called her Flora. She seemed healthy, and Sophia
appeared to have recovered – and then developed a high fever. She

did not lose all her vitality, writing on 3 October to 'My dearest Maryanne' to reassure her about the wellbeing of Charley Boy: 'I have crept out of bed before anyone is up.' But on 1 November Raffles told Wallich that 'it was only last night that we were forced to apply thirty leeches, and have recourse to warm baths and laudanum, to keep down inflammation.' For a while, he despaired of Sophia's life. He himself was 'still subject to the same attacks which so often and so completely overpowered me at Singapore.'

In mid-November, Sophia was still 'confined to her couch,' he wrote to Thomas Murdoch, saying that if he reached England alive, 'I am certain that no inducement shall ever lead me to revisit India.' Towards the end of November four of his Bencoolen friends died, including Captain Francis Salmond, 'as dear and intimate with us as our own family… Charley's "funny man".' Raffles found that he himself ('my *only* friend Sir Stamford Raffles'), had been appointed Salmond's sole executor. 'How is it,' Raffles asked Wallich, 'that those we love and esteem…are thus carried off, while the vile and worthless remain?'

Then, on 28 November, baby Flora died. Raffles told McQuoid that Sophia was still in bed recovering from 'one of those dreadful fevers which are the scourge of this land…when the dear Babe which had hitherto been most promising and thriving was carried off in a few hours.' He wrote to Peter Auber at India House that the loss of a child only a few months old was normally 'one of those things that might soon be got over' – but this loss, of their fourth and only remaining child in the East, 'has revived all former afflictions and has been almost too much for us.' Their spirits were 'completely broken', and still they could not get away from Bencoolen, detained for want of a ship. 'How often do we wish the *Fame* had come out direct' – she was on some circuitous itinerary – 'we might have [been] saved this last misfortune – but we have neither seen nor heard of her…Either I must go to England, or by remaining in India *die.*'

The *Fame* was a Company ship, specially chartered for them.

Raffles in his misery was lambasting Peter Auber for not organiz-
ing a direct sailing to Bencoolen from England. He wrote again on 4
January 1824: 'We have entered the new year, and as yet no accounts
of the *Fame*.' Every day's delay was dangerous for Sophia 'and night
and day we cannot help regretting that you have not ensured a ship
on the strength of my letters to you – I relied exclusively on what
you would do.'

Sophia, broken-hearted and ill as she was, was more controlled,
writing to Maryanne the previous day: 'Before I begin my own sad
story I must speak of dear Charles.' He was no trouble, 'a delightful
Boy,' who slept on her bed with her for two hours every day, and 'has
never had an hour's illness.' Only then did she write about her fresh
grief, and her joy and regret at leaving Bencoolen – regret, because
in Bencoolen the spirits of 'my dear departed children' seemed
always to be hovering, just out of sight, 'blooming and smiling as
if in life.' She was hardly able to hold up her head. 'The loss of my
dear Baby – so glowing with health and strength' had rekindled the
earlier sorrows; and the leeches, and the inevitable 'salivation' had
reduced her system. 'I am more like the shadow of an earthly being
than anything possessing life.' Her whole aim was '*acquiescence*'. She
had a gold chain bracelet made, from which hung five small gold
lockets containing a scrap of hair from each of her children, with
their names and dates inscribed on the reverse. Only Ella's did not
have the date of death as well as of birth.

Since the *Fame* did not appear, and the *Borneo* had put in at Bencoolen on its way to England, Raffles decided to take the opportunity of sailing with her. The accommodation on the *Borneo*, he told
McQuoid, was 'wretched, but I now incline to cut and run at all
costs.' The day the loading was completed, the *Fame* finally turned
up. The boxes were removed from the *Borneo* and loaded on to the
Fame.

It is worth noting, while the labourers are manhandling the
wooden chests from one ship to another, that the little *Borneo*
reached England safely and without incident.

Everything seemed suddenly hopeful. In his last letter to Maryanne, Raffles told her the *Fame* would be ready to sail within a week.
Charley Boy, who was 'all and everything that we or you could wish,'
was kitted out for the voyage with 'a Fur Cap and Blue Cloth Jacket
trimmed with lace and ornamented with gilt buttons with a pair of
Dutch Trousers.' He and Sophia were also in charge of David Scott,
the little son of a Singapore merchant friend, and they had a medical
man with them, Dr B. Bell. The *Fame* was 'a nice little ship with
excellent accommodation and room for all my plants Tigers Bears
Monkeys etc of which I can assure you I have no small family. We
shall have a second Noah's Ark, and I only wish I could loose a little
dove by the way who might light on your little island and restore
you to peace and harmony.'

For in Singapore the Flints, predictably, already had issues with
John Crawfurd. Raffles conceded to Maryanne that 'I never placed
much confidence in his judgment or experience...He is however no
longer under my *direct* authority and I cannot interfere at present
to any great extent.' (Crawfurd was not under Raffles' authority in
any way at all.) 'Above all things, I beseech you not to let Flint have
any personal Quarrel or discussion with him... You may be certain
that it will end in Flint's discomfiture, however right he may be.'

He would be more useful to them in London, he said and, expansive
in relief at his imminent departure, expressed a wish that 'you should
all consider yourselves as still under my protection. I have not deserted
Singapore and never will, and perhaps one day when you least expect
it, better luck may happen to the place than any of you dream of.'

Shortly before they sailed, Raffles wrote to the Court of Directors about his personal finances. The Company were looking for
a refund of his salary as Lieutenant-Governor of Bencoolen for
the years 1816 to 1818, when he was in England. He quoted back
to them the letter from Lord Minto authorising him to claim the
allowances 'from the date at which I shall cease to draw those of
Lieut-Governor of Java,' and hoped for a favourable decision.

The *Fame*, that 'nice little ship', with all Raffles' collections safely stowed – 135 hefty crates, apart from the live creatures – set sail in the early morning of 2 February 1824 with a favourable wind. His cargo took up much of the ship, and there was a load of saltpetre in the hold. This was, Raffles said, one of the happiest days of his life. 'We were, perhaps, too happy.'

That evening, fifty miles south-west of Bencoolen, the *Fame* caught fire. The alarm was given at about twenty past eight, and within less than ten minutes the ship was ablaze.

'Sophia had just gone to bed, and I had thrown off half my clothes, when a cry of fire, fire! roused us from our calm content, and in five minutes the whole ship was in flames!' A steward had gone below with a naked light to draw brandy from a cask, which caught fire, starting the inferno. Raffles wrote a vivid account of the catastrophe, and later published a version of it as a pamphlet. Sophia wrote her own account to Maryanne, and between the two one gets a graphic impression of their ordeal. This is Sophia:

> I had just laid my head down on my pillow and Tom was in
> his little dressing cabin when the cry of Fire made me rush to
> the door – where I saw a man spring up the hatchway covered
> with flame – Tom flew to see what was the matter – and "Fire
> – Water – Water" resounded thro' the Ship – the next minute
> Tom returned to say it was all over, we must perish – the next
> cry was "Lady Raffles to the Boats" – I had only time to throw
> on my pelisse (she had 'nothing but a wrapper,' wrote Raffles,
> 'neither shoes nor stockings'), wrap Charles in a shawl, and get
> David Scott whose cabin was in flames when he was dragged
> out of bed – and we got into the boat – the flames bursting thro'
> our windows as we descended the ship's side, and the whole
> vessel a sheet of flame – the rest of the party left the other side
> of the ship and in ten minutes every soul had quitted her – there
> was not even time to get a drop of water, or refreshment of any
> kind – fortunately the Captain seized a compass and this was
> everything to us.

The live animals and birds were not saved, but by half-past eight, according to Raffles, everyone was off the ship and into boats, and less than ten minutes afterwards the *Fame* was 'one grand mass of fire.' She blazed until around midnight, when the saltpetre exploded, 'and sent up one of the most splendid and brilliant flames that ever was seen, illuminating the horizon in every direction, to an extent of not less than fifty miles, and casting that kind of blue light over us, which is of all others the most horrible.' Finally they lost sight of the ship as she went down in a cloud of smoke.

Then their boat was adrift in the dark ocean. 'Fortunately the sea was smooth,' wrote Sophia, and 'the Boys slept soundly.' Raffles' account adds the detail that neither Nilson Hull nor Dr Bell had saved their coats; but the tail of his own coat, plus a pocket-handker-chief, 'served to keep Sophia's feet warm, and we made breeches for the children with our neckcloths.' The crew 'rowed manfully', back in the direction of the Sumatran coast. As Sophia said, if they had not had the compass, and if the disaster had happened the following night, when they were further out to sea, they could not possibly have survived.

Morning came. 'I felt perfectly convinced,' wrote Raffles, 'we were unable to undergo starvation and exposure to sun and weather many days' – they had no food and no water – 'and aware of the rapidity of the currents, I feared we might fall to the southward of the port.' Then they saw Rat Island, and knew they were on course for Bencoolen.

This last stretch was the worst, especially for Sophia: 'The sun was on the meridian and I felt nearly exhausted for we had nothing to shelter us from its rays and the boat was so small we could only take care of the children.' A ship standing in Bencoolen roads came out to rescue them and take them back into port. 'By this time,' wrote Raffles, 'Sophia was quite exhausted, and fainting continu-ally.' They were on dry land by two o'clock in the afternoon. 'If any proof had been wanting, that my administration had been satisfac-tory, we had it unequivocally from all; there was not a dry eye...'

They were driven straight back to their old house, were all four in bed within an hour of landing, and slept through until the next morning.

They had lost everything except their lives. 'All our *plate*,' Raffles wrote to Maryanne on 8 February, 'including that from Java – all Sophia's jewels without exception – all our gold work – my valuable collections of all kinds;' all his papers, correspondence, notes, memos, the records of his administration of Java, 'all my *beautiful* drawings – in short the cream and best of everything I had collected and attained during my residence in India – all – all has gone.' They had no clothes at all, and were 'engaged in renewing our Wardrobe, no easy matter in such a place as this – poor Sophia's laces! No finery now, we are glad to get hopsacks to cover our nakedness.' They were very weak. Raffles underwent 'a severe salivation' during February, and Sophia a less severe one; the infernal mercury treatment in which doctors placed such confidence left them weaker than they had been before.

'Every exertion I had the power of making was required to collect a few comforts for those around me, for we were destitute of everything, I had not even a pair of stockings on... We have now covering,' Sophia wrote to Maryanne on 22 March, 'clothes I cannot call them.' Unfortunately Charles' English nurse had left when they sailed, to get married. Although Sophia had found a 'very good Malay attendant,' Charles 'never leaves me and is very much attached to me.' She was taking him to church, and keeping up his lessons and his nap routine. Raffles assured his mother that Charley treated the *Fame* catastrophe as a joke. But Sophia said he had 'hesitations of speech' and was 'quite naughty'.

The strain of looking after him for Sophia, who admitted to having 'very little strength,' is obvious. She went on to urge Maryanne, even more desperately than usual, to make provision for the future and for her children's education, even if it meant sacrificing her arrangements for their new house on the Hill. Her children had to be educated and 'put out into the world... Let me hear that you are putting by half your income.' But that was never the Flints' way.

'Tom,' she wrote, had 'submitted to the loss...the fruits of the labour of his whole life – with the most wonderful patience and good spirits – without a single murmur. I really could not withhold my admiration the day after our sad return on seeing him sit down with his usual energy and pleasure and perseverance' – starting all over again on the great map of Sumatra he had made for William Marsden, which had gone down with the ship. 'He sent for the draftsmen and set them to work as if nothing had happened.'

In his own account of the fire, he lamented not only the loss of the map, and other treasures, but 'all my splendid collections of drawings, upwards of *two thousand* in number – with all the valuable papers and notes of my friends Arnold and Jack; and to conclude, I will merely notice, that there was scarcely an unknown animal, bird, beast or fish, or an interesting plant, which we had not on board: a living tapir, a new species of tiger, splendid pheasants, etc, domesticated for the voyage.'

The *Fame* itself was insured. Raffles' collections and personal property were not. He wrote a report on the loss of the *Fame* to the Court of Directors, giving an account of the lost documentation of the Eastern Isles, which would have been of great value to the Company. 'In a pecuniary point of view, my loss has not been less extensive.' Much was of personal value 'which no money can replace.' Money could compensate for other losses: 'It rests solely and exclusively with the Court, to consider in how far my claims, on account of services, may be strengthened by the severity of misfortune.' On returning to Europe, 'I shall throw myself on your Honourable Court, to enable me to end my days in honourable retirement.'

In the hope of compensation from the Company he appended an inventory of his and Sophia's personal property:

Plate The Service of plate presented to Sir Stamford Raffles by
the inhabitants of Java. First Cost £3000. Added to, £1,500.
Private plate, another £1,500.

Jewels Diamonds presented to the Family of Sir S. Raffles by the Captors of Djojocarta £1,000. The sapphire and diamond ring presented by Princess Charlotte £1,000; another diamond ring, £500. Lady R's family jewels, watches etc £3,500.
Gold In dust and coinage of the country, of antiquarian significance £4,200.

He jotted down disparate things as he and Sophia thought of them: 'China, Japan articles for presents and household, Malay manufactures, embroideries and cloths of all kinds and patterns intended as samples for British industries, likewise drugs, ivories. Lady R's harp and music. Furniture etc. Shawls, muslins, curiosities. £2,000 of wines. Family table linens, Lady R's wardrobe £1,600, Sir S. Raffles' ditto £200.' They had paid in advance £1,200 for their passage.

Raffles estimated the total loss at £29,180, 'in 135 packages marked TSR and described in ship's manifest entered at Bencoolen before sailing'. This sum did not include 'the expenses of the drawings and other subjects of Natural History, books, sketches of costume and a variety of articles of very considerable cost and value.' All gone, to the bottom of the Indian Ocean.

'I cannot tell you the horror with which I think of the voyage and the dread I have of going to sea again,' Sophia confessed to Maryanne. After one false hope – they were all set to leave on the *Wellington*, but the Captain went 'raving mad' – they embarked on the *Mariner* on 8 April 1824 and set sail once more two days later. To the Address of sympathy and praise which his colleagues in Bencoolen presented him, he replied (his script shaky, with a few crossings-out): 'It may be that I placed too high a value on my Collections, that I was too confident in my future career, perhaps I was too much attached to the things of this world. The lot of man is a mixture of good and evil, and we must be content with it – and at all events we know that all worketh for good in the end.'

With a determination bordering on the crazy, Raffles set himself a rigorous programme of work for the voyage. He set out his daily timetable – mathematics, logic, Greek, Latin, Hebrew – in a note-book, like a schoolboy. He cannot have kept this up. The *Mariner* was thrown about by fierce gales for three whole weeks around the Cape, 'the ship nearly torn to pieces and ourselves nearly worn out'. Raffles recorded in his notebook: 'The gale was so severe that during this period we were unable to leave our cots, the sea poured through the decks into our cabin, and the roar of the wind was such that we could not hear each other speak. Lady Raffles, though boarded up in her couch, was obliged to have ropes to hold by to prevent her knocking from one side of it to the other.' They had been at sea eleven weeks before, on 25 June 1824, they reached St Helena for a scheduled stopover.

Lieutenant-Colonel Farquhar had hung on in Singapore, waiting and hoping for a reversal of his dismissal as Commandant of the Garrison from the Supreme Government, which Palmer assured him would be forthcoming. But the Supreme Government, having endorsed Raffles' decision, could not reverse it without appearing to be in error, and let it lie. By an unfortunate coincidence Farquhar, bound at last for retirement in Scotland, and on board the *Maitland*, anchored at St Helena just a few hours before Raffles and Sophia – 'but we did not land till evening and the Colonel was anxious (as I conclude) to avoid an interview, he sailed the next morning and we did not see him.'

No Napoleon on St Helena this time; he died in 1821. The Raffles family stayed with the Governor at Plantation House, and while there Raffles received the news that his mother had died. It was not a surprise. In his final letter to Maryanne from Bencoolen, he wrote: 'My last accounts of our poor Mother are melancholy, and I can hardly expect to see her alive.' But it was, as he wrote to the Duchess, 'a sad stroke at such a moment, just as I felt the possibility of once more embracing her... Pray excuse this hasty scrawl; my eyes are quite blinded with tears, and my hand is so nervous that I can scarcely hold my pen.'

Raffles would not learn until they reached England that, while they were on the high seas, the Treaty of London between the British and the Dutch was ratified, after four years of negotiations. It had been signed when Raffles was in Bencoolen between the fire on the *Fame* and his final departure. As part of the Treaty, Britain ceded Bencoolen and all other stations in Sumatra to the Netherlands. Malacca was again ceded to the British.

The great news was that the Netherlands withdrew all opposition to the occupation of Singapore. George Canning, one of the British signatories of the Treaty, recognised Singapore as the '*unum necessarium*' for the future of the British Empire. This outcome was a triumph for Sir Thomas Stamford Raffles.

The *Mariner* left St Helena on 3 July and landed safely at Plymouth on 22 August 1824, a Sunday. They were home.

Chapter 14

Endgame

England 1824–1826

T he Rev. Thomas Raffles was in the West Country, preaching
and doing a little tourism the weekend that the *Mariner* anchored
at Plymouth. On the Sunday, his sermon was in Devonport, beside
Plymouth, so he was there to meet Raffles and his party when they
landed. 'Lady Raffles looks better than I expected,' Cousin Thomas
wrote to his wife, 'but my cousin is much reduced, and exces-
sively weak.' Raffles admitted to 'a sad headache from the effects of
landing.' They all spent that first night with Sophia's sister Alice
Mudge and the Rosdews at Beechwood in Plympton St Mary.

From there Raffles and Sophia went by post-chaise to Sophia's
parents in Cheltenham – Raffles urging the post-boys to go faster
because of Sophia's 'impatience to see her child' – achieving about
thirteen miles an hour 'until our front wheel caught fire,' as he
reported to the Duchess. They were celebrities because of the fire
on the *Fame*, which had been reported sensationally in the British
press. When they stopped, people crowded round the carriage to
get a glimpse of them, and landlords of inns waived the bill. When
Sophia gave her name in a shop, the shopman said, 'Lord, Ma'am,
you aren't the lady that was burnt in the *Fame?*'

In Cheltenham they were at last reunited with Ella. They did not move in with Sophia's parents, but took 'a snug house' of their own at 2 Wellington Place. Raffles was as ever projecting himself into the future, confiding to the Duchess his dreams of how his life might develop. 'I confess that I have a great desire to turn farmer' – about two hundred acres, he thought. 'With this, I suppose I should in time become a country magistrate; and if I could eventually get a seat in Parliament...'

He and Sophia made a ten-day foray to London a month after their arrival. Raffles had interviews with the Chairman and Deputy Chairman of the Company and saw friends at India House, and conveyed to Cousin Thomas that the feeling seemed 'very much in my favour.' They also saw on this trip 'the dear children from Ireland' – Maryanne's teenaged son Acheson and daughter Charlotte by her first marriage to Quintin Dick Thompson. Their guardians, the Baron and Mrs McLelland (Quintin's sister), hearing that Raffles was in London, brought the young people to see him. Acheson, Raffles told Maryanne, was tall, 'strikingly handsome and elegant' and very like his father. Young Charlotte was 'everything you could wish but by no means as handsome as Acheson,' with 'more of the Raffles face than any other... We will keep up a continuous communication with Ireland.' Raffles and Sophia were more conscientious about Charlotte and Acheson than their mother was.

The most important task for Raffles in the autumn of 1824 was to negotiate with the Company for compensation for his losses on the *Fame.* He was also expecting a pension. He could count on about five friends among the Directors, and contacted other well-disposed – as he thought – and influential figures, asking them for support.

Lord Hastings, who had been summarily recalled from Calcutta, could not help: 'On the strange terms existing between me and the India House, such an inconsistency would not fail to be taken up and distorted... It would rejoice me to be serviceable in any way without involving this dilemma, though I fear that I have at present little influence.' Charles Williams Wynne, President of the Board of

Control, wrote: 'You appear to be unaware that in the award for services rendered to the Company we possess at the India Board [the new name for the Board of Control] only negative powers – we may refuse or curtail but we cannot originate or increase… I assure you that there is seldom a disposition to allow us by recommendation… to exceed those limits.' Raffles' lobbying may have been something of a misjudgement.

He was 'drawing out a brief review of my public administration during the last twelve years' in Java, Sumatra and Singapore, for the Court of Directors. He wrote to the second Earl of Minto, son of the late Governor-General, asking whether he might avail himself of his father's papers. He wanted, to judge from the younger Minto's reply, anything 'tending to prove the very high opinion that my Father entertained of your merit and services'. Raffles also enquired about documents relating to the invasion of Java, since his own were lost with the *Fame*. Raffles had never met the late Governor-General's eldest son and heir, and he proved unhelpful.

Raffles, characteristically, made up his mind that the loss of his records only rendered compiling his Statement of Services 'the more interesting,' and was optimistic about its reception: 'I expect the Court of Directors will make some compensation for my losses in the *Fame*, and I think it likely that by Christmas my Public Services will come under review of the General Court.' Predictably, nothing happened by Christmas. He and Sophia were gathering strength for, as Sophia put it, 'our winter campaign.'

William Marsden, apprised of the campaign, wrote a kindly letter saying he had 'talked over very thoroughly with W.A. [William Astell, Chairman of the Company] the grounds and circumstances of your claims,' and had some advice: 'You will of course become, if you are not already, a Member of the Asiatic Society.' Raffles would also be asked to join the Oriental Club, 'but this (tho' highly respectable) you may take time to consider of.' Raffles did the following year become a member of the Asiatic Society, and of the Society of Antiquaries; and a Vice-President of both the Language Institution and the African Institution. He took Marsden's hint and kept away from the Oriental Club – founded that same year, with a membership confined chiefly to past and present senior civil servants of the East India Company.

The Archipelago was being reconfigured, and Raffles submitted his views. C. Williams Wynn told him that 'the plan of Government has been formed very much in conformity with your suggestions and those of Governor Phillips.'

The Foreign Secretary, now George Canning, wrote to say he was 'greatly pleased and gratified' that Raffles was satisfied with the new agreement with the Netherlands: 'No one more competent than you to judge.' He added: 'I cannot deny that your extreme activity in stirring difficult questions, and the freedom with which you committed your Government without their knowledge or authority to measures which might have brought a war upon them, unprepared, did at one time oblige me to speak my mind in Instructions of no very mild reprehension. But I was not the less anxious to retain the fruits of your policy which appeared to me really worth preserving – and I have long forgotten every particular of your conduct in the Eastern Seas except the zeal and ability by which it was distinguished.'

This was typical of authority's ambivalent attitude to Raffles. No one could fail to recognise his zeal and, especially as regards Singapore, his peculiar genius – yet so much of what he did outrageously exceeded his remit.

Raffles explained to Maryanne the imminent 'arrangement for Singapore and the union of the 3 settlements under one Government.' This tallied with his previous impassioned recommendation to Lord Hastings. Penang, Singapore and Malacca, under a single Governor and Council, were 'each to have a Resident and be independent of each other.' None of this, he assured his sister, should affect William Flint, but he must 'keep quiet and save all he can.' On 1 August 1826 the Straits Settlements, which lasted until 1946, came into being.

In Cheltenham Raffles was hampered in the writing of his Statement of Services by illness, and in late October 1824, Captain Thomas Otho Travers made the crossing from Cork to visit him. He found Sophia 'looking uncommonly well. Indeed I was surprised at her appearance. She complained of loss of weight but I have never seen her look better.'

Sophia's life, miraculously it must have seemed, was back on track. She was with her little daughter, and her parents were just around the corner. She made light of Raffles' troubles to Maryanne – and perhaps to herself as well – his headaches were '*bilious* not *nervous*.' Luckily Charley Boy and Ella played together nicely. 'Ella is as pretty as the most perfect regular features can make her, as well as the most intelligent of expressions.' She was like her father, 'with strait, chestnut hair, but not a very fair skin.'

With the arrival of Travers, Raffles rallied and became positively 'energetic'. This was more than a reunion, it was a reconciliation. 'Tot and I have burnt the papers, as the saying is,' Raffles wrote to Maryanne. For they had parted badly, with recriminations from Travers after he was sent by Raffles to be Resident at Singapore, only to find that Farquhar had no intention of leaving. Tot worried that Raffles' constitution was so thoroughly undermined. 'He seemed a complete Skeleton with scarcely enough skin to cover his bones – his head tormenting to a sad degree.'

Raffles said he was putting on some weight and 'gaining strength daily and sometimes fancy I am growing young again.' Yet one may wonder, as he shivered through that dull, dank English autumn, wrapped up in his worsteds and woollens, whether his imagination did not conjure up the tropics with something like nostalgia – the humid warmth, the fierce, short-lived afternoon rains, even the reliably scorching sun.

He and Sophia left Cheltenham before Christmas, moving to London for their 'winter campaign'. Raffles thought the cost of placing himself at the centre of London life was money well spent.

He rented 104 Piccadilly 'next door to the Marquess of Hertford's', but it was too small. Sir Humphry and Lady Davy were moving out of 23 Lower Grosvenor Street in Mayfair, and Raffles took it from Sir Humphry on a thirty-year lease, planning to move in February 1825 'when the London season will be commencing.'

Sophia's parents left Cheltenham too, and bought what their daughter called 'a most delightful house in a most beautiful part of the environs of London.' Their new home was a large villa in rural Hornsey called, by mischance, Farquhar House. Charley and Ella spent much time at Farquhar House when Raffles and Sophia were away on visits.

Raffles' youngest sister, Ann, was never part of the Hulls' family parties at Farquhar House. She was always 'difficult', and had led a restricted life as companion to their mother. Since their mother's death, Ann lived in Edinburgh with their cousin Mary Anne Wise, daughter of the Rev. John Lindeman, and Raffles paid her an allowance of £150 a year. On 23 May 1825 she died, aged thirty-two, 'carried off by a rapid consumption'.

'Poor thing,' wrote Sophia, 'it seems to have been a mercy to herself and all those connected with her, for her weaknesses and waywardness increased every day – till at last they were by all accounts beyond endurance.' Sophia could be acerbic. When Uncle William, Cousin Thomas's father, died in November 1825, Sophia's comment was, 'No great loss. It is a pity his wife did not die too.'

Raffles and his replacement creatures and collections, although fewer than those lost, were, as before, much in demand among fellow naturalists, and specimens were swapped and compared. He assured the Duchess that he was following her advice – 'idling and playing the fool with my time as much as possible,' but that was not in his nature. The idea of a Zoological Society was still alive, and had been reviewed by the Zoological Club of the Linnean Society in 1823. The first meeting of Friends of a proposed Zoological Society was in July 1824, and Raffles had been appointed Chairman in anticipation of his return.

He and Sir Humphry Davy together moved things forward; the first circular was sent out on 1 February 1825, with no mention of live animals, only 'preserved specimens'. A meeting of 26 February was chaired by Raffles, and the prospectus of 1 March was the first to posit a collection of live animals. Davy, going out of town, left Raffles with the job of writing to influential people to solicit subscriptions. In his application to Sir Robert Harry Inglis on 28 April Raffles said that he hoped to have a hundred names 'within a day or two'. He had Robert Peel, the Home Secretary (secured by Davy), on the top of his list. 'In the first instance, we look mainly to country gentlemen…but the character of the institution must of course depend on the proportion of men of science and sound principles which it contains.' His own insistence on 'the scientific aspect', he said, put him 'a little at issue with Sir Humphry Davy.'

Raffles' social life was correspondingly febrile. On 18 May 1825 he told Cousin Thomas: 'Necessity has compelled me to go much into society: and I am almost surprised that, at this gay season of festivity, I have been able to carry on the war – seldom a day passes without an engagement for dinner and for many weeks I have not been able to command an hour's leisure.' Everything was 'so new varied and important in the Metropolis of this great Empire, after so long an absence in the woods and wilds of the East, that like the bee I wander from flower to flower and drink in delicious nutriment from the numerous intellectual and moral sources which surround me.'

At the same time, he was negotiating a country house purchase. Though Lower Grosvenor Street 'suits us exactly,' he and Sophia had been 'in search of a cottage to retire to in the summer in preference to the wandering life of Watering Place visitors.' They found what they wanted through William Wilberforce.

Raffles was in touch with Wilberforce as soon as he moved to London, but his social whirl was not Wilberforce's style. He was living with his wife out at Uxbridge Common 'for the very purpose of not being tempted out after dinner,' which they took at 'a rather early hour,' so he was 'sadly unsociable in the Dining way.' But if Raffles and Lady R would come and see them in Uxbridge, and if a 'homely' reception was acceptable, they would be more than welcome. Wilberforce became very fond of 'my dear Lady R.'

Wilberforce was projecting a final house-move – to a property called Hendon Park, ten miles out of London, with more than a hundred acres. It was on Highwood Hill on the northern edge of Mill Hill, a farming hamlet on the borders of Middlesex and Hertfordshire. Mill Hill was a favoured retreat for the prosperous on account of its elevation and proximity to London.

Adjacent to Hendon Park on Highwood Hill was another property, Highwood House. This too was for sale, and at Wilberforce's suggestion Raffles decided to acquire it. Once more, he would have a Hill. Highwood was a two-storey white-stuccoed house, its façade featuring two rounded bays flanking a central portico. An earlier mansion on the land had belonged to Lord Russell, executed for his part in the Rye House plot to murder Charles II, which added a certain frisson.

When Cousin Thomas' father died in November 1825 and was buried at Christ Church, Spitalfields, Raffles was present – and straight after the funeral the cousins sped up to Mill Hill so that Cousin Thomas could see Highwood. He reported to his wife that it was 'a lovely place… The views are most extensive and the diversity of hill and dale, wood and lawn, truly delightful.'

Raffles was on a high now, writing to his merchant friend A.L.Johnstone in Singapore: 'My friends assure me that the Direction [of the East India Company] is open to me, and that I have no reason to expect difficulty in getting into Parliament.' He asked Johnstone to remit all the moneys left with him 'as soon as you can, as I am anxious to invest my little property as early as possible,' since shares were soaring, and people were making quite astonishing sums of money on speculations abroad.

Too late. There was a financial crash in 1825. The Bank of England was chiefly to blame, with its expansionist monetary policies, irresponsible lending, poor supervision, and obfuscated operations. Bursting bubbles were followed by panic selling, falling share prices and a credit squeeze. Bail-outs came too late to prevent six London banks and seventy country banks from folding. Property values fell. Fortunes were lost. Notes were printed to ease the money supply. Lord Liverpool, the Prime Minister, told the Commons that 'the law as to the constitution of banks was absurd and ridiculous in its nature, futile in its construction, and dangerous in its effects.'

In late 1825 Raffles' man of business sent him the bad news that 'the run upon our bankers all the week was very great in consequence of false reports and probably improper management.' Payments had been suspended. 'Our balance in their hands is only about £1,200,' but would have been more if a payment due on Highwood had not been made shortly before. 'We have removed our accounts from the Bank of England,' which was then a commercial bank.

Raffles' financial misfortunes did not stop there. He lost 'some thousands' in Bencoolen after it was returned to the Dutch, from his investment in a sugar plantation. In addition, a particularly 'distressing and unlooked-for event' was the commercial failure of Thomas McQuoid, in whose agency house in Batavia he had invested £16,000, now lost.

The seeds of recovery were there but not yet recognisable. In his letter to Johnstone in January 1825, Raffles enthused about 'the *Locomotive* Steam Engines, which are to propel carriages without horses from one part of the country to another at the rate of ten or twelve miles an hour!' In September that year the first railway in the world was opened between Stockton-on-Tees and Darlington. 'Steam packets' were already churning round the British coastline. In April 1826 the steam vessel *Enterprise* made the voyage between Falmouth and Calcutta for the first time, although they ran out of coal at the Cape, and continued by sail. But a steam vessel was built in 1826 which would cut the voyage from Singapore to Calcutta from five weeks to about eight days; and a steam-vessel company in Singapore was formed to establish rapid transit between the ports of the Archipelago. The world Raffles knew was being transformed.

The first General Meeting of the Friends of the proposed Zoological Society took place on the premises of the Horticultural Society in Regent Street on 29 April 1826. Sir Stamford Raffles was appointed President of the Society by acclamation. He gave an opening address, and a letter was read from the Commissioners of His Majesty's Woods, Forests and Land Revenues agreeing to lease to the Society five specified acres of the Regent's Park, the Commissioners being at liberty to require the removal of any animal 'which may be deemed likely to become a nuisance or objectionable in the neighbourhood.'

At the first Council Meeting on 5 May 1826 Raffles nominated four Vice-Presidents, and it was agreed that everyone on the list of subscribers should be considered Members of the Society. Sir Stamford, in the chair, was requested to look for a suitable house for the accommodation of the Society. Six sub-committees were formed, four of them to be chaired by Sir Stamford.

Raffles and Sophia moved into Highwood with the children and Nurse Grimes. He wrote to Cousin Thomas on 15 June 1825: 'The house is small but compact and the grounds well laid out for appearance and economy, and I am assured I have not paid too much for it.' The estate comprised 112 acres, mostly laid down to grass, and Raffles had bought the standing crop of hay. There was a working farm; the outdoor and indoor staff required must have been considerable, but Raffles made no mention of the numbers – or cost – of his establishment. He saw Highwood as an investment. It cost him 'upwards of £20,000' and thought it would yield in the long run more than the three per cent available on the market. 'What the East India Company will do is uncertain, but if their liberality keeps pace with their delay, I ought to expect something handsome – tho' I confess I do not look for much.'

He 'farmed the ground' himself – which means he micro-managed the farm, not that he wielded a scythe – and 'Sophia takes care of the poultry and pigs. We brew our own beer and bake our own bread and lead an entire country life...I devote my time almost exclusively to the farm and grounds.' There was happiness at Highwood, not only for Raffles but for Sophia: 'You don't know what a sweet pleasure Highwood is and what a delightful pretty yard and dairy I have.' They were self-sufficient, she told Cousin Thomas, producing enough to have some left over to sell. Wine and fish were all she had to buy in.

Wilberforce, the old campaigner, still had one more crusade in him. That summer he recruited Raffles as a partner in his plan to 'build a Chapel of Ease in our neighbourhood.' He was obsessed with the project, writing Raffles long and increasingly illegible letters on the subject. A Chapel of Ease – a satellite place of worship within a large parish – was desired because St Mary's at Hendon, the parish church for Mill Hill, was four miles away. The Vicar of Hendon, the Rev. Theodore Williams, was a choleric gentleman who – on account of the sources of his own income – deplored the abolition of the slave trade. Wilberforce and Raffles were not the sort of people he liked. On 7 February 1826, Raffles reported to Cousin Thomas: 'We have not yet come to any conclusion and the difficulty seems to rest with our Vicar who is of a very peculiar character... My recommendation is to set about building the Chapel at once and discuss the government of it afterwards.' Controversy was such that the building of St Paul's Church, as it became, was not begun until 1829.

Raffles made his Will. Dated 5 September 1825, the witnesses were the Rev. Thomas Raffles, Sir Everard Home, and Mary Grimes. Sophia was an executrix, along with her brothers, John Watson Hull and William Hull, and Gerard de Vismes, an artist who was married to Sophia's sister Ella. The male executors were left in Trust Raffles' two houses and all his 'stocks, funds and securities' to provide for Sophia and their daughter Ella, with immensely complicated arrangements for all conceivable eventualities. Surplus funds were to be invested in real estate. Any children he had subsequent to the writing of the Will were to be treated equally with Ella – and if twins or triplets, 'on the same principle of division'. Maryanne's share of dividends was to be put into her own hands 'for her own separate and peculiar use and benefit exclusively of her present or any future Husband and without being subject to his debts control interference or engagements.'

Given the state of his finances in late 1825 the provisions of his Will were Utopian. Meanwhile he had every intention of involving himself in local life, writing to Sir Robert Harry Inglis on the last day of 1825 that 'my neighbours' – that is, the Wilberforces – urged him strongly to become a magistrate, though he feared that although he had spent his life 'directing others how to execute similar offices, I might myself be deficient in the details.' But he would put himself forward, not only from a desire to be useful, but because of the opportunity it would give 'of becoming *practically* acquainted with the real state of our society,' which he knew only 'theoretically'.

Lieutenant-Colonel William Farquhar was in London, though he and Raffles never met. He composed a long Memorial, submitted to the Court of Directors, setting out his complaints against Raffles' treatment of him and requesting to be reinstated to the command of Singapore. He claimed that Singapore as a settlement had been his choice, and that it had 'matured under his personal management'. Early in 1825 the Court asked Raffles for his comments. Both Farquhar and Raffles had a case, and each exaggerated his claim in the course of making that case.

Farquhar's mistake was making his Memorial hinge on his request to be reinstated as Commandant in Singapore. That was impossible. The clock could not be turned back. The Court rejected his Memorial. Raffles gave his version to Maryanne on 13 November 1825: 'Colonel Farquhar has had a very *long* and of course a very *hard* case before the Court ever since he has been at home, complaining of course in no very decent or moderate terms against me and petitioning to go back to Singapore, but it was only decided last week, and in a manner not I believe very much to his satisfaction. It was my wish, poor man, that he should be let off as easily as possible, but he seems to have failed in all he has attempted, and if he has not been so severely handled as he might have been, he may thank me for it.'

If Raffles had any remorse about how he had behaved he would never admit it to anyone, not even to himself. The unhinged state of his own mind being as it was in those last weeks in Singapore, he maybe hardly remembered the brutal way he got rid of Farquhar. He felt vindicated. 'The Court took the same view as the Bengal Government,' and 'there this mighty affair has finished.' Both Farquhar and Crawfurd 'are now *hors de combat*, and god grant you may do better under the new dynasty,' he said to Maryanne. (Crawfurd was replaced by Robert Fullerton that month.)

In February 1826 they closed up Highwood – 'carpets being taken up etc' – and returned to Lower Grosvenor Street for the London season. With the Farquhar affair resolved, Raffles was anticipating good news from the Company, 'now taking up my case and granting me an annuity – but I fear it will be very moderate and £500 a year is the largest amount I hear of.'

The Court of Directors finally delivered their response to his Statement of Services on 12 April 1826.

On Java, the Court conceded the success of the invasion force was 'promoted' by his plans and information, and that he was correct in his assessment of the financial difficulties that he encountered as Lieutenant-Governor, increased by 'inevitable' hostilities in Palembang and Yogyakarta. His sale of lands however was judged to be 'a questionable proceeding'. His other measures might have proved financially efficacious had the colony remained in British hands. In Sumatra, his internal reforms were approved. But his political measures 'incurred the strong disapprobation of the Court'.

The occupation of Singapore was 'approved by the Bengal Government,' and the measures 'ultimately carried into effect are to be attributed to his instrumentality, and to him the country is chiefly indebted for the advantages which the settlement of Singapore has secured to it. The Court considers this to be a very strong point in Sir Stamford Raffles' favour.'

The summing-up was mainly positive, but with pull-backs: 'The Government of Sir Stamford Raffles appears with sufficient evidence to have conciliated the good feelings of, at least, the great majority of the European and Native population; his exertions for the interests of literature and science are highly honourable to him, and have been attended with distinguished success; and although his precipitate and unauthorised emancipation of the Company's slaves, and his formation of a settlement at Pulo Nias, chiefly with a view to the suppression of a slave traffic, are justly censured by the Court, his motives in these proceedings, and his unwearied zeal for the abolition of slavery, ought not to be passed over without an expression of approbation.'

But there was no mention of compensation for the losses on the *Fame*, and no mention of a pension. There would be neither. The Accountant's Department had been doing sums. On the same day, Raffles was invoiced by the Company for £22,272, for immediate payment.

This debt, which was itemised, included repayment of his Bencoolen salary claimed while he was in England, plus interest; 'Loss in respect of discount' plus interest; 'Commission on exports' (£6,194); 'Extra charges at Acheen and Singapore', and a little afterthought of £592 for losses on spices from Borneo.

It was shattering. In a dignified letter to Secretary Joseph Dart written on 29 April, Raffles said he had already made arrangements for the disallowed Bencoolen salary, plus interest, to be paid from the Bengal Treasury out of Government securities in his name, the balance to be covered by an order on his agents. As for the 'Commission on Exports', the commissions were sanctioned by the

Bengal Government, subject to the approval of the Court of Directors. Until now, the Court had made no reference at all to the sums drawn, which led him to assume there was no objection. Because of the failure of his agents and bankers he was unable to meet their demands. He asked for time.

There was an abyss between Raffles' successful public life and his private circumstances. Just how dire the circumstances were can be judged by what Sophia wrote to Maryanne: 'We mean to go abroad next year, everything here is in such a dreadful state you are well out of the way. People starving, merchants failing, bankers ruined – in short, nothing can be more melancholy… We thought ourselves so comfortably settled, and now we shall be obliged to dispose of Highwood to meet the loss at Batavia.'

After the first General Meeting of the proposed Zoological Society, General Hardwicke, a retired Calcutta friend, sent Raffles a warning: 'Remember this is your first season of your Change of Climate; and bear in mind, that if you run into all that gaiety of the society in which you move, and yield to the many flattering invitations your friends will press upon you, you must not expect in one summer to renovate a constitution much shaken by long residence and arduous labors in an enervating clime.'

Raffles should have heeded General Hardwicke. He collapsed in the street after visiting Thomas Murdoch in Portland Place, and was brought home to Lower Grosvenor Street by a doctor who happened to be passing. He was unconscious for an hour. The episode was reported in the newspapers of 24 May 1826, but he was well enough to write to Cousin Thomas that day assuring him that although he was 'still rather weak and nervous, I am getting about again. My attack was sudden and unexpected, but fortunately was not apoplectic as was first feared… I am afraid of writing too much as my head is not quite what it should be.' His confidence was shaken. Sophia talked down his seizure as a 'fainting-fit'. Travers walked round the Regent's Park with him to look at 'the numberless new buildings which astonished me to see erected in so short a space of time' – the Nash terraces – after which they went to hear Weber's new opera *Oberon* at Covent Garden. But Raffles was changed. 'Although his spirit and animation was great, his articulation was at times heavy, thick and inarticulate.'

Wilberforce had not moved into Hendon Park full-time as he was having work done on the house. Raffles supervised the laying out of his grounds. Cousin Thomas recalled 'the glee with which he said, taking me to a long mound which he had raised and planted with shrubs and flowers, "There, I have raised this mound that the little man may enjoy his daily walk, sheltered from the north winds which would otherwise be too severe for him."' (Wilberforce, the 'little man', was a good deal shorter even than Raffles.)

On 30 June 1826 Raffles attended the second Council Meeting of the Zoological Society, chaired this time by the Duke of Somerset. As President, Sir Stamford Raffles laid before the meeting 'a sketch [by Decimus Burton] of the proposed plan for laying out the grounds in the Regent's Park,' and £1000 was voted for proceeding. Sir Stamford undertook to negotiate terms with Mr Burton. Sir Stamford reported that he had found a house, 33 Bruton Street, suitable for offices, the museum and the library. He was requested to close on the lease on the best terms available.

Sir Stamford also reported a proposal from James Cross, owner of the old Exeter Change menagerie, offering his services in the management of the Society's animals, plus his own present collection. The Council declined. The previous February, an elephant in the menagerie had run *amok*, maddened by pain from a poisoned tusk, and his death had been mismanaged. It took more than a hundred musket balls, followed by a thrust from a sabre, to bring him down.

Why did Raffles get up in the small hours of 5 July – five days after that meeting, the day before his forty-sixth birthday? He had been suffering for some days from a 'bilious attack' but went to bed at his usual time, between ten and eleven. Was his head giving him so much pain that he could not stay in bed? When Sophia woke at five o'clock and found him gone, she got up to look for him. She found him senseless at the bottom of the stairs. Medical help was called. But he was dead.

Sir Everard Home came straight to Highwood and performed an autopsy on the spot. He found a gross abnormality inside Raffles' head, but it was neither a tumour nor an abscess. He wrote an immediate draft report, expanded into a formal one: 'Upon removing the cranium, the anterior part of the right frontal bone was twice the thickness of the left... The outer covering of the brain was in a highly inflamed state, which had been of long continuance, from the thickness of the coats of the vessels. In one part, immediately upon the sinciput, this vasculosity exceeded anything I had ever seen.' (In his draft, he wrote that 'a space two inches long and one broad was so loaded with blood vessels as to appear of a different organisation from the rest of the membrane.')

In addition to this swollen tangle of blood vessels, there was in the right ventricle of the brain a coagulum of blood 'the size of a pullet's egg'. From this mass, four or six fluid ounces of bloody serum escaped during the autopsy. In the draft, Home said this occurred 'in sawing the sheaths' – the meninges protecting the central nervous system. The 'extravasion of blood,' or haemorrhage, 'which had been almost instantaneous, was the cause of immediate death, so far as the faculties of the brain are concerned.' There was no evidence of disease in any other part of the body.

The seizure Raffles suffered outside Thomas Murdoch's house, and his subsequently impaired diction, were doubtless caused by a less catastrophic bleed. A modern neurosurgical review of Home's autopsy, analysed in conjunction with descriptions of his symptoms, established a diagnosis of 'cerebral arteriovenous malformation'. The usual form develops in early embryonic life. The rarer form is acquired in adult life, sometimes due to trauma or infections (such as tropical fevers). In addition to severe headaches, common symptoms are nausea and vomiting – which accounts for Sophia's description of his attacks as 'bilious'. Thickening of a portion of the skull is associated with the condition.

The funeral was private, at St Mary's Church, Hendon. Owing to the intransigence of the vicar, nothing marked the place where Sir Stamford Raffles was buried. By the end of the century, there was no one left who knew.

In *The Times* of 1 March 1912 there appeared a notice from the vicar and churchwardens of St Mary's intimating that 'all persons interested in the remains of deceased persons interred within that portion of the churchyard adjacent to the south side of the church, proposed to be covered by the enlargement of the church, should apply for directions with regard to the reinterment of such remains.' A question was asked in the House of Commons about Sir Stamford Raffles' unmarked grave. The Straits Settlements Association contacted the vicar and the architect in charge in vain, because Raffles was not buried in the churchyard.

In April 1914, when workmen were taking up the floor of the south chapel of St Mary's, they uncovered a vault containing a single coffin. The wood had rotted, and a metal plate lay loose on the interior lead casing: 'Sir Stamford Raffles Knt. Died 5th July 1826. Aged 46.' ('46' was not a mistake for '45', but followed an old convention of counting the date of one's birth as one's first birthday.)

The vault was closed up again, and the new sanctuary was built above it. In 1920 the Association of British Malaya arranged for Raffles' coat of arms to be carved on the stone floor immediately over the vault, with an inscription memorialising Sir Stamford Raffles as Lieutenant-Governor of Java and Founder of Singapore.

Apart from the East India Company's claim, Raffles left debts of around £6,000 – mainly unpaid bills relating to the furnishing of Lower Grosvenor Street and Highwood. Sophia applied to the Company, explaining that after the claims on the estate were met 'there is little more than £10,000 to meet the demands of the East India Company.' She offered to transfer to the Company monies deposited in Bengal, and Raffles' India Stock, and a parcel of Consols, which would leave a balance of around £600 to make up the £10,000, to be made good 'on the first realization of the estate.' The Committee of Correspondence masticated the information, and recommended that the Court of Directors accept £10,000 'in satisfaction of all claims by the East India Company on the estate of Sir Stamford Raffles.' The Court accepted the recommendation.

Raffles' death was not a public event. His fame was, initially, entirely due to Sophia. She was not only the keeper of the flame but the one who ignited it; and the curator not only of his collections, but of his memory and reputation.

With unusual immediacy *The Gentleman's Magazine* of July 1826 carried an obituary article (unsigned) of twenty close-printed quarto columns summarising his career positively and in detail. No reader could have been left in doubt as to Sir Stamford's significance. Sophia surely had a hand in the drafting, even the writing of it. The article carries an account of the manner of his death, and quotations from his letters and reports, which could only have been supplied by her. A burst of triple exclamation marks, following a quoted piece of governmental cant, bears her stamp.

Only a month after Raffles died, Sophia was planning a memoir of him. She assumed Cousin Thomas would take it on, and conceived it as a compilation, instructing him to seek contributions. At the end of the year Cousin Thomas confessed he just could not undertake the work, so Sophia faced up to doing it herself. Friends and colleagues let her use their own material and extracts from their correspondence with Raffles. But she lacked anything about his life before he went out to Penang – 'the time is a perfect *blank* to me.' Little survived on paper about his childhood, or his years in India House, or the circumstances of his first marriage – and although Cousin Thomas helped out with 'early habits, character etc etc,' Olivia remained 'a perfect *blank*' which he may not have dared to fill. At the same time, Sophia prepared a new edition of *The History of Java.*

In April 1830 she was able to send Cousin Thomas a finished copy, bound in pink boards, of the *Memoir of the Life and Public Services of Sir Stamford Raffles F.R.S Etc, Particularly in the Government of Java, 1811–1816, and of Bencoolen and its Dependencies, 1817–1824; with Details of the Commerce and Resources of the Eastern Archipelago, and Selections from his Correspondence,* 'By His Widow'. With 723 pages of text and another 100 pages of appendices, it incorporated not only correspondence but also many of Raffles' voluminous reports, despatches, speeches, minutes, memos and extensive expository letters, lightened by linking passages by 'the Editor'. The *Quarterly* reviewer was about right when he wrote, 'On the whole, then, Sir Stamford Raffles is his own biographer.'

A positive, twenty-page overview of the book appeared in the *Edinburgh Review* in July 1830. The (anonymous) author, Captain Basil Hall, indicated that 'although it is not in human nature to suppose there should be perfect impartiality in such a case,' the humanity and feeling in the book removed it from the 'proverbially dull' category of books on Indian subjects which engaged 'none but the members of the Oriental Club.' The *Quarterly Review* carried a long and eulogistic notice: the book was surely 'a proud thing for the much-calumniated East India Company.' There were doubtless men in India House and the Oriental Club shifting in their chairs and adjusting their estimate of Sir Stamford Raffles.

When Raffles was in England in 1817, Francis Chantrey executed a marble bust of him. Chantrey was an extremely successful sculp-tor who 'did' all the great and the good – including, for St Paul's Cathedral, Major-General Robert Rollo Gillespie. Chantrey's origi-nal bust of Raffles went down with the *Fame*, but he had the plaster cast. Sophia commissioned several more – one for Cousin Thomas, one for the Zoological Society, another for the Singapore Institu-tion. There survives Chantrey's signed receipt to Lady Raffles for

£1,500, dated 7 May 1833, for 'a monumental statue of Sir Thos. Stamford Raffles in Westminster Abbey.' This is a life-size seated figure in white marble on a tall inscribed plinth. It was through Chantrey, Sophia told Cousin Thomas, that she contrived to have the statue placed in Westminster Abbey.

This statue is 'among the private and public memorials to his greatness…if none of them existed, the name of Stamford Raffles could still never be removed from the list of England's great statesmen.' So wrote Demetrius Charles Boulger, whose *Life of Sir Stamford Raffles* was published in the 'Makers of Empire' series in 1897, at the height of a British Empire assembling its myths and marshalling its heroes. Sir Stamford Raffles took his place in the parade, his name more resonant than ever it was in his lifetime, an exemplar of much that was great about the Empire – and then, in the postcolonial period, of much that was wrong and bad. 'Raffles' became a projection – like a shadow-puppet.

The materiality of him survives in a private collection – in a polka-dotted yellow silk waistcoat, thirty-seven inches round the chest, with a turn-up collar and embroidered trim, his dark sweat-stains under the arms. And a careful unwrapping of two folded papers reveals a handful of his hair – fine as a child's, light bright brown with foxy glints, fresh and shining as if cut yesterday.

Chapter 15

What Happened to the Others?

Maryanne's husband William Flint died of dysentery on board the *William Fairlie*, bound for Canton, in 1828. He died intestate, leaving Maryanne in difficulties. She returned to Europe with her daughter Sophie, visited her two elder children in Ireland, and spent time in France where the living was cheap. Her younger son Charley, aged fourteen, went with Sophia and Ella to see her there: 'Found mamma much better looking than I expected, and Sophie growing pretty and tall' – but 'shockingly spoilt by mamma.'

Charley's half-sister, Maryanne's elder daughter Charlotte Raffles Drury Flint, brought up by the McLellands in Ireland, married in 1835 the Hon. Charles Knox, who became the fourth Earl Castle Stewart in 1857. A niece of Raffles' old enemy William Robison, by coincidence, became the sister-in-law of Raffles' niece Charlotte. As the Dowager Countess Castle Stewart, Charlotte died near Torquay in 1906 – the last person living who had known Thomas Stamford Raffles. Charlotte's brother, Acheson, inherited Annaverna, the McLelland property in Ravensdale, Co. Louth and became a JP. He died in New Zealand in 1883.

Sophia found lodgings for Maryanne, until she moved back to Cheltenham to live with Sophia's widowed mother and Sophia's unmarried sister Emily in 1831. Maryanne was 'one of those gentle spirits that bends to all circumstances,' Sophia wrote, and it was Sophia who, after strenuous efforts, managed to extract from Singapore the modest property of William Flint on behalf of Charley and Sophie. Mrs Hull died in 1836, and the following year Emily Hull and Maryanne Flint died within two days of each other, both 'seized by spasms'.

When in 1824 John Palmer was away from Calcutta, his partners took control of Palmer & Co. and curtailed the personal expenses he took from the firm. He could not adjust to commercial discipline. The East India Company declined to bail him out. Palmer & Co. survived until 1830 largely on the strength of his personality and social standing. He died in 1836.

Thomas McQuoid tried his luck in Australia and became Sheriff of New South Wales in 1829. Money troubles continued to dog him and he took his own life in Sydney in 1841.

Dr Thomas Horsfield lived in London from 1819, as Curator of the East India Company's Museum, and then its Library, where he was visited by Alfred Russel Wallace, the future author of *The Malay Archipelago* and pioneer of the theory of natural selection. Horsfield's collections survived, but his executors destroyed his papers. Unassuming and retiring, he never received the recognition he deserved. He died in 1859 aged eighty-six.

Lieutenant-Colonel William Farquhar retired to Scotland, and lived at Early Bank Villa in Craigie on the outskirts of Perth – a large detached house with a gardener's cottage and, across the lane at the back, a coach-house, stables and peach-house. In 1828, at the age of fifty-four, he married Isabella Loban, with whom he had five surviving children. His Eurasian children were provided for, as was their mother, and some of his grandchildren came to Scotland. He was promoted by reason of seniority to full Colonel in 1829 and to Major-General in 1837.

Raffles' treatment of Farquhar in Singapore, and the failure of his Memorial to the Company, never ceased to rankle. In 1825, a year before Raffles died, 'the principal part of the gentlemen of the settlement' in Singapore founded a 'Raffles Club' in honour of Sir Stamford as 'founder of the settlement and as a lasting testimony to… the impulse and spirit created by his energy and activity during the short period of his residence here, to which is mainly to be ascribed its present flourishing and respectable appearance.' The first annual dinner, ball and supper of the Raffles Club was held at the Singapore Hotel on 6 July, Sir Stamford's birthday.

Hearing of this, Farquhar wrote under the pseudonym 'A Singaporean' a letter to the *Singapore Chronicle* (founded by his son-in-law Francis Bernard, who in 1827 abandoned his wife Esther and left Singapore), which was reprinted in the *Asiatic Journal*. It was an error, wrote 'A Singaporean', to designate Sir Stamford as the founder of Singapore. It was 'founded by the Supreme Government, at the representation of the Penang Government, acting on the suggestions of Lieut.Col. Farquhar.' The latter had been authorised to proceed alone when 'Sir Stamford altered his views' and joined the expedition. The Carimons having been judged unsuitable, it was Captain Ross who advocated checking out Singapore. Sir Stamford's 'presence and agency' at the momentous landing were 'purely adventitious'. He was not 'the sole founder of Singapore'.

Farquhar could not evade the fact that the civil branch was senior to the military branch, but if the title of founder 'can be claimed by subordinate officers, Lieut.Col F. had an equal claim.' Military success, he wrote, was always attributed to the General of an army, not to the commanding officer of a division, so by analogy 'the Marquess of Hastings is the real founder of Singapore.'

When Farquhar read in 1830 the article in the *Quarterly Review* on Lady Raffles' *Memoir*, he wrote to the *Courier* to protest against her attribution of the sole credit for establishing Singapore to her husband. Captain Basil Hall, the author of the review, snapped back in defence of Sir Stamford's primacy in the matter. Farquhar published his own account in the *Asiatic Journal* later the same year, making a good case for claiming at least 'a large share' of the credit.

After he died in 1839, the large stone mausoleum erected over his grave in Greyfriars burial ground in Perth carried an inscription detailing his thirty-three years in the service of the East India Company:

> Having in addition to his military duties
> served as resident in Malacca
> and afterwards at Singapore
> which later settlement he founded.

That is unequivocal.

The case of the Malayan Tapir represents another resentment Farquhar could have held against Raffles. Farquhar sent a drawing of it, plus a skeleton of its head and a detailed description, to the Asiatic Society of Bengal in 1816. But the drawing and his account were not published until five years later, in Paris, by Pierre Diard, the French naturalist who had seen the drawing and skeleton in Calcutta, and also a living specimen. He made generous acknowledgment to Farquhar, whose own account was published in 1821.

Raffles wrote about the live Tapir he saw in Calcutta in the 'Descriptive Catalogue' of his Sumatran collection in the *Transactions* of the Linnean Society of London for 1821–3. He claimed with truth that he had first known the Tapir (just a head) in Penang back in 1805; he tried to block Farquhar's 1821 paper by suggesting to Nathaniel Wallich that the Asiatic Society of Bengal might prefer to substitute his own account for Farquhar's. Wallich did not pursue this.

The rights and wrongs and anomalies, in Raffles' lifetime, of discoveries, taxonomies, attributions and first publications of exotic beasts, birds, fishes and plants, are a subject for specialists. Ambition, vanity and competitiveness all played a part. So did the extreme slowness of communications and of translations, and the lack of a functioning international community of naturalists. Not all the creatures or plants bearing the tag *rafflesi, rafflesii, rafflesia* or *rafflesiana* may, strictly speaking, be correctly designated, and that is not always his fault.

Farquhar's collection of more than four hundred natural history drawings went to the Asiatic Society in London in his lifetime. In 1993 the Society sold them, and they were donated by the purchaser, Goh Geok Khim, to the National Heritage Board of Singapore. A selection, along with a portrait of William Farquhar, is on permanent display in the Singapore History Museum; and there is a fully illustrated descriptive catalogue in two volumes of what is now named the William Farquhar Collection of Natural History Drawings. As a naturalist, Farquhar has received his due in Singapore.

But although 'Stamford' and 'Raffles' (not to mention 'Flint', 'Napier', and other familiar names), are remembered in streets, buildings and institutions, there is no memorial to William Farquhar and no Farquhar Street in Singapore. There was one, but it was insignificant and disappeared in redevelopment.

Raffles' own large and heterogeneous collection of natural history drawings form part of the Raffles Family Collection now in the British Library. Most but not all of them date from the brief period when he was in Bencoolen following the loss of around two thousand precious drawings and all the other treasures on the *Fame*. The surviving drawings have been finely reproduced, annotated and put in context by Henry Noltie in *Raffles' Ark Redrawn*.

The 'Minto Stone', the tenth-century inscribed stele presented by Raffles to Lord Minto, was shipped back to Scotland when Minto left India – though he, dying on the way home, never placed it as he had fancied 'on our Minto craigs' or saw it *in situ*. The Minto mansion no longer stands, and its land is built on. The Stone is in the garden of a modern house. The inscription on the exposed side is badly weathered. Negotiations have been ongoing since 2003 for the return of the Stone to Jakarta.

Lady Raffles, as she had always feared, remained financially responsible for Charles and Sophie Flint. She placed Sophie in a clergyman's family in Blackheath. She vacated Highwood and let it out, then tried to sell it. Finding no takers, she decided in 1835 to go back and live there. Financial strictures forced her to give up her horses and carriage. Charles was boarding with an expensive tutor, preparing for entry to Trinity College, Cambridge. 'He is not gifted with first rate talents – but I hope to see him a useful Minister of Christ,' she told Cousin Thomas, to whom she remained close and with whom she shared family news and religious animadversions.

Before returning to Highwood, travelling in Europe, she became a friend of Madame de Staël's daughter-in-law Adèle, through whom she met Frances, the young wife of Baron de Bunsen, the Prussian Minister in Rome. The Baron and Baroness de Bunsen became her intimate friends and admirers, and later suggested living with her at Highwood and sharing expenses, a proposal which she declined. Her second edition of the *Memoir* (1835) was dedicated to Baron Bunsen.

One can no longer refer to her as Sophia. She was Lady Raffles, 'the former Queen of the East among her relics, and surrounded by the remains of her station... In the midst she moves so queenlike, and so humble, so serious and so spirited, so intelligent and so full of kindness.' So she seemed to Frances de Bunsen. A visit to Highwood impressed upon this friend 'the dignity, the order, the quiet activity, the calm cheerfulness with which Lady Raffles rules the house, the day, the conversation...' Charles Flint's son, Stamford Raffles Flint, remembered her from his boyhood: 'Her tall and stately figure and quiet dignity are fixed in my mind.' He was impressed by 'the manner with which, after dinner was announced, she led the way alone into the dining-room.' She did not designate any gentleman to take her arm and accompany her in, as was the convention. Stamford Raffles Flint recalled a watercolour portrait of Lady Raffles by George Richmond (its whereabouts now unknown), painted around 1850, which represented her just as he remembered.

Highwood became a shrine. In the dining-room hung the portrait of Raffles by G.F. Joseph, now in the National Portrait Gallery in

London. A second portrait of Raffles by Joseph at Highwood had originally belonged to Thomas Otho Travers, who died in 1844. Lady Raffles used when in evening dress to carry a little scent bottle set in gold filigree attached by a chain to a ring on her finger. Her guests sat at a table of mottled Amboyna wood which extended to take twenty places. They ate with the King's Pattern silver forks and spoons which Raffles bought in 1824, each piece engraved with his griffin crest. There were silver-gilt dessert forks, spoons and servers, and fruit knives with agate handles. (No wonder Raffles left debts.) The guests took coffee or tea from the Duchess of Somerset's porcelain.

A gamelan orchestra was displayed in the hall. In a room known as the Museum were artefacts brought home from Java on Raffles' 1816 visit to London. The whole of Highwood was a museum: family portraits on the walls, including a miniature of Maryanne in a tawny-coloured dress and another of Lady Raffles in a jew-elled headdress, festooned with pearls. This was a small replica by E.A.Chalons of the watercolour he did in 1817, which went down with the *Fame*. Its companion piece of Raffles himself, in an identical frame, shows him with fine, light-reddish hair. All other portraits render his hair and eyes – which were large and light – much darker than they were.

Pudgy-faced William Flint hung there, and William Hull painted by Gerard de Vismes. There was a bust of Ella, showing her deli-cate profile; a bust of Napoleon by Canova which had belonged to Marshal Daendels, liberated by Raffles from Buitenzorg; and the original plaster cast of Raffles' bust from Chantrey's studio. In the ante-room to the drawing room stood a brass-inlaid round table made of the fine tortoiseshell William Flint procured for Raffles in Singapore. On this table lay a silver and tortoiseshell box with a key, lined in red silk and containing the remains of a human bone and a silver coin which had been found inside a fifteen-foot alligator. Also on the table were intricately worked gold boxes, and a *kris* in a gold sheath.

There was another and round Amboyna-wood table which, like the fourteen miniatures of the Mughal emperors from Tamurlane to Tippoo set in green velvet in a glass case, may have been in the drawing-room; likewise the ivory Chinese box fitted with intricately carved smaller boxes, containing tokens for various games made of mother-of-pearl and ivory filigree, every delicate piece engraved with the coat of arms on one side and 'TSR' on the other; and the folding chessboard of brass, tortoiseshell and mother-of-pearl. There were small fragile objects in ivory filigree – fan-holders like miniature umbrella stands, to be fixed to a wall; a visiting-card holder, a toothpick-case.

Most of the ethnological collection must always have been 'kept in boxes' in the outbuildings of Highwood. One which travelled with them from Bencoolen has survived, with LADY RAFFLES stencilled on the side. It is made of thick, heavy wood, iron-bound, with a coved top, and is the size of a large travelling trunk, fitted inside with drawers and compartments. It would have weighed a ton even before anything was put in it, and they sailed with scores of such containers. Some were custom-made for individual objects, such as their bulgy silver tea-urn (engraved with the coat of arms).

The bulk of the Raffles Collection was presented by Charles Flint to the British Museum after Lady Raffles' death. Another consignment was deposited in 1939 by Muriel Rosdew Raffles-Flint (Mrs J.H.Drake), Charles Flint's granddaughter. There are around 1,500 individual objects associated with Raffles in the British Museum's collections.

Of those items which are on display, some are in the Department of Asia, some in the Enlightenment Gallery, and a handful in other departments. The pick of the collection can be seen – Raffles' table-top model gamelan orchestra and sets of gongs, the bird-woman and the heads of the Buddha from Borobudur, masks and puppets, small bronze Javanese deities. The items in the Coins and Medals Department were mostly donated by Lady Raffles in her lifetime.

There remain around 800 objects stored in boxes and drawers, both on the BM's main site and in its off-site depositories. (Raffles did not want his collection to be 'kept in boxes'.) They include *inter alia* his Javanese puppets, masks, *kris*es, musical instruments, the Dutch torture instruments Raffles salvaged in Malacca, some textiles, and a quantity of miscellaneous artefacts chiefly of value by accumulation. Raffles was concerned with the materiality of life, 'the habits of man' – what the Enlightenment called *'res humanae'*. His obsession with collecting was sympathetic and systematic. Everything was labelled. Not only original objects, but models and miniatures commissioned by him, served his primary purpose – which was to bring home, in both senses, to the United Kingdom the complexity and ingenuity of south-east Asian culture and civilisation.

Ella, pious like her mother, growing up among artefacts from countries she never knew and in the sunlight and shadow of her father's memory, became engaged in late 1839 to the newly ordained John Sumner, eldest son of Lady Raffles' friend Charles Sumner, the Bishop of Winchester. She was small like her father – 'little Ella will always be *little* Ella' said her mother, who believed that 'tall people are seldom as strong as short ones.' Soon after her engagement she succumbed to tuberculosis. In February 1840 she declined rapidly, 'reduced to a skeleton'. She was taken to the south coast for the sea air, and died at St Leonard's on 5 May 1840, aged nineteen. Her mother was devastated. Her grief was terrible and uncontrolled. She had lost her last child and her last link with her husband.

The Bunsens, when the Baron was Prussian Minister Plenipotentiary to the Court of St James, moved to Oak Hill at Barnet, four miles from Highwood. At Oak Hill Lady Raffles met James Brooke, the Rajah of Sarawak in North Borneo. The Sultan of Brunei had granted him this hereditary title, with total sovereignty, in return for services rendered by him against the Sultan's enemies. Brooke was back in England in 1847, being lionized and feted (rather as

Raffles was in 1817) while campaigning, successfully, to gain recognition of his kingly status from the Government.

Brooke was an army officer in the Company's service who, after his father died leaving him £30,000, bought his own schooner, which he converted into a small warship. His plan – consciously following Raffles' example and Raffles' expansionist aspirations – was to stymie the Dutch by establishing a chain of British settlements from Singapore to North Borneo to northern Australia. He knew Singapore, and was inspired by what Raffles wrote about Borneo's potential in his *History of Java*. He shared Raffles' liberal and reformist views and his fantasy of being 'the great Mogul' – although his harsh measures against the indigenous people were, in 1851, the subject of an enquiry in Singapore. But in 1847, talking with dashing James Brooke, a man after her own heart, and one who appreciated the genius of her husband, would have been most agreeable for Lady Raffles.

A year and a half before Lady Raffles died, she bade a formal farewell to her friends, explaining that she was no longer in a fit state to write letters. Her sister Mary Jane, widow of Peter Auber, came to look after her at Highwood. She died in December 1858, aged seventy-two, and was buried in the graveyard of St Paul's, Mill Hill, the new church built at the instigation of Sir Stamford Raffles and William Wilberforce, to whom she had remained close, sharing his religious piety, until his death in 1833.

Frances Bunsen, learning of Lady Raffles' passing, thanked God 'for the termination of such a living death as she had existed through for years.' She did not mean just mental and physical decline, but the burden of grief and loss that Lady Raffles – that 'astonishing person' – had borne. Lady Raffles left a small annuity of £30 to Mary Grimes 'as a reward for her kindness and faithfulness.' Highwood was left to her sister Alice Mudge's daughter, Jenny Rosdew Mudge, who had married Maryanne's son – transformed, by the taking of holy orders, from Charley Flint into the Rev. William

Charles Raffles Flint. They sold Highwood and its land in 1859. The Rev. Charles Raffles Flint became Vicar of Holy Trinity Church at Sunningdale in Berkshire, to which he added a chancel and a chapel in memory of Sir Stamford Raffles, his uncle and guardian. He died in 1884.

Cousin Thomas, the Rev. Thomas Raffles, retired in 1861 on a pension of £400 a year. He died in 1863 and his funeral in Liverpool was, unlike his cousin's, a public event.

The year in which Sophia Raffles died also saw the end of the East India Company, following what was called in England the 'Indian Mutiny' of 1857. It started with a rebellion of the Company's sepoy soldiers in Meerut and spread through native states, with British retribution of the most severe kind. It was a case of 'something must be done'. The Government of India Act of 1858 – properly, the Act for the Better Government of India – provided for the liquidation of the East India Company and the transfer of all its functions and property to the British Crown.

Lord Grenville had advocated such a transfer during the debates on the 1813 Charter renewal. Five years before Raffles was even born, Adam Smith in *The Wealth of Nations* (1776) argued against monopolies on the grounds that they worked against the nation that set them up:

> Since the establishment of the East India Company…the other inhabitants of England, over and above being excluded from the trade, must have paid, in the price of the East India goods which they have consumed, not only for all the extraordinary profits which the Company must have made upon those goods in consequence of their monopoly, but for all the extraordinary waste which the fraud and abuse inseparable from the management of so great a company must necessarily have occasioned.

With free trade, Smith suggested, merchants would find it in their interests 'to reside in the East Indies and to employ their capital in providing goods' for Europe. The Company's settlements 'should be put under the immediate protection of the Sovereign.'

And so, more than eighty years later, they were. India House in Leadenhall Street, and its furniture and fittings, was sold in 1861, and the buildings were demolished the following year. Nothing is to big to fail.

Note on Sources

William Dalrymple in *The White Mughals* says that there are fifty shelf-miles of East India Company papers in the India Office Records in the British Library. I can well believe it. No one in a lifetime could read them all. Every researcher, within a relevant topic and period, reads what he or she can. Fortunately we are all in search of something different; I extracted material on what most preoccupied me, and have benefited, and quoted, from previous writers on Raffles who published letters, official despatches and documents which I have not myself read. In those hours in the Asian and African Studies Reading Room, battling with recalcitrant microfilm-reading machines, I was particularly concerned with the Raffles-Minto Collection, the Raffles Collection, and most of all with the Raffles Family Papers which had not been available to previous biographers.

Chief among those previous biographers is the grandfather of Raffles studies, Charles Edward Wurtzburg who, on his death in 1952, left a manuscript of 450,000 words. Clifford Whitting edited it down to 788 pages, and it was published as *Raffles of the Eastern Isles* in 1954. The work remains so dense that you cannot always see the wood for the trees, but I have constantly consulted Wurtzburg, also his copious research papers deposited in the Cambridge University Library. The research papers also include miscellaneous copies of letters, including those from Raffles to his friend in Penang David Brown and to Thomas McQuoid. Wurtzburg should really be mentioned in the endnotes for every chapter, but my debt to him is acknowledged here once and for all so as to avoid endless repetition.

The other principal Raffles biographies are by D.C. Boulger, *The Life of Sir Stamford Raffles* (1897); H.E. Egerton, *Sir Stamford Raffles and the Far East* (1900); J.A. Bethune Cook, *Sir Thomas Stamford Raffles, Founder of Singapore*

(1918), specially strong on missionaries and the Singapore Institute; Sir Reginald Coupland *Raffles 1781–1826* (1926); Emily Hahn, *Raffles of Singapore* (1946), which is useful for the Dutch view of Raffles and Dutch documents; H.F. Pearson *This Other India: A Biography of Sir Thomas Stamford Raffles* (1957); Colin Clair, *Sir Stamford Raffles, Founder of Singapore* (1963); Maurice Collis, *Raffles* (1966).

If C.E. Wurtzburg was the grandfather, then Professor John Bastin is the father of Raffles studies. Since the early 1950s he has been publishing articles, monographs, pamphlets, editions, introductions and short books about every aspect of Raffles' life and career, his policies, his family, friends and colleagues, his collections, and South East Asian culture and geopolitics. The footnotes to the books and documents edited or introduced by him constitute a Raffles encyclopaedia. My bibliography and endnotes testify to my enormous obligation to this body of work.

An essential, if partisan and partial source, incorporating many letters, documents and despatches, is Sophia Raffles' *Memoir of the Life and Career of Sir Thomas Stamford Raffles* (1830): 723 pages of text, plus 100 more of additional material, appendices and index. It can be read in the 1991 facsimile edition with an introduction by John Bastin.

I have not loaded the narrative with footnotes, but have appended for each chapter the principle texts and documents consulted, listed in the order in which they were drawn on or quoted, with comments where required. Readers who want more detailed particulars can enquire on the website rafflesbook. co.uk.

All letters from Raffles to his sister Maryanne, and all letters to or from Sophia Raffles (other than those to the Rev. Thomas Raffles) are from the Raffles Family Papers in the British Library, a collection which also includes many letters from non-family members.

The inflammatory correspondence between Raffles and Colonel William Farquhar was read in the National Archives of Singapore.

Raffles' letters to his mother, to the Rev. Thomas Raffles, to his Uncle William Raffles, and Sophia Raffles' letters to the Rev. Thomas Raffles, are in the Tang Holdings Collection in Singapore, edited with commentary and holograph facsimiles by John Bastin as *The Letters and Books of Sir Stamford Raffles and Lady Raffles* (2009).

The letters and papers of John Palmer are in the Bodleian Library, Oxford, as is the letter from Raffles to Alexander Hare about meeting Napoleon on St Helena.

The Indian Papers of the First Earl of Minto, which include Captain William Taylor's manuscript journal and letters, are in the National Library of Scotland.

Endnotes

Introduction

Patrick O'Brian, *H.M.S. Surprise, The Thirteen Gun Salute, The Nutmeg of Consolation*
T.M. Devine, *Scotland's Empire*

Chapter 1

Wa Hakim's reminiscences recorded by H.T. Haughton in 1882 and published in Sheppard, *Singapore 150 Years*. The Malay historian quoted in translation is Raja Ali Haji ibn Ahmad, see Matheson and Watson, *The Precious Gift*
Capt., J.G.F. Crawford's unpublished Diary is quoted in Wurtzburg
Thomas Sadler (ed) *Crabb Robinson*
Thomas Stamford Raffles B.A, etc (ed) *Memoirs of the Life & Ministry of the Rev Thomas Raffles*
For Walworth: *Survey of London* Vol.. 24 1955; various websites. The Cuming Museum is now at the Old Town Hall, 151 Walworth Rd
Peter Wilson Coldham, *Child Apprentices in America from Christ's Hospital*
Thomas Faulkner, *The History and Antiquities of the Parish of Hammersmith*
Sophia Raffles, *Memoir ...*
John Bastin, *Letters and Books* Chapter 1
D.C. Boulger, *Life of Sir Stamford Raffles* for 'the letter of 14 October 1819'. The original is in private hands
C.H. Phillips, *The East India Company 1784–1834*
John Keay, *The Honourable Company*

H.V. Bowen, *The Business of Empire*

Sir Frank Swettenham, *British Malaya*

C.B. Buckley, *Anecdotal History of Olden Times in Singapore* Vol. 1

A.E.H. Anson, *About Others and Myself* (for the Ibbetson story)

Captain Thomas Williamson, *The East India Vade-Mecum*

John Bastin, *Olivia Mariamne Raffles*

John Evans, *The Gentleman Usher*

James Fergusson (ed) *Letters of George Dempster to Sir Adam Fergusson*

London Metropolitan Archives for the Old Bailey report

Burke's Landed Gentry

Charlotte Louisa Hawkins-Dempster *The Manners of My Time*

Robert J. Devenish and Charles H. McLaughlin *Historical and Genealogical Records of the Devenish Families of England and Ireland*

Brian Harrison, *Holding the Fort*

Karl Marx 'Primary Accumulation' *Capital* Vol. 2

David Gilmour, *The Ruling Caste*

Chapter 2

Captain Thomas Williamson, *The East India Vade-Mecum*

Sir Evan Cotton, *East Indiamen*

Frank Swettenham, *British Malaya*

Alfred Spencer (ed) *Memoirs of William Hickey* Vol. IV

John Bastin, *Olivia Mariamne Raffles*

Jan Dalley, *The Black Hole*

John Bastin, *John Leyden and Thomas Stamford Raffles*

Sophia Raffles, *Memoir ...*

Rev. James Morton, *The Poetical Remains of the late Dr John Leyden*

Elisha Trapaud, *A Short Account of Prince of Wales's Island in the East-Indies*

Prince of Wales Island Gazette

Stephen Tomkins, *William Wilberforce*

Chapter 3

Isabella L. Bird, *The Golden Chersonese*

M.C. Ricklefs, *A History of Modern Indonesia*

Brian Harrison, *Holding the Fort*

A.H. Hill (ed) *The Hikayet Abdullah*

John Bastin, *William Farquhar*

Prince of Wales Island Gazette

John Bastin, *John Leyden and Thomas Stamford Raffles*

Rev James Morton, *The Poetical Remains of the late Dr John Leyden*
Edward Robarts's 'Narrative' is quoted in Wartzburg
Countess of Minto (ed) *Lord Minto in India*
Lord Curzon *British Government in India*
Sir George Elliot, *Memoir* ...

Chapter 4

John Bastin, *John Leyden and Thomas Stamford Raffles*
Annabel Teh Gallop, 'Raffles and the Art of the Malay Letter', BL lecture
Annabel Teh Gallup 'Illumination: The Art of the Malay Letter', Sydney
    lecture
Ahmat Adam (trs and notes) *The Letters of Sincerity*
Major William Thorn, *The Conquest of Java*
Captain William Taylor's manuscript Letters and Journals
Sophia Raffles *Memoir* ... for Raffles' letters to Minto from Malacca
Wurtzburg for translation of the 'Proclamation to the People of Java'
C.A. Gibson-Hill, 'Raffles, Acheh, and the Order of the Golden Sword'
Lee Kam Hing and Ahmat Adam 'Raffles and the Order of the Golden
    Sword'
A,H, Hill (ed) *The Hikayet Abdullah*
Countess of Minto, *Lord Minto in India*
Sir George Elliot, *Memoir* ...
Anthony Webster, *The Richest East India Merchant*
Syed Hussein Alatas, *Thomas Stamford Raffles: Schemer or Reformer?*
Joseph Conrad, *The Shadow Line*

Chapter 5

John Bastin, *John Leyden and Thomas Stamford Raffles*
John Bastin, *Olivia Mariamne Raffles*
John Bastin (ed) *The Journal of Thomas Otho Travers 1813–1820*. Post-1820
    extracts from the Journal are from Wartzburg. Original not seen.
Major W. Thorn, *The Conquest Of Java*
Major W. Thorn, *A Memoir of Sir R.R. Gillespie*
Christopher Hibbert, *George IV: Regent and King 1811–1830*
Henry Newbolt's 'Gillespie' in *Collected Poems 1897–1907* (1910)
John Blakiston *Twelve Years' Military Adventure in Three Quarters of the Globe*
Syed Hussein Alatas, *Thomas Stamford Raffles: Schemer or Reformer?*
Peter Carey (ed) *The British in Java 1811–1816*
Peter Carey 'Sexuality and Power'

M.C. Ricklefs, *A History of Modern Indonesia*
John Bastin, 'Raffles's [sic] Aides-de-Camp in Java'
Tim Hannigan, 'Sultans, Sepoys and Englishmen'
John Bastin, *The Natural History Researches of Dr Thomas Horsfield*
W.C. Mackenzie, *Colonel Colin Mackenzie*

Chapter 6

John Bastin, *The Native Policies of Sir Stamford Raffles in Java and Sumatra*
John Bastin, 'The Working of the Early Land Rent System in West Java'
John Bastin (ed) *The Journal of Thomas Otto Travers 1813–1820*
Karl Marx 'Division of Labour and Manufacture' in *Capital* Vol. 1
Emily Hahn, *Raffles of Singapore*
Dirk van Hogendorp, *Berigt* …
Sir George Elliot, *Memoir* …
Major William Thorn, *A Memoir of Sir R.R. Gillespie*
W.C. Mackenzie, *Colonel Colin Mackenzie*
Java Government Gazette
Utbe Bosma and Remco Raben *Being 'Dutch' in the East Indies 1500–1920*
Nigel Bullough, 'The Minto Stone'
Countesst of Minto (ed) *Lord Minto in India*
Rasheed El-Enany, *Arab Representations of the Occident*
Peter Carey (ed) *The British in Java*

Chapter 7

John Bastin, 'The Raffles Gamelan'
Ronan Kelly, *Bard of Erin: The Life of Thomas Moore*
Marchioness of Bute (ed) *The Private Journals of the Marquis of Hastings*
W.C. Mackenzie, *Colonel Colin Mackenzie*
J.E. van Lohuizen-de Leeuw, 'Which European First recorded the Unique
　　Dvarapala of Barabudur?'
John Miksik, *Borobudur: Golden Tales of the Buddha*
Nigel Barley (ed) *The Golden Sword*
Clifford Geertz, *The Religion of Java*
R. Kowner, *Skin as Metaphor*
Utbe Bosma and Remco Raben *Being 'Dutch' in the East Indies 1500–1920*
Jean Gelman Taylor, *The Social World of Batavia*
Tim Hannigan, 'Sultans, Sepoys and Englishmen'
John Bastin, *Olivia Mariamne Raffles*
The Countess of Minto (ed) *Lord Minto in India*

David Mitchell, *The Thousand Autumns of Jacob de Zoet*
Arnold Chapman, *A St. Helena Who's Who*

Chapters 8 & 9

John Bastin (ed): *The Journal of Thomas Otho Travers 1813–1820*
Lady Gwendolen Ramsden, *Correspondence of Two Brothers*
Alfred Spencer (ed) *Memoirs of William Hickey* Vol. IV
Christopher Hibbert, *George IV*
Thomas Stamford Raffles Esq. B.A. etc (ed) *Memoirs of the Life and Ministry*
    of the Rev. Thomas Raffles
Rev. Thomas Raffles, 'Reminiscences of Sir Stamford Raffles' in John Bastin
    (ed) *Letters and Books*
Richard Holmes, *The Age of Wonder*
John Gascoigne, *Joseph Banks and the English Enlightenment*
John Bastin, *Sophia Raffles*
Andrew S.Cook, 'William Marsden 1754–1836' *ODNB*
Sir Reginald Coupland, *Raffles of Singapore*
The Rev. Thomas Raffles, *Letters, During a Tour ...*
Thomas Sadler (ed) *Crabb Robinson*
Anna Letitia, le Breton *Memoir of Mrs Barbauld*
Thomas Stamford Raffles, *The History of Java*
John Bastin, *Sir Stamford Raffles's History of Java: a Bibliographical Essay*
    (which includes Raffles' letters to Elton Hamond from Falmouth, from
    the Baker MSS at the Royal Asiatic Society)
Catalogue of the Antiquarian Book Fair 1990 (for the presentation copy
    of *The History of Java* to Mrs Sophia Hull, and Raffles' inscription. The
    asking price was £35,000.)
Felix Felton, *Thomas Love Peacock*

Chapter 10

G.F. Davidson, *Trade and Travel in the Far East*
John Bastin (ed) *The British in West Sumatra 1685–1825*
Alan Harfield *Bencoolen: The Christian Cemetery and the Fort Marlborough*
    Monuments
John Bastin, *Sophia Raffles*
John Bastin (ed) *The Letters of Sir Stamford Raffles to Nathaniel Wallich*
    1819–24
John Bastin, 'Sir Stamford Raffles and the Study of Natural History in
    Penang, Singapore and Indonesia'

H.J. Noltie, *Raffles Ark Redrawn*

'Vegetable Titan' (signed 'B.') *The Saturday Magazine* Vol. I 1833 (for Dr Arnold's letter about the Great Flower)

Annual Register 1919 (for Salmond in Palembang and Raffles' 'Protest' letters)

Anthony Webster, *The Richest East India Merchant*

John Anderson, *Acheen and the Ports on the North and East Coasts of Sumatra*

Chapter 11

C.R.,Buckley, *An Anecdotal History of Olden Times in Singapore* Vol. 1

C.D. Cowan (ed) *Early Penang and the Rise of Singapore*

Thomas Stamford Raffles B.A. etc (ed) *Memoirs of the Life and Ministry of the Rev Thomas Raffles*

John Anderson, *Acheen and the Ports on the North and East Coasts of Sumatra*

John N. Miksic, *Archaeological Research on the 'Forbidden Hill' of Singapore*

Lee Kip Lin, *The Singapore House 1819–1942*

The letter from TSR to John Taylor 9 June 1819 is in the National Library of Singapore

John Crawfurd, *History of the Indian Archipelago*

Sir John Barrow, *An Autobiographical Memoir of Sir John Barrow*

The online archive of the *Quarterly Review* is edited by Jonathan Cutmore

Chapter 12

The letter from TSR to Joseph Dart February 1822 is in the National Archive of Singapore

Lee Kip Lin, *The Singapore House* 1988

Tan Sri Dato Mubin Sheppard (ed) *Malaysian Branch of the Royal Asiatic Society: Singapore 150 Years* (reprints of *JMBRAS* articles, mostly undated)

John Bastin (ed); *The Letters of Sir Stamford Raffles to Nathaniel Wallich 1819–24*

Anthony Webster, *The Richest East India Merchant* 2009

T.H.H. Hancock, *Coleman's Singapore*

John Crawfurd *Journal of an Embassy from the Governor-General of India*.1828

The Mission to Siam in the years 1821–2 from the Journal of the late George Finlayson

A.H. Hill (trs) *The Hikayat Abdullah*

Marchioness of Bute (ed) *The Private Journal of the Marquess of Hastings*

C.B. Buckley, *An Anecdotal History of Olden Times in Singapore* Vol. I

Nicholas A. Joukovsky (ed): *The Letters of Thomas Love Peacock* Vol. 1

Chapter 13

A.H. Hill (ed) *Hikayat Abdullah*
J.Bastin, *William Farquhar*
Singapore National Archives
Baron H.G. van Burgst Nahuis: typescript translations of extracts from his book are in the India Office Papers, BL
H. Temperley, *Foreign Policy of Canning*
Mrs A. Prinsep, *Voyage from Calcutta to van Diemen's Land*

Chapter 14

John Bastin (ed): *The Journal of Thomas Otho Travers 1813–1820*
Documents concerning the founding of the Zoological Society and minutes of early meetings are in the Library of the Royal Zoological Society of London.
Thomas Stamford Raffles Esq. B.A. etc (ed) *Memoirs of the Life and Ministry of the Rev. Thomas Raffles*
P. Chalmers Mitchell, *Centenary History of the Zoological Society of London* 1929
Victoria & Albert Museum
J.C.M. Khoo, C.G. Kwa, L.Y. Khoo 'The Death of Sir Thomas Stamford Raffles' Singapore Medical Journal Vol. 39 1998

Chapter 15

Castle Stewart Papers, Public Record office of Northern Ireland
'The Red Book': unpublished manuscript notes and family memories compiled by Stamford Raffles Flint (1847–1925), son of Jenny Rosdew and the Rev Charles Raffles Flint. In private hands
Augustus J.C. Hare, *The Life and Letters of Frances Baroness Bunsen*
John Bastin, *William Farquhar*
John Bastin, *Sophia Raffles*
Ivan Polunin and Kwa Chong Guan, *The William Farquhar Collection of Natural History Drawings*
H.J. Noltie, *Raffles Ark Redrawn*
Adam Smith, 'On Colonies' *The Wealth of Nations* 1776

Bibliography

Abbreviations:

Journal of the Malayan Branch of the Royal Asiatic Society   JMBRAS
Bijdragen tot de Tal- ,Lan- en Volenkunde   KITLV
Selected documents   sel. docs

Printed Books, including monographs

Date of first publication is given unless a later one is materially significant. Though many of these books have never been reprinted, some – even the earliest and most obscure – are available as downloads. Place of publication is not given since this is easily determined on the internet if required, as are any later editions with notes and/or introductions. In the endnotes I have given only short titles.

Adam, Ahmat (trs. and notes) *The Letters of Sincerity: The Raffles Collection of Malay Letters (1780–1824) A Descriptive Account MBRAS* monograph 2009
Alatas, Syed Hussein *Thomas Stamford Raffles: Schemer or Reformer?* 1971
Anderson, John *Mission to the East Coast of Sumatra in 1823 under the Direction of the Government of Prince of Wales Island* 1826
—*Acheen and the Ports in the North and East Coasts of Sumatra* (1840) with intro by A.J.S. Reid 1971
Anson, A.E.H. *About Myself and Others* 1920
Barley, Nigel *The Duke of Puddle Dock: In the Footsteps of Stamford Raffles* 1991
—(ed.) *The Golden Sword: Stamford Raffles and the East* 1999

Barrow, Sir John *An Autobiographical Memoir of Sir John Barrow, Bart. Late of the Admiralty* 1847

Bastin, John *The Native Policies of Sir Stamford Raffles in Java and Sumatra: An Economic Interpretation* 1957

—*The British in West Sumatra 1685–1965* (sel. docs) 1965

—*The Letters of Sir Stamford Raffles to Nathaniel Wallich JMBRAS* reprint 1981

—*Olivia Marianne Raffles* (monograph) 2002

—*Sophia Raffles* (monograph) 2002

—*Sir Stamford Raffles's The History of Java: A Bibliographical Essay* 2004

—*William Farquhar: First Resident and Commandant of Singapore* (monograph) 2005

—*The Natural History Researches of Dr Thomas Horsfield* (monograph) 2005

—*John Leyden and Thomas Stamford Raffles* (monograph) 2006

—(ed.) *The Letters and Books of Sir Thomas Stamford Raffles and Lady Raffles* 2009

Bird, Isabella L. *The Golden Chersonese and the Way Thither* 1879

Blagden, C.O. (ed.) *One Hundred Years of Singapore* 1931

Blakiston, John *Twelve Years' Military Adventure in Three Quarters of the Globe, or, Memoirs of an Officer* 1829

Bosma, Utbe and Remco Rabem (trs. Wendie Shaffer) *Being 'Dutch' in the Indies 1500–1920* 2008

Bowen, H.V. *The Business of Empire: the East India Company and Imperial Britain 1756–1833* 2006

Boulger, Demetrius Charles *Life of Sir Stamford Raffles* 1897

Buckley, C.B. *An Anecdotal History of Olden Times in Singapore* Vol. I 1902

Bute, Marchioness of (ed.) *The Private Journals of the Marquess of Hastings* 1858

Carey, Peter *The British in Java 1811–1816: A Javanese Account. A text edition. English synopsis and commentary on BL Add Mss 12330* 1992

Burgess, Anthony *The Malayan Trilogy* 2000

Chapman, Arnold *A St Helena Who's Who; or, a Directory of the Island during the Captivity of Napoleon* 1914

Chaudhuri, K.N. (ed.) *The Economic Development of India under the East India Company 1814–1858* 1971

Coldham, Peter Wilson *Child Apprentices in America from Christ's Hospital 1617–1778* 1990

Collis, Maurice *Raffles* 1966

Conrad, Joseph *The Shadow Line* 1917

Cook, J.A., Bethune *Sir Thomas Stamford Raffles Founder of Singapore 1819 and Some of his Friends and Contemporaries* 1918

Cotton, Sir Evan (ed. Charles Fawcett) *East Indiamen* 1949

Coupland, Sir Reginald *Raffles of Singapore* 1897, 3rd edn. 1946

Crawfurd, John *History of the Indian Archipelago. Containing an Account of the Manners, Arts, Languages, Religions, Institutions, and Commerce of its Inhabitants, with Maps and Engravings* 3 vols 1820

Curzon, Lord *British Government in India* 1925

Dalley, Jan *The Black Hole: Money, Myth and Empire* 2006

Dalrymple, William *The White Mughals* 2002

Davidson, G.F. *Trade and Travel in Far East* 1900

Dempster, Charlotte L. Hawkins *Memoirs of My Time* 1920

Devenish, R.J. and C.H. McLaughlin *Historical and Genealogical Record of the Devenish Families* 1948

Devine, T.M. *Scotland's Empire 1600–1815* 2003

Dowden, Wilfred S. (ed.) *The Letters of Thomas Moore* 2 vols 1964

—(ed) *The Journals of Thomas Moore* 3 vols 1984

Egerton, H.E. *Sir Stamford Raffles: England in the Far East* 1900

El-Enany, Rasheed *Arab Representations of the Occident: East-West Encounters in Arabic Fiction* 2006

Elliot, Sir George *Memoir of the Honble Sir George Elliot, Written for his Children* 1853

Evans, John *The Gentleman Usher: The Life and Times of George Dempster (1732–1818) Member of Parliament and Laird of Dunnichen and Skibo* 2005

Faulkner, Thomas *The History and Antiquities of the Parish of Hammersmith* 1839

Felton, Felix *Thomas Love Peacock* 1973

Fergusson, James (ed.) *Letters of George Dempster to Sir Adam Fergusson 1756–1813 with Some Account of his Life* 1934

Finlayson, George *The Mission to Siam ... in the years 1821–2: from the Journal of the late George Finlayson, Esq., Surgeon and Naturalist to the Mission. With a Memoir and Introduction by Sir S. Raffles FRS* 1825

Flower, Raymond *Raffles: The Story of Singapore* 1984

Gascoigne, John *Joseph Banks and the English Enlightenment* 1994

Geertz, Clifford *The Religion of Java* 1960

Gilmour, David *The Ruling Class: Imperial Lives in the Victorian Raj* 2005

Hahn, Emily *Raffles of Singapore* 1948

Hancock, T.H.H. *Coleman's Singapore* 1986

Hare, Augustus J.C. *The Life and Letters of Frances, Baroness Bunsen* Vol. 1 1879, Vol. 2 1880

Harfield, Alan *Bencoolen: The Christian Cemetery and the Fort Marlborough Monuments* 1985

Harrison, Brian *Holding the Fort: Melaka Under Two Flags 1795–1845* 1985

Hibbert, Christopher *George IV: Regent and King 1811–1830* 1973

Hogendorp, Dirk van *Berigt vanden Tegenswoordigen Toestand der Bataafsche Betzittingen in Oost-Indien* 1799

Holmes, Richard *The Age of Wonder* 2008

Joukovsky, Nicholas A. (ed.) *The Letters of Thomas Love Peacock* Vol. 1 2001

Keay, John *The Honourable Company* 1991

Kelly, Ronan *Bard of Erin: The Life of Thomas Moore* 2008

King, Dean *A Sea of Words: A Lexicon and Companion for Patrick O'Brian's Seafaring Tales* 1995

Knight, David *Humphry Davy: Science and Power* 1992

Kowner, R. *Skin as Metaphor: Early Racial Views on Japan 1548–1853* 2004

Le Breton, Anna Letitia *Memoir of Mrs Barbauld* 1874

Lewis, Samuel (ed.) *A Topographical History of England* 1831

Liu, Gretchen *Singapore: A Pictorial History 1819–2000* 1999

Lee, Kip Lin *The Singapore House 1819–1942* 1988

Mackenzie, W.C. *Colonel Colin Mackenzie: First Surveyor-General of India* 1952

Madden, Paul *Raffles: Lessons in Business Leadership* 2003

Marsden, William *The History of Sumatra* 3rd edn 1811

Matheson, Virginia and Barbara Watson (annotated trs.) *The Precious Gift* by Raja Ali Haji ibn Ahmad 1982

Marx, Karl *Capital* Vols 1 & 2 1867 & 1885 (trs. Eden and Cedar Paul) 1928

Miksic, John N. *Archaeological Research on the 'Forbidden Hill' of Singapore: Excavations at Fort Canning 1984* 1985

—*Borobudur: Golden Tales of the Buddha* photographs Marcello Tranchini 1990

Milton, Giles *Nathaniel's Nutmeg* 1999

Minto, Countess of (ed.) *Lord Minto in India: Life and Letters of Gilbert Elliot, First Earl of Minto, from 1897 to 1814* 1880

Mitchell, David *The Thousand Autumns of Jacob de Zoet* (novel) 2010

Mitchell, P. Chalmers *Centenary History of the Zoological Society* 1929

Morton, Rev. James *The Poetical Remains of the late Dr John Leyden with Memoirs of his Life* 1819

Nicolson, Adam *Men of Honour: Trafalgar and the Making of the English Hero* 2005

O'Brian, Patrick *H.M.S. Surprise* 1973 (novel)

O'Brian, Patrick *The Thirteen-Gun Salute* 1989 (novel)

O'Brian, Patrick *The Nutmeg of Consolation* 1991 (novel)

Pearson, H.F. *This Other India: A Biography of Sir Thomas Stamford Raffles* 1957

Philips, C.H. *The East India Company 1784–1834* 1940

Prinsep, Mrs A. *Voyage from Calcutta to Van Diemen's Land* 1829

Raffles, Lady (Sophia) *Memoir of the Life and Public Services of Sir Thomas Stamford Raffles* 1830; facsimile edition with intro by John Bastin 1991

Raffles, Thomas Stamford *Review of the Administration, Value and State of the Colony of Java with its Dependencies: As it was, – as it is, – and as it may be* 1816

—*The History of Java* Vols 1 and 2 1817. Facsimile reprint 1988 intro John Bastin.

Raffles, the Rev. Thomas *Letters, during a Tour through some parts of France, Savoy, Switzerland, Germany, and the Netherlands, in the Summer of 1817* 1818

Raffles, Thomas Stamford BA, of the Inner Temple, Stipendiary Magistrate for the Borough of Liverpool *Memoirs of the Life and Ministry of the Rev. Thomas Raffles, D.D., LL.D, etc* 1864

Ramsden, Lady Guendolen *Correspondence of Two Brothers: Edward Adolphus, Eleventh Duke of Somerset, and his Brother, Lord Webb Seymour, 1800 to 1819 and After* 1906

Ricklefs, M.C. *A History of Modern Indonesia* 1981

Sadler, Thomas (ed.) *Crabb Robinson (1775–1867) Diary, Reminiscences, and Correspondence* 2nd ed. 1869

Scherren, Henry *The Zoological Society of London: A Sketch of its Foundation and Management* 1905

Said, Edward *Orientalism* 1978

Sheppard, Tan Sri Dato Mubin [*sic*] *Singapore 150 Years* (sel. docs) 1973

Smith, Adam *An Inquiry into the Nature and Causes of the Wealth of Nations* 1776

Smith, Cecil Woodham *Queen Victoria: Her Life and Times* Vol. 1 1972

Solomon, Eli *Sir Thomas Stamford Raffles: A Comprehensive Bibliography* 1997

Spencer, Alfred (ed.) *Memoirs of Sir William Hickey* Vol. IV 1925

Stern, Philip J. *The Company-State: Corporate Sovereignty and the Early Modern Foundations of the British Empire in India* 2011

Stockdale, John Joseph *The Island of Java* 1811

Sweet, Michael J. and others *Raffles: Book of Days* 1993

Swettenham, Sir Frank *British Malaya* 1907

Talfourd, Thomas Noon *Letters of Charles Lamb with a Sketch of his Life* 1849

Tarling, Nicholas (ed.) *The Cambridge History of Southeast Asia* 2 vols 1992; 4 vols (with supplementary material) 1999

Taylor, Jean Gelman *The Social World of Batavia: European and Eurasian in Dutch Asia* 1983

Temperley, H. *The Foreign Policy of Canning* 1925

Thorn, Major William *The Conquest of Java* 1815 (reprint with intro by John Bastin 2004)

—*Memoirs of Sir R.R. Gillespie* 1816

Tomkins, Stephen *William Wilberforce* 2007

Trapaud, Elisha *A Short Account of Prince of Wales Island in the East-Indies given to Capt. Light by the King of Kedah* ed. and intro John Bastin 1962

Wallace, Alfred Russel *The Malay Archipelago* 1869

Wathen, J. *Journal of a Voyage in 1811 and 1812 to Madras and China* 1814

Webster, Anthony *The Richest East India Merchant: The Life and Business of John Palmer of Calcutta 1767–1836* 2009

Williamson, Capt. Thomas *The East India Vade-Mecum* 1810

Walford, Edward *Old and New London* Vol. 6 (Deptford) 1878

Wurtzburg, C.E. *Raffles of the Eastern Isles* 1954

Periodicals

Bastin, John (ed.) 'The Journal of Thomas Otho Travers 1813–1820' *Memoirs of the Raffles Museum* No. 4 May 1957

—'The Western Element in Modern Southeast Asian History' *Papers on Southeast Asian Subjects* No 2, U. of Malaya in Kuala Lumpur 1960

—'The Working of the Early Land Rate System in West Java' *KITLV* Vol. 116 1960

—'The Raffles Gamelan' *KITLV* Vol. 127 1971

—' Dr Joseph Arnold and the Discovery of Rafflesia Arnoldi in West Sumatra in 1818' *Journal of the Society for the Bibliography of Natural History* Vol. 6 October 1973

—'The Letters of Sir Stamford Raffles to Nathaniel Wallich' *MBRAS* Reprint No. 8 1981

—'Sir Stamford Raffles and the Study of Natural History in Penang, Singapore and Indonesia' *JMBRAS* Vol. LXIII Part II December 1990

—'Raffles's Aides-de-Camp in Java' *JMBRAS* Vol. 65 June 1992

—'Abdullah and Siami' *JMBRAS* Vol. 81 June 2008

Carey, Peter 'Sexuality and Power' *Newsletter*, International Institute for Asian Studies (Leiden) 2010

Cowan, C.D. 'Early Penang and the Rise of Singapore 1805–1832' (sel. docs) *JMBRAS* Vol. XXIII Part 2 1950

Gibson-Hill C.A. 'Raffles, Acheh and the Order of the Golden Sword' *JMBRAS* Vol. XXIX May 1956

Hill, A.H. (trs. and notes) 'The Hikayat Abdullah: an annotated translation' *JMBRAS* Vol. XXVIII June 1955

Hoffman, John 'A Foreign Investment: Indies Malay to 1901' *Indonesia* (Cornell) Vol. 27 1979

Khoo, J.C.M, C.G. Kwa and L.Y. Khoo 'The Death of Sir Thomas Stamford Raffles (1781–1826)' *Singapore Medical Journal* Vol. 39 1998

Lee, Kam Hing and Dr Ahmat Adam 'Raffles and the Order of the Golden Sword' *JMBRAS* Vol. LXIII December 1990

Lohuizen-de Leeuw J.E. van 'Which European first recorded the unique Dvarapala of Borobudur?' *KITLV* Vol. 138 1982

Shelford, W.H. 'Raffles' Grave' *British Malaya* July 1926

Weatherbee, Donald E. 'Raffles' Sources for Traditional Javanese Historiography and the Mackenzie Collections' *Indonesia* (Cornell) Vol. 26 October 1978

Prince of Wales Island Gazette

Java Government Gazette

Asiatic Journal and Monthly Miscellany

Oriental Herald (Calcutta)

Journal of the Indian Archipelago and East Asia

Burke's Annual Register

Cobbett's Parliamentary Debates

Edinburgh Review

Quarterly Review

National Register

The Literary Gazette

The London Magazine

The Gentleman's Magazine

The Saturday Magazine

*

Oxford Dictionary of National Biography

Victoria County Histories

Survey of London Vols 24 & 25

Burke's Landed Gentry

London Metropolitan Police Archives

And a great many websites, with special appreciation of British History Online

Lectures. Papers, Dissertations

Gallop, Annabel Teh 'Illumination: the Art of the Malay Letter' University of Sidney June 2007

—'Raffles and the Art of the Malay Letter' British Library June 2009

Hanson, Ingrid 'Raffles' Drawings at the BM: An Analysis' School of Oriental and African Studies, U. of London 2009

Knapman, Gareth 'Race, Empire and Liberalism: Interpreting John Crawfurd's History of the Indian Archipelago' Asian Studies Association of Australia, Melbourne July 2008

Mault, Natalie A. 'Java as a Western Construct: An Examination of
Sir Thomas Stamford Raffles' The History of Java' Louisiana State
University 2005

Wright, Nadia 'Sir Stamford Raffles – a Manufactured Hero?' Asian Studies
Association of Australia, Melbourne July 2008

Illustrated and Descriptive Catalogues

Archer, Mildred, and John Bastin *The Raffles Drawings in the India Office
Library, London* 1978

Noltie, Henry J. *Raffles' Ark Redrawn: Natural History Drawings from the
Collection of Sir Thomas Stamford Raffles* Botanic Garden, Edinburgh 2009

Polunin, Ivan and Kwa Chong Guan with introduction by John Bastin *The
William Farquhar Collection of Natural History Drawings* Goh Geok Khim 2
vols 1999

Sloan, Kim (ed.) *Enlightenment: Discovering the World in the Eighteenth Century*
British Museum 2003

Unpublished

Bullough, Nigel 'The Minto Stone: its History and Significance and a Plan
for its Restitution' Internet post 3 May 2005

Hannigan, Tim 'Sultans, Sepoys and Englishmen: Stamford Raffles and the
Invasion of Java'

List of Illustrations

Frontispiece: Sir Thomas Stamford Raffles (1781–1826), by James Lonsdale, (1777–1839): Private Collection/The Bridgeman Art Library

Colour plate section

1. Portrait of Raffles by George Francis Joseph (1817) (© National Portrait Gallery)
2. Raffles' father Captain Benjamin Raffles (private collection)
3. A drawing of his mother Anne, courtesy of the Trustees of the Estate of Athene Sanders
4. The Rev. Thomas Raffles, first cousin. Engraving by E. Bocquet, 1814
5. Raffles' first wife Olivia, miniature by Nathaniel Plimmer, 1805
6. India House, headquarters of the East India Company in Leadenhall Street, from Ackermann's *Views of London*
7. Raffles' sister Maryanne (private collection)
8. Maryanne's second husband, Captain William Flint (private collection)
9. 'Charley Boy', aged five (private collection)
10. Raffles' second wife Sophia, copy of oil by A.R. Chalon (private collection)
11. Sir Thomas Stamford Raffles, copy of oil by A,R, Chalon (private collection)
12. Bust of Ella Raffles (private collection)
13. Princess Charlotte (1796–1817), only daughter of the Prince Regent, bust attributed to Peter Rouw
14. William Farquhar, first Resident and Commandant of Singapore by J. Graham, 1832, courtesy of Mrs Wendy Lumsden

Index